Victory in Jesus

Victory in Jesus

Equipping Christian Families
for Foster Care or Adoption

Cheryl Sasai Ellicott

Sweetwater Still Publishing
Colcord, Oklahoma USA

Visit Sweetwater Still Publishing at
www.sweetwaterstill.com

Notice: This book is designed to share personal experiences as well as insight and encouragement with families who have adopted or are considering foster care, adoption or ministry to street children. It's not the purpose of this book to reprint all of the information that's otherwise available. Families are encouraged to read all of the available material and learn as much as they can. Every effort has been made to make this book as accurate as possible, nevertheless there may be mistakes, both typographical and in content. Likewise, information may become outdated; things change rapidly. The author and publisher do not claim to know what's best for your church, your family or the children under your care. Only God knows where He's called you and what His will is for you there.

Disclaimer: Identifying information and some names have been changed throughout the book where needed to protect children and families.

ISBN: 978-0-9843599-7-4
LCCN: 2016905348
Published by Sweetwater Still Publishing
Colcord, Oklahoma USA
Printed in the United States of America
20 19 18 17 16 / 10 9 8 7 6 5 4 3 2 1

To Sam and Joe Sasai:
If I could, I'd give you a happy end.
May God use your stories to bring many home,
whether they be lost upon the earth
or within the darkness of their souls.

Table of Contents

From the Author:

"'You are our God.' Indeed, in you the orphan finds mercy."
(Hosea 14:4b ISV)

This book is meant to educate, prepare and encourage Christians who are called to bring God's mercy to the fatherless. But it's also an alarm (see Ezekiel 33:7-9.) I'll explain that later.

Christians, to be victorious on this mission, you'll need information and preparation You deserve to hear from Christian parents who've gone before you—and you need the whole story, not only the happy highlights. That's why *Victory in Jesus: Equipping Christian Families for Foster Care or Adoption* was written. If you're not yet a believer in Jesus, you're welcome to glean what you can. For a fuller understanding of this message, ask God to explain it. Most of what I write is only discerned with the Holy Spirit's assistance, when our spirit is in union with Christ.

For parents who are familiar with my previous writing, I have praise reports for you, along with some new warnings. The landscape has changed much since I first began caring for the world's neediest children. The challenges of raising abused and neglected children are now acknowledged and discussed more openly than they used to be. However, with this progress have come some negative trends; I'll address those as well, later on.

This book is a compilation of things I've learned and also stories shared with me by others who minister to fatherless children. Some of the information appears in my previous book; it's vital to your well-being, so I've included it again as a reminder and also for those who haven't read it. Some of the stories in the section "War Stories" were first printed years ago; they now have updates for those who wondered what happened next. Other stories in the book are new, including my own: "Lord Prepare Me."

Since 1989, I worked with approximately fifty children in need. Shortly after our wedding, my husband and I became house parents through the *Teen Challenge* ministry. Thus we were Mom and Dad to about twenty-five teens or pre-teens in a shelter home. In subsequent years we were foster parents to an another twenty-five children in our own home. We already had three biological children, in addition to a daughter lost to cancer, before we adopted through the foster care system. We've also experienced the anguish of adoption-dissolution (not a simple disruption). In 2001 I founded a support group for foster and adoptive mothers; these women were a blessing to me and to each other. My husband also worked with disabled adults for over fifteen years; together we did in-home care for them as well. In the years since our children became adults, we've begun to reach out globally, supporting ministry to orphans and street children wherever the Lord leads and provides.

However, even parents (like us) who know we're called to this, and who entered this arena with healthy support-systems, have—in wonderful, idealistic zeal (with *rose-colored glasses* firmly in place)—waltzed in over their heads and made lasting mistakes. Therefore, allow me to warn you of the greatest pitfalls ahead.

Yes, you're envisioning the joy of making a difference, loving an unloved child. And you should be! You believe it's more blessed to give than to receive. You're correct! You believe God's version of love never fails (correct again). You know you'll reap a harvest if you continue to do good and do not give up. God bless you; I love your heart. Really, I do! You inspire and encourage me. But may I remind you that there's an unseen battle to fight? I want you to persevere long enough to see the victory and the harvest. Your enemy is invisible, but he's very, very real. When you reach out to these children, their enemies become *your enemies.* Oh, certainly, your God is stronger—He's Almighty. *But He's a jealous God!* Were you aware of that? He tolerates no rivals in your heart or your home.

> *"You have persevered and have endured hardships for my name, and have not grown weary. Yet I hold this against you: You have forsaken your first love." (Rev 2:3-4)*

If you learn only one thing from this book, let it be this: it's easy to get caught up in the work of a humanitarian and forget the *Lover of your soul.* But you were created to love God—with all of your heart, mind, body and soul. And the only way to succeed is to remain as a branch connected to the vine [Jesus]. Good works cannot take the place of adoring your Savior. They aren't an adequate substitute. Keep your relationship with God, through Jesus, as the most important thing—the *only* thing that matters—and He will pour out His spirit on the children... in His time.

"Even youths grow tired and weary, and young men stumble and fall; but those who hope in the LORD will renew their strength. They will soar on wings like eagles; they will run and not grow weary, they will walk and not be faint." (Isaiah 40:30-31 NIV)

My Story

"Lord Prepare Me"

Dear Children,

My story is for you.

I don't have all the answers to your questions, nor to my own. But I know this for sure: Jesus is God, and He gave His life so that I could know Him. If that's all I ever know for sure, it's enough.

Because of this one absolute and unchanging conviction, regardless of cost, I've "set my face like flint" to seek God, through the atoning work of His only begotten son, Jesus. The power of His Holy Spirit within me both compels and carries me in this direction. I might never know my exact purpose or calling, but if I know the God of my purpose, that's more than enough.

I hope to know more tomorrow, but today I can promise you this: He sparkles more brightly; His beauty alone is unspoiled; He beckons gloriously, without guile or guilt; He rends the heavens to come down, rescuing all who cry to Him; He purifies hearts and carves new channels for our lives; He brings floods of living water from piles of stone.

I'm bathed in his dazzling light and drenched with His beautiful love time and again. Therefore, I've determined to follow hard and present Him with the fruit that is rightfully His, despite the many foxes that sneak in to devour time, weaken devotion and extinguish love. I've failed, some; this doesn't surprise me. But I'm deeply astonished at how often I've not failed; it's an astounding miracle — a result of His power extended through His amazing grace.

Children, imitate me as I endeavor to imitate Christ; He knows you're but flesh — He'll help you. Love your Creator with all that you are, and then some. Cherish what He cherishes, despite the little foxes in your life.

"Tremble, O earth, at the presence of the Lord,
at the presence of the God of Jacob,
who turned the rock into a pool,
the hard rock into springs of water."
Psalms 114:7-8 NIV

Testimony

My daddy was an orphan; his father was a lost boy. I didn't learn their stories until many years later, but as a young girl I had a recurring dream that I was lost. Maybe we're all born with a certain fear of being lost, but I had more.

In the late summer of 1988, I was a young adult, a mother of one. I remember waiting for an appointment one particularly hot day. As I sat in the waiting room, enjoying the breeze from the air-conditioner, I flipped through a magazine and stopped on a certain article. Photos of wailing infants, pitifully unhealthy, stared back at me as I read about an epidemic of abandoned drug-babies. It hurt my mother-heart in so many ways. Not only were they suffering, they were unwanted and alone. They were lost . . .

I was overcome with emotion, a passion to jump up and do something. Yet I was powerless. What could I do to help an *epidemic* of suffering children? However, I'd read in the Bible that I should care for the fatherless, the foreigner and the widow. Since He commanded it, couldn't I at least try? As I sat there, grieved and praying, I came to a decision: *Lord willing*, I would show these children that someone wanted and loved them: His name was Jesus.

I might begin my story there, saying that's why *I am who I am* and why *I do what I do*. But it leaves questions unanswered. I'm not sure I have the answers; sometimes I still wonder who I am and how I got here. I've never forgotten my name, birth date nor address, yet. But is the date I was born into a certain family, my current location and activity *my identity*? Is the path that physically brought me here *my story*?

I watched my brother Arturo preach a glorious message the other day, each sentence first in his native language (Spanish), then in thickly-accented English for the few Anglos in the crowd and for the Micronesians in the back row.

It was over ninety degrees outside, with close to one-hundred-percent humidity, and the little church building wasn't air-conditioned. The small crowd sat quietly on the worn pews, wearing their best clothes, smiling and sweating. Some fanned themselves. Arturo read his Bible to the crowd with passion, then humbly taught what it meant. The love of Christ shone from his warm, tan face. I thought, *What a compassionate person my brother is! How strong are his smile and his faith!*

"After I was saved," Arturo said, "I saw a man I used to know before I was saved." He paused, then continued, "He was drunk." Heads nodded all around the room. Across the aisle from me, the old man with the wheelchair smiled from beneath the thick, black glasses that blind men wear. When he smiled the dirty bandages on the side of his head wrinkled up. And Arturo continued, "When my friend saw me he said, 'Sing me a song, Arturo!' So I said, 'Of course, my friend!'—and I picked up my guitar." Arturo made the motions of picking up a guitar, cradled it and tipped his head back and said, "I sang for him like this: *'My dear friend, you need Jesus! Jesus can pull you out of the pit you are in. Jesus can save you! If Jesus saved me, then he can save you too!'"* Arturo translated, sang the lines in Spanish, then grinned widely and said, "But my friend stopped me and said, 'No, Arturo! I cannot be saved! Don't sing that song anymore!' and I said, 'Oh yes you can be saved, my friend!' But again my friend said, 'I don't want to be saved! I will never be saved, Arturo!' So I said to him, 'I'm going to pray for you!' My friend shook his head and said, 'No! Don't pray for me, Arturo!'" Grinning, Arturo shook his head woefully and then continued the story, "I said, 'My friend, I am going to pray that Jesus makes a special day for you to get saved! If he saved me, then I know he can save you too!'"

Again Pastor Arturo smiled widely. The faces in the pews around me beamed back; heads nodded. Arturo finished by saying, "So I prayed for him! The next time I saw my friend, it was a few years

16

later. Can you guess what he was doing? He was preaching the gospel!"

It was a wonderful message. Then the blind man asked to go up front and give a testimony. His grown daughters gathered around and helped him into the wheelchair, then took him down front so he could proclaim the goodness of God in Spanish. The small crowd listening had the same lovely faces, some lined from age and the hard life of poor immigrants—most were thousands of miles from their homeland. Other faces were new and filled with the wonder of youth. I thanked God for allowing me to attend such a simple but precious family reunion. I regretted it would be over soon.

After the blind man's testimony, we all ate potluck dinner together. The very, very big pot looked like *menudo*. The cooks didn't speak English, and it sounded like the Anglos didn't know what they were eating; I certainly didn't tell them. It wouldn't hurt them. They enjoyed it and ate heartily; I had just the rice and raw cabbage.

Later, as I left church to return home, I regretted that I never try the menudo and also that I don't know my brother Arturo's full name. I've never spoken to him, and he doesn't know me. I don't have one drop of Hispanic blood, but we're brothers and sisters *in Christ*. Since we're family, I should have had some of his soup. I don't avoid it only because I'm afraid of boiled animal intestines, but I have food allergies.

So is that my story? Not that I have food allergies and don't want to eat boiled animal intestines, but the fact that I experienced spiritual birth—was *born again*—and exited the dominion of the natural-only, becoming adopted by God and part of His diverse family? I think that's part of it.

The Bible declares I have a firm obligation to both my brothers and sisters *in Christ* and also to my blood relatives. So the story of me must start with both births. If you're a born-again believer, you also have two birthdays and a *testimony*. You might have written your testimony down or shared it in public. I have a short version that I can read in front of crowds in 3 or 4 minutes; it goes like this:

I grew up mostly in the Pacific Northwest and rural Alaska. Dad was a pipe-fitter/welder with a union, so we moved with the jobs (every six months to a year). I had two sisters, and I was the most fearful child—shy and scared of almost everything, especially of moving. My parents cherished us; they were capable, accomplished and excellent providers—for that I'm thankful. But it didn't help my fears that they drank often and were extremely adventurous. We camped in the wilderness every weekend for years, banging coffee cans with spoons to chase bears away. Dad's boat was the fastest and loudest around (built by his *scary* cousin who pioneered jet boats on the rapids of the Snake River). Dad's vehicles were even faster and louder. Dad didn't drive, he passed traffic! We didn't sightsee, we roared over the logging-roads, catching air on the other side of the mud-holes—the music blared, the tires skidded, spun and slipped along the mountainside, and I stared out my window at wrecked cars in the canyon below. I had an ulcer by the time I was in my teens.

But there was a time I wasn't quite so fearful. We weren't Alaskan Natives, but when I was 7 or 8 years old I first heard the gospel from a family who ministered to Athabascan Indian children in Gakona, Alaska. This was the brightest, most peaceful point of my childhood. Mom dropped us off at mission outreaches and even sent me to Bible camp. There was only one television channel in town: the PTL (Praise the Lord) Network. It was weird, but soothing; it gave me hope. When I was 9 years old I confessed Christ as my savior. I was very excited about Jesus. In daydreams my adult-self stood (fearlessly!) before crowds, imploring them to embrace Christ and beware of communism. Someone gave us a pile of comic books: *The Hiding Place, The Cross and the Switchblade, God's Smuggler* and others. (Most were about Christians martyred under communistic governments). I read them over and over again; I too wanted to bring the light of Jesus to a dark world.

We lived in Gakona longer than most places. But we moved again when I was about 10. Along the way I lost my comic books; soon I completely forgot about Jesus. (Not only did I forget to follow Him, my memory of who He was, and of ever being in church, was plucked from my mind.)

Without Jesus, my overwhelming fears collaborated with the other quirks of my nature to turn me into a liar and a thief—and a serious chain-smoker. I started having boyfriends, and my preaching daydreams were replaced by a desire for a handsome prince on a white horse to come and carry me away. When I was eleven I went to an evangelical outreach to Eskimos for a short time (in Bethel), but I was no longer listening. By the time I turned eighteen I was a weary atheist, a stubborn *know-it-all* and a single mother trying to get away from a violent, alcoholic boyfriend.

But then when I was nineteen, by the mercy and grace of God, while on a short trip out of Alaska (trying to escape, but failing), I met a young stranger whose passion was street-witnessing; he was really good looking, so I let him read his Bible to me. He explained *the Four Spiritual Laws* and (I think) *the Roman's Road*. Afterward the Scriptures haunted me. Through God's mercy, I was suddenly aware that God was real and near. It was frightening, but comforting as well. I didn't deserve God's love, but He'd given His only son as a ransom for me anyway. He paid my penalty so I could be forgiven and brought near to Him—as His body and bride. I was overwhelmed with shame, but also with fear and a strong desire to repent and accept His offer. So I gave my heart and life to Jesus, and my daily goal became to *know Him*, at all costs. Right away my lost childhood memories of Him returned, and He began freeing me from my habitual sin (and the violent boyfriend). He also freed me from my many fears; they were all replaced by just one thing: *Fear of God.*

Since then my understanding of the gospel and of Christ has grown, but my goal is unchanged. I want to know Him and (with the strength He gives) serve the rest of the body of Christ—even if that puts me before crowds, *fearlessly imploring them to embrace Christ.*

I want to walk worthy of being what He calls me: I am His bride, who waits for him to come on a white horse and carry me away.

Pieces of Me

Now you know my brief testimony, but I owe you more. God has a plan for your life—He has a mission for you. Therefore, I'm going to do something you might not like, but that you need. I'm going to tell you a longer story; it might make you learn some history. Don't groan—you can do this, and you'll get the point at the end. You're a missionary, so you need to know about those who've gone before you. Ready, set, take a deep breath . . . go!

When my sisters and I grew up, we eventually settled thousands of miles from each other. On those rare occasions when the family gets together, I wish our visit would never end—I've missed them. We love each other and get along well, but being together reminds me that we're different. In fact, I've only had the kindred-spirit sort of connection with one of my biological relatives, and, wouldn't you know it, she's known as our *crazy-aunt*.

Aunt Ginny and I aren't exactly alike, by any means. I have never hissed and meowed at people—not even in jest. I adore books, but I don't dream of living inside a book-mobile someday. I agree that social-security numbers could be part of a sinister plot, but I have one anyway. And I do not have piles of neatly tied and stacked trash bags stowed throughout my home. I'm not worried about the people who sort through what I put into the dumpster (now that I live in the rural south, I know this man. He finds a lot of cool stuff.) But are Ginny's ways wrong? She might have some very important secrets in her trash.

I've heard that Ginny's white hair goes down past her waist, but I've never gotten up early enough to see it; by the time I rose it was always neatly rolled into a bun. Anyone watching Ginny walk would never guess she's elderly; her pace is brisk, even when the temperature tops 110 degrees. She's small and lean, but strong. Her olive-complexion gives her an exotic look; rightly so.

When she's home, Ginny sits in one spot, the same exact spot every day. She sits and reads, mostly her Bible, but also history and books about natural cures to health problems. She owns almost as many books as I do. She rarely speaks; if she does, her voice is low and soft. She sits peacefully, reading and peeling her raw onions. Aunt Ginny drinks a lot of water and eats one raw onion every day, along with her garlic and a small cup of soup. She avoids other people's food, just in case. Ginny has food allergies; one bite of beef-contaminated food puts her in the hospital. Ginny writes a lot of long letters; she's been around the world and knows many people. Her letters offend some; there's not much of a personal greeting, they're just one long section of Scripture after another. I love Ginny's letters.

When I was in my mid-twenties, Aunt Ginny lived with us for a year or so. The spot she chose on the sofa soon had a permanent imprint, despite her feather-weight, and it forever smelled of onions and garlic. Ginny was with me when my fourth biological child, Caleb, almost died. At about twelve-days-old, baby Caleb mysteriously contracted an *ecoli* bacterial infection in his blood. It was impossible, they told me, for ecoli to be in his blood when it existed nowhere outside of his bloodstream. Nonetheless, it was there. A few days before he ever got sick, I had a dream that my perfectly healthy newborn suddenly became ill and had to return to the hospital. In my dream he was admitted to the hospital, but soon I needed to return home to care for my other children, who were toddler and preschool age. "Don't worry," the nurses said, "We'll watch Caleb. Go on home and take care of your children."

Later, in my dream, I got a call from the nurses. "Come to the hospital," they said. "Your baby is missing!!"

The dream seemed to last all night long. We frantically searched for our newborn in every place imaginable.

He was never found.

I woke up in tears, shaking, gripped with near panic.

Oh, I told myself, *Silly girl! It was only a dream!* I calmed a bit. Still the sadness of the dream weighed on me all day long.

A few days later baby Caleb suddenly developed a dangerously high fever (such young infants do not get fevers, they told me), and he was admitted to the hospital. Just in time, they said . . . Our precious newborn was in for a long hospital stay, and we had a dilemma. His siblings were at home with their father. Eventually my husband had to go to work. If he didn't work, we couldn't pay our bills. I didn't have a babysitter, and my young children weren't allowed into the ICU.

"Don't worry," the nurses said. "We'll watch Caleb. Go on home and take care of your children."

I was suddenly in the middle of my nightmare.

But I prayed and God had an answer. My eccentric aunt had recently ended up at my house. "I'll sit with Caleb," Ginny said. "I won't leave him alone for an instant." So Ginny came, with her peaceful smile and her quiet voice, and her onions, and she chose a spot right beside the crib where Caleb lay attached to wires and tubes. Incidentally, his room was at the end of a long deserted hallway, right next to the unlocked door to the parking lot—and the nurses rarely made it to his end of the hall.

When my husband worked, Ginny sat at the hospital with baby Caleb; then when he came home, I went to the hospital. Another dear friend, one of my sister-in-laws, took shifts with Ginny. We worked it like this until Caleb came home. My relief, as I walked out of the hospital with my baby in my arms, was beyond explanation.

God sent me Ginny for many reasons, more than I can explain or know. But what if I told you that Ginny has a mean-streak? Sometimes she's downright disturbing. I've wanted to take her by the shoulders and say, *Auntie! You're scaring the children! Where is your faith?*

Like me, Ginny is human. If we listen to God's Holy Spirit and let Him lift us up, we'll do just fine. But if we forget to guard against our human-tendencies, it's our own fault when people are estranged from us. What if I told you that the reason Ginny doesn't live with us anymore is because I kicked her out? It wasn't her fault. In those days my marriage was floundering. The pain of that and the stress of having young children, got the better of me. I thought my problems would decrease if I didn't have an onion-eating aunt perched on my sofa, staring at us and listening to everything we said. So I kicked her out, but sweetly. She went to live in a run-down studio apartment on the south side of Tucson. She did all right; she's a tough old bird, as they say. Of course I didn't like the places she ended up. Each one was worse than the one before.

What would you say if I told you that I've lost track of Ginny, and it was my fault? After awhile I let my bitterness and anger get the better of me and I got my elderly aunt kicked out of her apartment. I got in her landlord's face, *not sweetly*. I called it righteous indignation—the place was a dump, and Ginny's landlord was treating her unfairly because she's an elderly, poor woman. So I gave him *the old what-for*, in my most impressive way. But the Bible says that man's anger does not bring about the righteousness of God—and boy is that true.

I should have just taken Ginny back into our home, I mean *God's* home that He shares with us. Ginny sent word to me, saying she'd been kicked out. I waited for her to come walking up the street to visit. She always shows up eventually. But this time she didn't come.

Some years earlier, my sisters were the ones who moved Ginny to the big city from a tiny country town in Arkansas. We all hoped our father might decide he really did like his sister, if she were closer. So they moved Ginny closer—right into Mom and Dad's house. Daddy tolerated her for a short time. He even let her hug him, once. But then she tried to hug him again. Not long after that, Ginny came to live with me . . . and that's where she stayed, on my couch, until I kicked her out. After a few years my sisters moved away from the city. Then my parents moved away. So I waited for Ginny to come to see me, because we only had each other, and it's hard to look for someone like Ginny who's always hiding. Surely she'd come soon and tell me where she was living. Surely she'd come soon, so I could apologize.

Surely she'd come.

Ginny never came. Eventually my family and I moved out of state too. A few years later we heard that Ginny had died. We grieved for her . . . and I grieved for my foolish actions. But not nearly as much as we grieved last year when we found out that we'd heard wrong. Ginny's obituary doesn't exist, and the person we thought the rumor originated with says *she never said any such thing*. It was a horrible misunderstanding. And now, not only did we lose Ginny somewhere on the bad side of the city, but we left her for dead years ago.

Our words and actions change the stories of those around us.

What if I told you that the people at the church, sitting in the pews listening to my brother Arturo preach, might only be there to con him (and the crowd) out of some money? Was the old man with the wheel-chair really blind? Did he really need that huge bandage on the side of his head, or was he playing a part? When he was wheeled up front to give a testimony, he admitted he'd never been to this church before—his many infirmities kept him homebound. Or, so he said. Then he gave a sob story and asked for money.

Would the fact that Arturo preaches to illegal immigrants change your opinion? For many years he shared the message of Christ's love and redemption with people who crossed the border in secret and were in the country illegally, taking jobs from American citizens. Every story has many sides.

The story of me isn't only about the good I've done, but also the bad. And I'm not the only character in the story. No one is born alone, without family or country. If they are alone, the families and countries *they are not a part of* are a huge piece of their story. Take, for example, my grandfather Samuel.

As far as I know, G. Samuel Sasai was not really a Samuel, nor a Sasai. Born to Japanese peasants at the turn of the century, my grandfather was destined for something more. Yet the path to this *something more* wasn't easy.

The Circus

Even as a tiny boy growing up in Japan, Samuel was quick-witted and uncommonly agile. He was a beautiful child. His soft, black hair lay in waves, and his olive skin was clear and smooth. Long lashes hooded his wide, dark eyes. If not for his strong chin and jaw, his full lips might have been too pretty for a boy. His looks and athletic tendencies attracted too much attention. Old enough to understand, but too young to defend himself, he was stolen away from his family.

Far from the protection of his parents, Samuel was trained to perform for crowds in a circus. Whether he traveled with The Great Sasai's Japanese Troupe of Gymnastic Wonders or one of the other Oriental troupes has been forgotten. Japanese acrobats were a popular draw near the turn of the century. A young child swinging high in the air made the act even more daring, thus more lucrative. With his small stature, strong limbs and good looks, Sam was perfect for the job. But he wasn't a thrill seeker, nor interested in fame and fortune. Sam was just a lonely boy who cried himself to sleep at night. He was at the mercy of strangers, and they were not merciful.

But there is a God of mercy, and He hears the cries of lost boys.

If the world was civilized, such behavior existed only in pockets. By 1900, when Sam was born, America believed itself to be on its way. In many ways it was; most Americans held some form of Christian doctrine, thus they were tamed. Meanwhile, other nations such as Papua New Guinea were still eating the missionaries America sent to them. But missionaries dared not even enter Papua New Guinea when the Japanese were in town.

Japan, a prince among heathens, had a long history with Christianity; most of it was bad. Japan's first Nestorian Christian missionaries arrived in 198 AD, coming to the inland seaport of Sakoshi, near

Himeji. The message spread and God blessed Japan with revival in 515 AD. But apparently the church grew cold and died out afterward.

Later, in the 1500s, Catholicism came to Japan. They taught *another jesus*, one who embraced Buddhism and Shinto to attract the people—not to draw people to the One True God, but to addict them to religious ceremonies and Western ways. This *jesus* even used feudal lords to brutally coerce his subjects to convert.

The Roman Catholic church might have started out right, sharing the biblical gospel message that Jesus and the apostles taught. But Jesus was killed for His message and then each of the apostles were killed for it—except for the apostle John. Efforts to kill John failed, and at last he was exiled to the island of Patmos.

It had never been an easy or safe message to preach.

By the time Catholicism came to Japan, the Roman Catholic church was thoroughly corrupt. They'd ruled with a strong arm for centuries, banning any translation of the Bible except Latin, which virtually no one understood. In the 1380s, a rebel named John Wycliff produced an English version Bible. Another *rebel*, Jon Hus, approved of this translation, declaring that everyone should be allowed to read the Bible in their own language! For this crime the Catholic church burned Hus at the stake, using Wycliff's Bibles as kindling for the fire.

Unfortunately, without a translation of the Bible, the Japanese people couldn't tell the difference between the glorious gospel of Jesus Christ, and a corrupt pretender. As the numbers of Christians and Catholics grew, the fear of them grew as well. Animosity intensified and, in 1597, twenty-six Japanese Christians were crucified for their faith. In 1614 anti-Christian edicts resulted in over 40,000 Japanese Christians being massacred. Japan completed their full-scale persecution and destroyed most of the Christian community by the 1620s. An official, stricter, ban of Christianity—complete with death penalty—was enacted in either 1627 or 1638. Catholicism and Christianity died out, leaving no permanent imprint upon Japanese society.

Despite efforts by brave missionaries, by the year 1905 Japan was still awash in darkness. But a little Japanese boy cried out, and he was heard. If God's message could not reach him, God would take him to the message.

While Sam was still quite young, his circus family crossed many waters and came to the other side of the world. In America this little troupe of Oriental acrobats traveled with the circus from city to city, performing before crowds. During the winter the circus companies stayed at winter quarters, training new acts. Each spring they set off again. But Sam grew, and in time he was capable of choosing for himself where he would travel and where he would not. There came a time when Sam refused to be a slave anymore. He determined to put that life behind him and to never look back. From now on, he alone was the master of his destiny! With that decided, he left the circus. Perhaps he meant to run away and return to his family, but the distance was tremendous, and too much time had passed. He no longer knew the way home. Thus Sam began his life in America, just another lost-boy grown up. But if immigrants had trouble surviving the American slums, an Oriental orphan had even more. Among all foreign groups, only the Asians were consistently denied citizenship in America. Americans enjoyed watching them in the circus, but they didn't want them as neighbors. America might have been civilized, even religious—but this religion didn't usually include loving or-phans and foreigners.

Sam may have drifted for awhile, an unwanted, orphaned for-eigner in the only country he knew. Orientals were banned from many neighborhoods, chased out of marketplaces and shunned from the beautiful churches; Sam wasn't good enough . . . not even for God, or so it seemed. Sometime before his 21st birthday, Sam suffered the effects of a broken heart. Circus life was harsh, but at least he'd had a family and a home of sorts. He even had fans who appreciated his talents and cheered him on. Now he was nobody, with nowhere to go. Sure, he was his own master! But what good is that, if no one wants you anyway? It wasn't the first time Sam ever cried out in the isolation of his heart. But this time he heard the answer. Sam wasn't so different from you and I. If we stop long enough to listen, we hear our heart cry: *No one cares if I live or die! Though surrounded by a sea of souls, I feel lost and alone.*

If we listen, ready to hear, a still, small voice replies:
YOU FEEL LOST AND ALONE?
Yes! our heart wails.
THAT'S BECAUSE YOU ARE.

We're stunned. It's not the answer we expected. We wanted comforting words. But Scripture declares we are spiritually dead and alone, separated from God. We were born with a nature to sin, therefore we sin. Just one sin separates us from God, and no amount of good works can restore us. God is perfectly holy; sin cannot enter His presence. The penalty for sin is death and eternal separation from God. Since we cannot escape our sin, nor pay for it (with anything but our death and eternal condemnation), we live apart from our Creator, drifting toward our end. Sam wasn't so different from you and I. But this time when he cried out, he was finally ready to hear the answer . . . Sam was created to know and love his creator. But sin made God look away from him. Even if everyone in the world had loved Sam, his loneliness would have remained. Human relationships couldn't fill his need for God. However, from the beginning of time, God announced that he would send a redeemer to save man from this fallen state. In time, Jesus Christ, God in flesh, came to earth. Though creator of all things, Jesus was an unwanted traveler too; rejected, mocked and spit upon. Jesus was tempted in all ways, but He never sinned. Jesus was totally innocent, but He died a sinner's death. Jesus suffered punishment for sin and the hell of separation from Father God. But after three days in a grave He came alive again, proving His triumph over sin and death. Therefore, He alone can forgive, cleanse and save all who put their hope in Him. He shares His righteousness with those who turn from their old ways to embrace His ways. Sam longed to know God's love and find his purpose; but it hurt to hear he wasn't worthy of it. Once again, he wasn't good enough. God was offering Sam charity . . . it stung. He knew he could resist this unflattering message and walk away, or accept God's offer of an exchange: life for life. Christ died for him and rose again. Would Sam now die to his self-ruled life and (through the power of the Holy Spirit) be *born again* as God's slave? Sam paused, for just a moment, then surrendered his pride. He put his destiny in more capable hands and turned toward the narrow path of a believer.

At last, Sam wasn't a lost boy anymore.

Pockets of Faith

"Jesus stood and said in a loud voice, 'If a man is thirsty, let him come to Me and drink! Whoever believes in Me, as the Scripture has said, streams of living water will flow from within him.' By this he meant the Spirit . . ." John 7:37b-39a

*J*ust as with civilization, untainted Christianity has long existed only in pockets. True believers bring hope to the hopeless, without asking for anything in return. They bring souls to Christ, not merely to a church.

One such believer was a red-headed, farm-girl named Christine Amalie Anderson. Christine was born in 1885 to Norwegian peasants who immigrated to America seeking a better life. The Andersens found America was a rich land for those who would work hard. Eventually they were blessed with eleven children, all born as American citizens! While only eight lived to see adulthood, their parents were overjoyed to give their children such a wealthy and free land to call home. Most of the children appreciated the opportunities, but Christine troubled her family. The Andersens worried about Christine's safety, among other things. As a young adult, Christine often put on a homely dress and made trips into the crime-infested slums to visit the poor. Not able to stop her, the family decided to do something about her shabby clothing. If nothing else, at least they could make her presentable—despite her lovely red hair, Christine was not a beauty; she required the help of a pretty dress. Therefore, one of her sisters made her a new dress. Nevertheless, the next time they saw Christine, she was dressed pitifully again.

"Christine, what's happened to your new dress?" her sister asked.

"I met a woman who needed it far more than I did," she replied.

By the year 1910, while Sam Sasai was still a child performing before crowds, Christine had dedicated her life to missionary work as a *deaconess*. It was the reformer Martin Luther (1483-1586 AD) who earlier expressed a need for the office of deacon (and deaconess) to be revived and for the Roman Catholic order of nunneries and monasteries to be done away with.

"Good, pious works never make a good, pious man, but a good, pious man performs good, pious works," Luther said. "Faith is a sure, desperately bold confidence in the grace of God. So sure of it, that it would for this trust die a thousand times. And for this reason, without any coercion, a man is made willing and eager to do good to every one, to serve all, to suffer many things, for the love and praise of God, who has shown him so much grace. Therefore it is quite impossible to separate works from faith, just as impossible, in fact, as it would be to separate heat and light from fire."

His words were vital for establishing this office, called Diaconate, and for destroying monasteries and nunneries. But at the same time he confessed he hadn't yet found the right people for an office whose duties were to care for the poor and sick of the congregation. "Therefore," he said, "I will not trust myself to begin it until our Lord God makes real Christians."

Three hundred years passed before the deaconess movement finally came to life. The rule of the corrupt Roman Catholic church ended, and an age of comparative religious freedom began. With this increasing freedom, the Bible became more readily available and many hearts were set on fire by what they read. A generation of believers rose up who were willing and eager to do good to every one, to serve all and to suffer many things for the love and praise of God, who had shown them so much grace.

The deaconess movement began in Germany in the 1840s, having been alive only in the Mennonite community prior to that. The office of deacon or deaconess, as described in the Bible and instituted by the early church, was very specific: deacons were to minister to the poor and the needy believers in the church. When relating to the lost world around them, they were to do the work of an evangelist. Combining these elements, the movement advanced the gospel through serving the needy. It quickly spread through Scandinavia, the Netherlands,

Britain and the United States. Lutherans were especially active, but between 1880 and 1915, various denominations opened sixty-two new training schools in the United States.

A deaconess dedicated her life to humble service in the name of Christ. She received no pay, but her needs were met and she was guaranteed a home. She was allowed to leave her vocation if she prayerfully decided to marry and raise a family. She did not wear a habit, as the nuns wore, but she was given the "deaconess garb" which was a cheap, unattractive, out-of-style dress. It didn't enhance her looks, but it protected her in dangerous places. It declared to all that she was a *woman of God*.

But later, with the arrival of the *Social Gospel* movement (1880s-1920s), the deaconesses branched out. They worked to improve life on earth for all poor, without evangelizing. They lobbied for new laws protecting women workers, establishing public health and sanitation services and improving welfare-support for poor mothers and their children. As their mission grew, volunteers were chosen for their energy and abilities more and less for their passion for Christ and His gospel. Thus the deaconess movement drifted away from the original objective and took their nursing out into the world—without a strong gospel message.

The deaconess movement peaked in about 1910, then slowly died. Women had realized they could serve in their own names and make money at it! Young ladies stopped enrolling in the deaconess schools, opting for nursing school instead. Gradually the deaconess missions changed their names as well; they became the hospitals of our cities today. St. Mary's Hospital, Deaconess Hospital—very few large cities escaped the imprint of the early work of these missionary women.

But when the movement waned, Christine continued serving in Christ's name. When offered the chance to make more money, Christine smiled, shook her head and said, "The Lord will provide." But some time after her thirtieth birthday, Christine Amalie Andersen met a young Oriental missionary named Sam Sasai. If she thought she would spend the rest of her life as a single deaconess, this handsome young man had other plans.

Sam Sasai asked Christine to become his wife.

Waiting for a Healing

In August of 1921, Sam and Christine walked into the Richmond County courthouse to ask permission to marry. He was 21 and she was 35 years old. She left her work as a deaconess, convinced that her Lord was leading her into a new life with Sam. But first, they had an obstacle to overcome. Sam was an Asian foreigner.

In 1921, if a woman married a foreigner, she lost her American citizenship. Loss of citizenship meant loss of many rights granted Americans, even the right to travel about freely. Had she waited until the Cable Act was passed in 1922, Christine could have married any foreigner, except an Asian, and kept her citizenship.

But she did not wait, and she chose Sam.

To make matters worse, they were in the state of Virginia. At this time many Americans—including the registrar of the state of Virginia—were fully bewitched by the teachings of eugenics. Virginia's registrar would later write to Walter Gross (director of Nazi Germany's Bureau of Human Betterment and Eugenics) praising his work and lamenting that Virginia hadn't yet accomplished as much as the Nazis had.

Many Americans considered interracial marriage *repulsive*. American lawmakers repeatedly proposed a nationwide law prohibiting intermarriage between whites and non-whites; so far it hadn't passed. Just one of the many defenders of this law was Representative Seaborn Roddenbery of Georgia. In his 1912 speech introducing his bill before the United States Congress, Roddenbery said:

> "Intermarriage between whites and" [non-whites] "is repulsive and averse to every sentiment of pure American spirit. It is abhorrent and repugnant to the very principles of Saxon government. It is subversive of social

peace. It is destructive of moral supremacy, and ultimately this slavery of white women to" [non-white] "beasts
will bring this nation a conflict as fatal as ever reddened
the soil of Virginia or crimsoned the mountain paths of
Pennsylvania .... Let us uproot and exterminate now this
debasing, ultra-demoralizing, un-American and inhuman
leprosy" (Congressional Record, 62d. Congr., 3d. Sess., December 11,
1912, pp. 502-503.)

Virginia law made it a felony for a white to marry any "non-white" between the years of 1691 and 1967. Nevertheless, Sam Sasai and Christine Andersen decided to try anyway. I suppose they prayed—a lot—on their way to the courthouse. On August 19th, 1921 this article appeared in the Richmond Times:

CUPID BRIDGES DIFFERENCE BETWEEN JAPAN AND U.S.

**Gen Sasai and Christina Anderson Happily Married When
Search of Statute Books Fails to Find Law to Prevent Union.**

"East is East, and West is West, and never the twain
shall meet," may be all right as poetry, but Rudyard
probably did not have romance and the Virginia law in mind
when he penned the lines. For while poetry is supposed
to be more lenient than law where love is concerned, the
Virginia law, stern and uncompromising in many respects,
has shot the bolt of poetic license and not only permitted
East and West to meet, but to marry at leisure.

When Gen S. Sasai, a Japanese missionary, 21 years old,
and Miss Christian Anderson, 35, also said to be engaged
in missionary work, sought a marriage license in this city
on Tuesday, it was deemed advisable to get a ruling from
the Attorney General's office before issuing the certifi-
cate. Leon Bazile, connected with the Attorney-General's
office, to whom the case was referred, could find no
statute prohibiting the union of an Oriental and an
Occidental.
Accordingly, the marriage license was issued and, it is
presumed, brought into existence another American-Japanese
entente cordiale, which may or may not have some effect
on President Harding's disarmament conference.

Apparently Sam and Christine received a mighty miracle, slipping into marriage under the radar. Meanwhile, the battle raged on. The state of Virginia passed a very strict eugenics law the next year, which allowed the forcible sterilization of racially-impure children as well as other classes of minorities. Then, just two-and-a-half years after Sam married Christine, the state passed the Racial Integrity Act, making laws against inter-racial marriage even stricter and the punishment more severe.

But now happily and legally married, Sam and Christine began their new life. They ministered together in a slum-mission and Sam found work washing windows. He might have lacked typical job skills, but he was an expert at dangling from ropes high in the air.

Later that year the couple was blessed with their first baby. If Samuel longed for a child with the fair Norse complexion, round rosy cheeks and pretty red hair of his mother—for the child's sake—he was disappointed. Little Sammy Jr. was even darker than his father, with eyes like coal and thick black hair.

In 1923 Christine was pregnant again. The family moved to Omaha that year; Nebraska was slightly less hostile toward inter-racial marriage. In Omaha a woman was only prohibited from marrying a Black or Oriental person; she could marry other non-whites, such as American Indians etc. Not that it was safe—about this time in Omaha, a Greek man was murdered by a mob for the crime of flirting with a white woman. And of course, Christine's husband *was* Oriental.

Life was hard. Perhaps Sam and Christine wished for a girl this time, a pretty little girl who might grow up and marry "White." At least their grandchildren could then escape this dangerous prejudice. Most likely they hoped their baby would have her mother's features.

But it wasn't to be.

On a hot, muggy night in July of 1923, Christine went into labor. After many long, painful hours, my daddy was born. They were blessed with another boy! He was strong and healthy, with smooth olive-hued skin and a wavy thatch of inky-black hair. They named him Joseph Andrew. Just a hint of his mother's looks softened his exotic features. If Christine noticed, her joy was brief.

Christine was sick. Each day her infection grew worse. But she wasn't a deaconess any longer, and a doctor's care and medicine were very expensive. Christine didn't have money. She had a busy toddler, a newborn baby and a foreign husband whose only skills were doing flips and swinging from ropes. And her husband was only 23 years old.

"If I'm meant to recover," she said, "the Almighty will have to heal me Himself." Christine gave her beloved husband his second son, and then she waited for her healing.

She died when my daddy was just three-months-old.

Sammy Jr. and baby Joseph were taken away from their father and put into the care of the Asylum for Orphans. They stayed just a short time until Christine's sister Hannah came from Wisconsin to take them home. With one mighty blow Sam lost his whole family, again.

Merry-Go-Round

When I was a child I went to a year of school in Idaho, in a logging town. One day after school I complained to my mother, "They call me an Indian and they push me down," I said. "They won't let me on the merry-go-round!"

My father was in the room. He looked up from reading the Wall Street Journal. He usually didn't comment; he was a very quiet man. However, this time he had something to say. "When I was a boy I fought my way to school every day," he said. "And at the end of every day, I fought my way home."

I never again complained about being picked on, at least not when my father was around. Less than six months later we moved to Gakona, Alaska; it was an Athabascan village at the junction of two rivers. In my first week at school the Indian girls, who all had the same last name, very seriously approached as a group, surrounded me and asked, "What are you?"

"I'm Hawaiian," I answered.

The group retreated, huddled and talked it over. After a few minutes they returned with broad smiles. "Hawaiians are Indians," the spokesperson said. That settled, we ran off to play together.

Daddy's childhood wasn't so simple. He was raised in Wisconsin, in a region filled with Norwegian dairy farmers. His Aunt Hannah and uncle Fred also ran a dairy farm, so he grew up milking cows. Daddy didn't like cows. The family tried to protect Daddy and Sammy Jr. by keeping their foreign father away and by hiding their heritage. They didn't adopt Daddy and Sammy Jr., but they changed their last name, giving them a French name. The boys were told to pretend they were American Indians. My father, always the rebel, told everyone he was Hawaiian instead. (I was eighteen-years-old when I finally found out I wasn't really Hawaiian.)

My father grew up bitter, angry and ashamed. He was ashamed of his mother's blind faith and angry that God didn't heal her. He resented his father even more—for leaving and for being Japanese. He didn't know how young Sam was when his sons were born, and he didn't know Sam's presence was seen as a danger to his sons. He only knew Sam was gone, and he wasn't respectable. Somebody told Daddy his father was a drunk bum. Maybe he was. Maybe Sam hit bottom and stayed there for a year or two. Sam's faith might have faltered after losing his little family.

Nevertheless, by 1925 Samuel Sasai was back in church. There he met a young woman named Pearl; they were married shortly after. Pearl was very different from Christine, but once again Sam's taste in women was unique. Pearl was so conservative and religious that many church-going people were offended by her—including my daddy's aunt Hannah, who was raising him. Hannah and Fred's family were respected churchgoers, but they once remarked that it was a shame Pearl didn't seem to understand that it was the 1920's— women were wearing their hair cut short and their dresses above their ankles now!

By the year 1930 work was hard to come by in America. The country was deep in depression and people were forced to move long distances to survive. Around this time Sam and Pearl set out for the coast of California, where there was a large Asian population and jobs. At the same time, Hannah heard there was work for Norwegians in Nova Scotia, Canada. She and Fred took my daddy and his brother Sammy to the neighbor's house, promised to return after making money in Canada and then drove away. Daddy was seven-years-old.

Daddy was a tender-hearted boy. Some people described Hannah as a *bear of a woman*, but daddy loved Hannah and called her *Mommy*. He looked up to Fred and called him Father. He'd never known anything but their love and their home. He told me later that the neighbor man was cold and cruel; he used his belt without reason. Daddy didn't understand the man and didn't know how to please him; he couldn't figure out why he and Sammy Jr. were punished so often and so harshly. Hannah and Fred were gone for a whole year. By the time Hannah and Fred came home, Joseph Andrew and Sammy Jr. were not soft-hearted boys anymore.

The next year, out in California, Pearl and Sam learned that they were going to have a baby. In 1933 their first and only child was born. They named her Virginia, Ginny for short. Ginny had her daddy's straight nose and tilted eyes and a lighter olive complexion. She was beautiful and strong; she was also born into a country in serious turmoil. Europe was engulfed in brutal unrest and America was quickly being drawn in. Americans distrusted Asians before, but now things were dire.

In 1936 Ginny was three-years-old and completely unaware of the chaos around her. She didn't know that it was often difficult for an Oriental person to make it safely down the street. She only knew she loved her daddy, and she missed him when he was out working. She waited cheerfully every day for her kind father to come home from work. Despite the weariness of a long day of work, he would walk in the door, pick Ginny up and carry her on his shoulders while she giggled. But then, a few days before Christmas, Sam was late coming home. Ginny cried, and Pearl tried not to worry. Pearl and Ginny waited . . . and waited some more. They prayed and eventually began asking around.

Has anyone seen Sam?

Did Sam come to work today?

They were told not to worry. Go back home and wait; he'll show up eventually. He was a reliable fellow. Surely he'd come soon; Pearl and Ginny were the light of his life. Sam adored his wife, and he was a devoted father; he wouldn't leave them. So they went back home and waited some more. But on December 24th, 1936, Sam Sasai was found under a bridge. He'd been murdered.

As soon as they could, Pearl and Ginny returned to the east, back to Pearl's family. If Pearl thought she'd raise Ginny alongside her brothers, she'd forgotten that Hannah was called a bear of a woman with good reason. Hannah's family now had more reason to be offended by ultra-conservative Pearl. Poor little Ginny's hair was also too long, and her dresses weren't cut short enough to be stylish. Hannah's family loudly pitied Ginny because she had to live with a killjoy like Pearl. In every photo of Pearl, her smile is wide, beautiful and welcoming. Nevertheless, Hannah's family coined a nickname for Pearl: *Old Stony Face.*

Unfortunately, Pearl and Ginny didn't spend as much time around the boys as they'd hoped to.

In 1939 Daddy turned sixteen-years-old, and Fred drove him south and put him on a bus. He went to stay with Hannah and Fred's grown son Hollis, so he could learn to be a welder. Meanwhile, Sammy Jr. had enlisted in the military (still calling himself an American Indian) and was preparing to go overseas. Less than two years later, Daddy joined the Air Force to learn to fly planes, and to kill *Japs.* Sammy Jr. was part of a huge invasion; he ended up freezing his feet in Italy, and I believe that ended his military career.

Eventually Pearl and Ginny realized that the eastern portion of America wouldn't tolerate a white woman who was the widow of a Jap, nor would they put up with her racially-impure child. So Pearl took Ginny and they moved back to the West Coast. Shortly afterward, the American government rounded up all of the known Asian and Asian-American families and put them into prison camps. Pearl and Ginny escaped notice, as did the little Indian boys, Joseph and Sammy Jr.

After the war ended, Sammy Jr. married, then became a widower and moved to Alaska where he pretended to be an Eskimo. At last he found relief from most of the racism that had plagued his and Daddy's lives. In Alaska Sam Jr. and a partner purchased a plumbing and heating company from the mayor, and they built it into the largest in the entire state. My father, handsome and charming Hawaiian Joe, also married—but he and his young wife were separated most of the time. Each time they decided to reunite (for a few weeks) his wife would get pregnant. They lived this way until they had six children, and then they stopped trying and got divorced. Daddy met my mother not too long after that; when they were sure it was true love, they took a motorcycle ride to the next state and got married. They had three girls; I was the middle child. Before I learned to read, Dad's brother Sam called from Alaska, saying he had a job for Dad. So we packed and prepared to move north.

By this time, Pearl and Ginny had settled in the desert of Arizona and Ginny was working at a military base, as a secretary. Or so she said. Ginny was a devoted daughter; she loved her mother and stayed with her until she buried her in 1960. After Pearl's death, Ginny wrote long letters to her brothers, saying goodbye. Then she set sail for Japan. She was going to be a missionary, or so the story goes. There are many sides to every story, and Ginny has a lot of secrets.

I love history and I also hate it. History teaches me that people are more complex than I could ever imagine. It teaches me to question my society and beware of the currents that it so readily floats upon. However, in so teaching, it warns me that I'm complex; I must question *even myself*, and beware of those popular currents that often send me drifting.

If I'm learning anything from my story, then (like Sam) I want Jesus to be my safety net if life knocks me down again and again. I want to have faith like Christine's, even if it doesn't seem to pay well. I don't want my life to repeat mistakes that have already done enough damage, so if ever I'm in Hannah's place, I'll use my *bear like* tendencies to protect the tender hearts in my care. I'll avoid judging others and seek to instill faith. hope, love *and understanding* into the hearts of children, even if their fathers truly are not safe to have around.

Someday, if I'm Arturo, I'll preach with a wide smile on my face and compassion in my voice, sharing the glorious gospel of God. I won't worry whether or not the blind man really wants to see. I'll share my soup with all who are hungry and brave. And I'll speak up, loud and clear, because the boys in the back might have crossed many oceans to hear this message!

And someday, if I happen to be me again . . . I pray Jesus will remind me what Spirit I'm of, before I call down fire. I'll swallow my pride and keep my beloved aunt perched on my sofa, staring at me. Sometimes life hurts, so I'll let her see me cry. And maybe, just maybe, I'll learn to *meow and hiss*, just to see what happens.

Grievous Appointments

So it happened that in 1988, just after my twenty-first birthday, I sat in the waiting room, waiting for some appointment, and I flipped through a magazine. As I read about the epidemic of abandoned drug-babies, their little faces stared back at me from the pages. It's hard to describe how much it hurt to read the article; I was the mother of one, but I'd just buried her. I was grieving the loss of my baby girl, my two-year-old daughter Holly who recently lost her fight with cancer.

I trusted God . . . I knew He was in control; I knew He was good; I knew He loved us. But Holly was gone; her body wasted away, and she had suffered . . . my kisses and hugs, even my prayers, didn't make the cancer go away. Oh, how she suffered . . . I was glad that her suffering had ended. Yet, now my arms were empty. Never again would I press my face into her soft brown hair and breathe in her beautiful baby-sweetness. Never more would I wake to the sight of her long-lashes resting on plump pink cheeks as we shared a pillow. I would never again hear her laughter, nor hear her crying for me; never be able to run to her, pull her into my arms and hold her near my heart. Never say again, "Hush, Mommy's got you. I'll protect you."

Meanwhile all those lovely little babies, withdrawing from drug addiction in cold hospital beds, stared from the magazine's pages, breaking my already broken heart. They were suffering alone. It was unfathomable. But what could I do to help an epidemic of suffering babies? I hadn t even been able to help my own child.

Maybe I had nothing to offer. I was powerless. But my Savior was powerful! The Bible that I'd begun reading commanded me to care for the orphan, the foreigner and the widow. Since He commanded it, shouldn't I at least try? I came to a decision that day: with

His help, I would do something to show these precious children that He wanted and loved them. Jesus created them to be His beloved friends, and I would bring them to Him.

I hadn't always been idealistic, but when I was nineteen I fell in love with Jesus. His love lit a fire in my heart; the darkness and fears that had been my childhood companions drifted away. He led me away from the old and familiar and into brighter paths. With my new perspective, I began ministering to pregnant teenagers, and I volunteered at our city's juvenile detention center. I had compassion on these kids in their rebellion and confusion. I also encouraged others in study of the Bible, and anytime I heard of a prison ministry meeting, I was there—taking notes! Oh, and I, who formerly was the black-sheep and rebel in my family, was now engaged to a young man who led worship, taught Bible studies and had a calling to be a pastor! No, none of this was the natural me. This new behavior and these concerns hadn't been part of me until I asked God's Holy Spirit to make my heart His home.

When Holly died I fell more fully into the arms of my only hope: Jesus. Life hurt; love hurt even more. I was barely an adult myself when I buried my baby girl. Nothing made sense except the love I felt when I prayed and the way the Bible beckoned to me. God loved us. He knew best. I had to believe this; the alternative was just too horrible. No, He hadn't forgotten about us, nor turned His back, nor found that His arm wasn't long enough to save. He was good. He was all powerful. He was the healer of my heart and the sustainer of my hope. I still had my life ahead of me; my daughter and I would meet again, when we both stood before the throne of God.

I determined to use my life to help the unloved children of the world and those behind bars. My passions were still burning brightly. This was a miracle. And with a devoted fiancé' who was in love with Jesus, I had extremely high hopes for a meaningful future.

Worse Things

$\mathcal{S}$ix months after Holly died, and just three months after I got married, I became a mother again. I was a shelter *house-mother* to six incorrigible teenagers.

When my husband and I married, we were young; almost any job would do. Neither of us had finished college yet, so I stood behind a counter making copies all day, and he washed rental cars. But after a few weeks, I begged God to find me a job with more purpose! I also wished to work with my husband. With this repeated prayer on my lips, I began hunting and we wound up in an interview to be house-parents at a Christian shelter for teenagers. The interview went well. Soon we moved into our new home-away-from-home. I was twenty-one, looked about fourteen and suddenly had six large teenagers calling me *Mom*.

It was the second time I'd ever found joy in my work. The first job I'd enjoyed had been teaching preschool. Not that I didn't like to work—when I first met my husband I was working three jobs. But I enjoyed those for their paychecks. Working with children brought me joy, even though it didn't pay well.

Imagine my shock when, just after my husband and I were married, he told me that he didn't want me to work outside the home. Could I go from three paychecks, *to none?* I wanted to make him happy, but how would I pay my bills? And what in the world would I do all day long while he was at work? Apparently there were many things we forgot to discuss before marriage. We both loved children, but I got another shock when he informed me that he hoped I'd have ten children with him! What had I gotten myself into? I responded by explaining that I wasn't planning to have any children; I was going to adopt! There were so many babies already born, waiting for loving parents! I expected him to understand and to feel the same way, once I explained it thoroughly a few times. When that didn't win him over, I tried explaining it thoroughly a few more times.

I was wrong. No matter how well I explained it, he didn't want to adopt; he wanted his own children, and he wanted me to be a stay-at-home wife, despite the fact that he had only a minimum-wage job. So (with much wrestling in prayer) I began a pattern of *giving my cares to Jesus* that I would later realize was one of the wisest choices I'd ever made. Longing to trust God and obey the Scriptures, I yielded my own desires and decided to do what my husband thought best—the Bible instructed me to *do marriage this way*. I let go of my fears about what we might eat and how we might pay the bills; God would provide.

Well, I thought I yielded. I suppose the house-parent position was a compromise. I was able to work with needy children, yet I was still there for my husband and still home, since we lived in the shelter. And with the tiny amount we were paid for the position, it was almost like I wasn't working at all! Yes, this was the perfect answer.

Yet, what a way to start life as a married woman. The children were very hard on our three-month-old marriage. These kids were pros, masters of the divide-and-conquer maneuver. I learned quickly to show a united front, to always support my husband 100% when the kids were listening. (We could talk about our differences in private.) Once they realized that he and I were always of "one mind" they gave up that tactic. However, I also learned (somewhat too late) that my husband's Bible knowledge far outweighed his trust in God. In my youth and ignorance, I had become *unequally yoked* without meaning to. (It would be many years before he stopped wrestling with God.) I was challenged on all sides to keep my eyes on Jesus and to see myself as the *bride of Christ;* Jesus loved me perfectly; this was what kept me going.

During my first month as a house-mom at the shelter, I drove fifteen-year-old Brandi to a run-down motel on the dirtiest side of the city to pick up her belongings. It was late at night and very dark; I prayed a lot while waiting for her to gather her things and say goodbye to the topless dancer she'd been sharing a room with. Brandi's time at the shelter was up, but the shelter-director and his family were taking her into their home. They had only a glorified porch to offer, but they'd transformed it into a charming, comfortable bed-room. Over the next six months or so, I watched the changes in Brandi and was encouraged. She was thankful to be included in their family and had put her faith in Jesus.

But we had countless teenagers come and go in the shelter, and Brandi was the only one who showed outward evidence of life-changing faith. Nonetheless, without any prompting or urging, most of the kids responded to at least one "altar call" and then gave their testimonies (on stage, before crowds) night after night at the churches we visited. The very convincing testimonies of these pre-teens and teens brought the crowds to tears and brought in large donations that were needed to keep the shelter running. It was a little disturbing; this was the first time I'd been around people who said all the right "Christian" phrases, but whose actions didn't align. As a fairly new believer myself, I begged God to make my faith real and cause me to bear much fruit.

Shelter life was always interesting; we attended countless churches, outreaches and Christian concerts. We went to see The Power Team give their evangelical show more times than I can remember. I learned to cook an army-sized meal in a tiny, sweltering-hot kitchen, while counseling sobbing teenagers and bandaging skinned knees. The kids laughed, cried, played many games and fell through walls (when roughhousing with my husband). Some kids fought; others snuck off together to make-out. We had teenagers who wet the bed every night and others who couldn't use the bathroom alone because they'd make themselves throw up their dinner. We had glue-sniffers and honor-students, runaways and throwaways, crimi-nals and innocents and many *in-betweens*. After our first year as full time house-parents, the group-home changed from a 30-day-shelter and became a long-term residential treatment center for girls only. During this transition, my husband and I also found out we were expecting our first child; we gradually became just part-time house-parents. After a few years we left for good. We had our own children to take care of, and the shelter environment wasn't ideal for babies.

During our time as house-parents, we had about twenty-five teens and preteens come and go. Each one was unique and memorable—each child taught me something that I needed to know. First on the list was Timothy, a cute, blonde twelve-year-old with movie-star looks. He taught me that (before I undress) I should thoroughly inspect the room, looking for gaps under or around the door, or a heater vent that might make me visible to whomever is lying on the floor, in the dark, peering into it from the other side. Timothy came to us because he molested the younger children in his adoptive family; I'm not sure how much he saw before we finally found out about the heater vent in our bedroom, but I promise it was much more than we meant for him to see.

Sixteen-year-old Kaliha taught me that not only the boys need to be watched. Kaliha was gorgeous, with exotic features. Her adoptive parents brought her to us after they caught her molesting their eleven-year-old son a few months after they brought her into their family. When she was in the group home, we put the couch across the hall to block travel between the girl's wing and boy's wing; the house-parents took turns sleeping on the couch. I don't know if that worked, but it was the best we could do.

I learned from fifteen-year-old Chantelle that even children who are adopted as infants might carry lasting baggage from their unfortunate beginnings. She came to us after her post suicide-attempt stay in the mental hospital. She blamed all of her problems on the fact that she was adopted, though she'd been in her adoptive family for as long as she could remember. She played the piano beautifully and was extremely well-articulated and well-educated. Her adoptive family may not have been everything she wanted, but it was obvious they'd imparted poise, excellent manners, education and a strong grounding in biblical knowledge. These qualities set Chantelle apart; if any of our shelter-kids have succeeded and had healthy lives, I believe she was the most likely candidate.

Sixteen-year-olds Aaron and George (who also came from an adoptive family) taught me that whether you're a tall, blue-eyed blonde whose brain damage is from taking acid and other drugs, or a short, sinewy Indian with Fetal Alcohol Syndrome, your reality is about the same. Both boys ran away from the shelter, which put them back in juvenile detention. A few years later, George got 25-years in prison when he tried to kill his girlfriend's family by burning their house down. I don't know about Aaron, but I wouldn't be surprised to hear that he's spent his life in prison, if he's survived this long.

From Teddy, a fourteen-year-old, skinny little blonde girl, I was reminded that children will do the stupidest things, even when they don't want to, just because nobody wants to challenge the coolest kid. One night Teddy coerced all of the children into running away, then made them sit in a parking lot all night, though they wanted to come home and go to bed. Being the ring-leader is all about attitude; brawn is rarely a factor.

Twelve-year-old Mikey taught me that nobody wants to stink; we should help them stop, if we can. Not only could Mikey's putrid shoe-odor clear a room in seconds, but he very frequently had even funkier gas (flatulence). Poor little Mikey, with his dishwater hair, clumsy body and average looks, wanted so badly for the older boys to like him; he began wearing deodorant—on his behind—hoping to mask the smell when he passed gas. Of course it didn't work, and when the boys found out, they had more reason to harass him.

Mikey was rare for shelter-life; he actually had a father, and he knew him well. However, since Mikey's mother had died, his dad remarried. The new wife didn't like Mikey. Although Mikey wanted to be a good boy, to please God and people, he became frustrated occasionally and then had rage issues. I really don't blame him; he was grieving the death of his mother. Mikey's life was probably more painful than if he hadn't had a father. His dad wouldn't bring him home—though Mikey begged with tears and great sobs. Dad wanted to keep his new wife happy and safe. Mikey stayed with us longer than most of the kids. At one point he left, because he was adopted by a family who had one child close to his age; they wanted a playmate for their son. Three months later, they brought Mikey back; their son didn't like him. However, when Mikey came back, he didn't stink anymore. We assumed it had been a dietary or other health issue. Regardless, the short-term adoptive mother cured Mikey of his stink, at least externally, and for that everyone was grateful.

Dark-eyed Sheena was very different from Mikey, but her story was similar. Her mother had remarried, and when Sheena accused her new stepfather of molesting her, Mom kicked Sheena out. I don't know if she was lying—it's not uncommon with troubled girls. But I learned from Sheena that there are things worse than living with an abusive step-parent; being rejected by your mother is one of those things.

Then ten-year-old Daniel came along, with his super-thick glasses and gap-toothed smile. This small boy taught me that some kids are unbelievably resilient. Though his mother was one of the craziest I've met, and she persistently made cruel parenting-mistakes, Daniel was unfazed; he was a smart, sweet, well-behaved kid. This cheerful, helpful boy got along with everyone he met; he didn't belong in a shelter for incorrigible children. Life isn't fair.

Sharing a Space

When our biological children were babies, we were licensed through the department of developmental disabilities as in-home caregivers for developmentally disabled adults (in our own home). It wasn't a calculated, career-driven decision; we already had Robby living with us. He was a twenty-something developmentally disabled man who had followed my husband home back in his college days (after my husband shared the gospel with him) and who we'd continued to take to church in the years since. Robby couldn't explain the gospel, or tell you *what* he believed, but he developed a very serious, strong belief in Jesus nonetheless.

After Robby's relatives all either passed away, couldn't or wouldn't look out for him, he came to live with us. I didn't mind sharing our space—he was a pleasant fellow—but he was literally eating us out of house and home. We were just a young couple with two small children and another on the way—and we lived in a one-bedroom apartment at that time. We decided to seek licensing for our sakes and for Robby's. Even though he should have been eligible for caretakers and group-home housing, Robby was not; his relatives neglected to sign him up with the state (as disabled) before he turned eighteen. Against odds, after many prayers and many months, and with the help of a Christian lawyer who volunteered his time, Robby was finally approved and funded; the state now guaranteed he would always have paid caretakers, even if we were not them.

We kept Robby, and a few other temporary visitors, during the next couple of years. Robby wasn't much trouble, as long as I kept the groceries hidden—if I wasn't watching him, he'd go through a week's-worth of food in one sitting, and then we'd end up with a clogged toilet and sewage flooding our apartment as Robby tried to "fix" his mess. Robby was friendly, quiet, and he loved our babies. However, he didn't understand why his little buddy, our toddler Corban, couldn't yet catch a softball when it was thrown right at him. Also, Robby knew I didn't want him picking up baby Caleb, who had just started crawling, so before I'd come around the corner and catch him holding Caleb, Robby would quickly put him down . . . the best he could. Robby had very poor large-motor-skills. He couldn't under-stand that babies won't land on their feet if you just let go in mid-air. Having Robby around required hyper-vigilance on our part. He also frequently woke me up in the middle of the night complaining that his shoulder hurt. I'd give him an Ibuprofen and send him back to bed. I figured he didn't really need it, but he'd keep asking (all night) if I didn't give in. When we weren't home, or if Robby was out around town, he'd call 911 if he had an ache or pain. If he were close to a hospital, he'd take himself to the Emergency Room. He called 911 frequently and spent even more time in the Emergency Room. If dinner wasn't ready on time, Robby went knocking door to door telling the neighbors that he was hungry. And . . . after he'd been with us for awhile, he started showing up for breakfast totally naked and then acting like it was an accident; he only did this when he was sure my husband had already left for work. These things were somewhat manageable, but when the police called because Robby was making obscene phone-calls and stalking a pretty little cashier, the mother in me was finally thoroughly unsettled. Although we loved Robby and he was like an endearing little kid (forever), we finally had to let him go to another caretaker. After that we kept in touch occasionally. A few years later he was diagnosed with Huntington's disease; eventu-ally he became very ill. I regretted the many times I hadn't taken his pain seriously. I was, however, glad to hear that Robby steadfastly held to his faith in Jesus, even though he couldn't say what he believed about Jesus. The disease finally took Robby's life when he was in his mid-thirties.

Around the time Robby left our home, we got a call from our old boss at the shelter. They had a thirteen-year-old girl named Maria who'd exceeded her time at the shelter, but still couldn't go home. "Can she come and live with you?" we were asked. So we brought home our first "foster daughter."

Maria was a joy to have around; she stayed only a few months and then went home. Parting with her was sad. She was a good girl, but her mother was mentally and morally deficient. Maria's mother was friendly, and she cared about her daughter, but she had a very low IQ and men-problems. What Maria's mom desired most in life was a man; any man would do. Because she couldn't get one to stay, Maria's mom had a series of rough boyfriends. Over the years I've seen this repeated many times. Dangerous men are drawn to women like Maria's mom; they want a free place to crash for awhile—no questions asked—and the creature-comforts included. I only hope this didn't include little Maria.

Maybe it's just my memory, but I can't remember a single thing that Maria ever did that needed correcting. She had large gaps in her education and asked many questions. But she was a fun, sweet child who got along very well with our small children. She cheerfully helped with chores, eagerly entertained our young kids with appropriate games and she seemed to genuinely like us. She thought I was cool and wanted to know if she could call me Mom when we were out in public.

Nonetheless, while Maria was still with us, maybe even a little before she came, I entered a dry time in my spiritual life. My husband had dropped-out of all ministry-activities a few years earlier, but I had continued, until now. My husband was a steady provider and a loving, devoted father; he enjoyed being a dad. Our children were adored, cheerful and healthy. I was very thankful for these things and more. Nevertheless, as a *husband* he wasn't doing well; marriage to this man made me very sad.

With much prayer that God would help me, I carefully followed the Bible's advice to me, especially to me as a wife, but one person following the recipe for a happy marriage does not make it so. I remember one year (as I was leading a women's Bible study group) I began to think I wasn't qualified to be a leader of anything. My marriage was heartbreaking, my home wasn't always happy, my kids were sometimes out of control. I thought maybe I was a hypocrite— although I knew of nothing against myself, no sin between me and God, I didn't want the women to have lives like mine! So I stopped leading the Bible study and stopped doing anything ministry-related, except for things like saying yes when asked to bring Maria home. Instead of looking for ways to shine the light of Jesus, I found other things to keep myself busy for a few years. I went to the gym to work out, and I played a lot of soccer. Then I formed a city-wide church basketball league and put myself onto a team that I felt might need the most help. I'm not a big help athletically, but I could encourage them; this one team consisted of mostly deaf women. However, it turned out that these deaf ladies were college basketball players. (I really hadn't known!) So my little team completely smoked the rest of the league and won the championship. It was a lot of fun, but God was trying to get my attention. He began showing me things and asking me questions . . . Yes, it was fun, but was it *edifying?* Yes, it was fun, but it was changing me, not in good ways. Being out playing, working-out and practicing much of the time put me in constant contact with young men who noticed me; there was always one following me around, being overly friendly and helpful. And then it got even worse; some of the women I played soccer and basketball with started showing an interest too. And my young husband was left at home with our children and new baby far too often; he was trying hard, but he wasn't a mom. For awhile I heard my Savior whispering that He wanted me to go home. It took me a moment or so, but at last I yielded.

When I stopped playing and went home, my spiritually-dry season ended. I was home schooling my children, doing 4-H with them (raising rabbits etc.) and back in college (distance-learning) when the Lord began to speak clearly to me again. Lo and behold, the Lord of Heaven and Earth filled my mind and heart with the very same things He'd shown me the last time we were in constant-contact. He rekindled my burden for the needy children of the world. I soon realized He was calling me to become a foster mother.

He'll Be Answering Soon

While I completed my foster-parent training, I gathered children's clothing and put it into little bins according to size. I had an extra bedroom, so I painted small teddy-bears on the walls, sewed cheerful curtains and filled the room with toys, dressers, a crib and a vintage wooden toddler bed with turned-legs. On the dresser I placed a lamp with teddy-bears that matched the walls. When the room was done, I was ready. Or so I thought.

I became licensed as a short-term foster home; children came to me first, and then if they didn't go back home, they'd move on to a regular foster home. Most of the time I only accepted children younger than my own; I was licensed for three, but usually took only one or two at a time, because we already had our own kids. Since we lived in a large city, our foster-home could have been filled to capacity at all times—but three was really too much; unless the need for a home was dire, and temporary, I declined.

As it had been at the shelter, now each foster child was unique, each with a different story and something new for me to discover. The joy of getting to know the children was constant, as was the sorrow of learning their needs. After a few years, I realized that foster parents were too isolated, so I began a support-group for them. We had *get-togethers*, a private/secure email sharing group and each other's phone numbers. For most of us, this was the first time we'd interacted with such like-minded people. The fellowship was incredibly encouraging.

Over the years I was licensed through more than one agency; each had their pros and cons. In my time as a foster mother I seldom grew weary; the interaction with the children and parents reminded me that my life and my story mattered. In the first ten years that I was licensed, about twenty-five children spent time in the little room with the teddy-bears on the walls; they slept in the crib or the wooden toddler-bed with the turned-legs. They played in the yard with our children, they accompanied us to church, and they sometimes slept in my arms—but only rarely. They were all unique, but most shared a few traits: they were traumatized because they'd just lost the only world they knew, and they wanted their mothers. Regardless of negative issues in their family, and regardless of how safe or fun my family and my home were, I was not Mom. They didn't want to be with me.

As sad as it sometimes was to see the trauma these children lived with, I never regretted fostering children. However, I do have two major regrets; I don't want to see others repeat these, so I'll share.

We once had a high-risk foster daughter; her father was a violent criminal (considered criminally-insane by his home-country who had deported him) with a history of kidnapping his very young daughter (the child in our care). This little girl's mother was a drug-addict and alleged prostitute. After the state accidentally published our home address (and sent the information to the biological father, who'd just been released from prison), evidence made us believe he began stalking us. We became highly cautious (maybe overly-paranoid) and I do slightly regret that our children had to live with "yellow alert" and "red alert" codes dictating their activities and where they could play each day. But I seriously regret that when this little girl's mother began calling me, I refused to speak to her. "Please talk to me," she begged, time after time when she'd call. "I'm not asking to talk to my daughter; I know I'm not good for her, and I'm very thankful that she's with you," she said. "But I'm dying, I just found out I have cancer. I hoped and prayed you would talk to me and tell me how my little girl is doing." Each time this poor woman called, I wondered if the girl's father was putting her up to the call, and if so, for what reason? What might their trick be? I let my paranoia get the better of me. The woman died of cancer soon after. I didn't talk to her about her child, and I didn't tell her about Jesus. I am so, so sorry.

My second regret is that when my biological children grew up, they had a very negative (and wrong) impression of babies and small children, because they hadn't spent enough time around happy, healthy babies and toddlers. Instead, my kids grew up amidst a steady stream of toddlers and preschoolers who were abused, neglected, born drug-addicted and screaming . . . they might not have been able to say the word, but my foster children were usually crying for their mothers. Because our biological children were close in age to each other, they couldn't remember what a healthy, nurtured baby or toddler in his own mother's arms looked like. This caused some confusion and hesitation when they were young-adults considering starting their own families.

If I could start over again, these are things I would try to correct. However, we rarely get do-overs.

But even amidst our mistakes and imperfect existences, there's beauty. There's always evidence that God is good and that He's moving mountains; His light is always shining, somewhere. Whether we notice it or not, it's there, waiting to be seen.

Yes, my daddy was probably an alcoholic, but he was the most caring, responsible alcoholic I've known. Someone instilled biblical principles into him early on, and he never let them go. He believed that our welfare deserved his body, heart and soul; while we were growing up, we never lacked for anything—meanwhile he constantly sent child-support to the many children from his broken first marriage. He was a reliable man, proving the rewards of hard work. The worst thing I ever saw my daddy do, even when *pickled out of his mind*, was when he opened the Gideon's Bible in a motel and read it to us. I think I was nine-years-old; it wasn't long after I'd gone to church camp and asked Jesus into my heart. When I got home from camp, I compared the message I'd heard there to what I knew about my father, and I concluded that Daddy was going to hell. So I started praying for him every night, although I didn't think he'd ever admit he needed a savior, or that he should stop sinning. I cried about it too. But then one night my handsome father stumbled into the motel room after a late night out, and he picked up the Gideon's Bible. "I'm going to read to my girls!" he announced, a little too loudly. Mom tried to pull him away from it; "Go to bed, Joe," she said. He refused. My sisters and I sat up in bed and listened intently; we'd never seen our daddy with a Bible before! Mom would often drop us off at church, or let the church bus come and take us—sometimes she even dressed up and went along. But not Daddy; he didn't like Christians. But now he picked up a Bible and opened it, then he started to read out loud. He grinned and shouted and waved his arms around; he jumped up and down in his snake-skin boots. He read with a booming voice and a strange accent. Mom rolled her eyes and shook her head. "Joe, go to bed," she said. Daddy didn't seem to like the first page he chose, so he stopped after a few sentences and tried another page, then another . . . just a sentence here and there . . . and then he stopped smiling, and he stopped reading. We squealed and giggled and jumped up and down like he had, encouraging him. But he remained silent. "Go to bed, Joe," Mom said. After a moment, Daddy set the Bible down and went to bed. I never saw him pick up a Bible again. That was the worst thing my dear, lost daddy ever did.

Dad's sister Ginny made peace with God, but their heritage haunted her. When Ginny went to Japan, she tried in vain to find her relatives. She searched for over ten years and then came home. No one but God will ever know my grandfather's true name, nor who his grieving parents were. We only know he wasn't exactly G. Samuel Sasai. Nor was Sammy Jr. an Eskimo, but it served him well until his death; then his wife and children finally learned that they weren't an Eskimo family. Daddy, charming and beloved Hawaiian Joe, who was no more Hawaiian than his Indian-turned-Eskimo brother, may have died a lost man. God is good and patient. He gave Daddy eighty-two years to notice Him; time and again the Almighty manipulated circumstances to shine the light for my dad. The Savior of the world was calling out to him, "I'm your Father, I'm your Creator, and I died to show you how much I care . . ." In his last years, Daddy's most frequent visitor was a man who just happened to move in next door and who just happened to be a pastor. God only knows if my rebel father changed his opinion, perhaps at his last breath. Only God knows many things.

Just as with physical identities—Eskimo, Hawaiian, Japanese etc.—a person's spiritual identity isn't always what they claim. The Bible says, "The sins of some people are plain to see, and their sins go ahead of them to judgement; but the sins of others are seen only later." (1 Tim. 5:24 GNB) We might suspect something's wrong, if we're looking for the fruit of the Spirit and seeing none, but only God knows what's really going on.

When our biological children were High School age, my dear wind-swept husband finally stopped wrestling with God. He'd always said the correct Christian phrases, so no one actually realized he was fighting, until he surrendered. It's impossible to grasp just how fiercely the whirlwind has been stalking your family, until it suddenly stops and everything grows still. Peace, calm and deliverance overtook our family when he raised his white flag to Jesus. There was an explosion of blessings and answered prayers. Since that time the Spirit of God took up residence inside my husband and transformed him; he's become the cheerful, humble and wise, servant-hearted man God wanted to create all along—of course, he wouldn't have gotten his hip knocked out of place if he'd thrown in the towel right away; you don't brawl with God and win, and you don't keep it up for that many years without getting a few scars.

Since that time our family has enjoyed restoration and rebuilding. We've gone many places hand in hand; we've seen revival and miracles, and hopefully we've spread some love and shone a little light.

My life, and especially my trials, have taught me many things. At the top of the list is that the best way to deal with worry is to stop running, turn around and look at it. Examine it, and then give it to Jesus. Most of the things I've been tempted to worry about actually ended up happening to me, after I followed God where He wanted me to go. Following Jesus requires sacrifice. When I worry, I'm telling God there are things I won't accept in MY life. Yet, it isn't my life; He bought me. Now this is HIS life. So I say, Yes, Lord. Whatever. I trust you; if you let me get hurt, I believe you'll heal me afterward. There's a huge difference between trusting God enough to pray about things and trusting God enough to step forward.

While we take forward steps, we've watched our children grow up, get married and produce lively little miniatures of themselves. We've traveled to sing and preach where we're asked to; I've stood fearlessly (with trembling hands and knees) before crowds, singing and proclaiming that they should embrace Christ. (I haven't yet warned them about communism; I'll get to that later.) I've met beautiful brothers and sisters in Christ from many nations (I didn't eat their food, but at least I didn't hiss and meow at them); I accidentally gave my favorite gloves to the homeless lady, when I only meant to give her my extra-coat. (My cherished gloves were clipped onto the coat's zipper. Yes, I repented of my selfish attitude; who needs the gloves more?) I've witnessed more miracles than I can remember, more than I could've imagined; I've watched God change demon-possessed drug addicts into serene Sunday School teachers; I've become bitter, and I've grown soft again; I've been warned in dreams about trials I was about to face, and I've walked through the fire with Jesus and come out the other side without smelling like smoke. I've watched God answer every one of my prayers, except those that I know He'll be answering soon.

And, I'm sorry to tell you, I've been to jail to sing about the grace of God to the Micronesians who didn't make it to church because they got caught beating their wives. That, my friends, is part of my story — but every story has many sides. As you live your own story, answering the cries of the world's neediest children, you might encounter the dark side. Therefore, if you forget everything else I've said, please remember these two things:

1. The circus doesn't turn out well-mannered children, but they need Jesus too.

2. Someone might have crossed many oceans to hear you share the message of Christ. So speak out loud and clear, smile widely, and don't worry if they're on the back row for quite awhile.

Your Story

Introduction to Part Two:

Some information in the following chapters also appears in my shorter adoption book, *This Means War*. If you've read it before, consider this a reminder; these biblical concepts are vital for the well-being of your family and they lay the foundation for the chapters which follow.

God Have Mercy:
Helping Children to Come Out

In Bible interpretation scholars often apply "the Rule of Firsts"-taking special notice of the first time something appears in Scripture. This mention is always significant; it sets the precedent for interpreting the concept when it appears again. Keeping the *Rule of Firsts* in mind, here's the first time the word *orphan* (or fatherless) appears in Scripture:

[The Lord says,] "Do not take advantage of a widow or an orphan. If you do and they cry out to me, I will certainly hear their cry. My anger will be aroused, and I will kill you . . . " (Exodus 22:22-24a NIV)

Over forty other Bible Scriptures outright proclaim, or clearly imply, that God defends orphans (along with widows). If we abuse, neglect or cheat the fatherless, we arouse God's wrath. However, one Scripture declares that Almighty God, *who is love,* will at some time turn away from even the orphans. He'll refuse to show them pity.

". . . he will not show pity on any of the widows and orphans, because all the people are godless and wicked and everything they say is evil."
(Isaiah 9:17b GNB)

This prophecy was fulfilled after the ancient nation of Israel turned away from their God, ignored His warnings and calls to repent and was eventually destroyed by enemies. Because of her covenant with the God of Abraham, Isaac and Jacob, Israel had been divinely blessed and invincible; she was surrounded by God's *hedge of protection*. But she turned away to follow idols, heaped up sins and ignored the prophets and warnings—even the obvious removal of the hedge. Total destruction of her northern kingdom followed (in 722 B. C.), and in 586 B.C. the survivors of Judah's decimation were carried into captivity.

But many years later, on April 30, 1789, another newly formed nation dedicated themselves to this same God. Intent upon patterning their nation after ancient Israel, they performed a ceremony and took vows binding them to be faithful to God. Inside a church—their *ground of consecration*—they prayed as Solomon had upon Israel's Temple dedication. This also was spoken over their new nation that day:

". . . the foundation of our national policy will be laid in the pure and immutable principles of private morality . . . . . . The propitious smiles of Heaven can never be expected on a nation that disregards the eternal rules of order and right which Heaven itself hath ordained." [1]

The results were tremendous: God placed a hedge of protection around this new nation; she became the most powerful and blessed of all. She was invincible. Yet in time, this nation also turned away from God and denied her vows. She shamelessly heaped up sins— mocking both *private and public morality*—spilled the innocent blood of her children and lusted after gold and other idols. Just as Israel before her, she entered a season of warnings, which were ignored. Next, the hedge of protection began to crumble. The first breaches were so tremendous, the collapse was heard around the world. On the exact ground where the founding fathers dedicated the nation to God, she was devastated by terrorists—it was "the worst terrorist attack in world history." In 1789 when this nation took her vows to God, it was within a small church called St. Paul's Chapel; at that time *Ground Zero*, the site of the future terrorist attacks, was an empty field next door, which belonged to the church. Unaware of these facts, the terrorists who staged the attack gave their plans a code-name: *The Big Wedding*.

The nation is, of course, the United States of America. "No people can be bound to acknowledge and adore the Invisible Hand which conducts the affairs of men more than those of the United States," the first president declared. [1] Not only was America bound by vows to acknowledge God, but also to *adore* Him.

In Isaiah Chapter Nine, when the Lord removed the hedge and stirred up Israel's enemies to attack her, instead of repenting, the leaders responded:

"The bricks have fallen, but we will build with dressed stones; the syca-more trees have been cut down, but we will replace them with cedars."
(Isaiah 9:10 ISV)

Likewise, on September 11, 2001, after the World Trade Center fell, America also failed to take this removal of protection to heart. Instead of calling the nation to turn from unfaithfulness and return to her God, leaders responded by publicly quoting the prophecy of Isaiah—*word for word, multiple times*. "The bricks have fallen, but we will build with dressed stones; the sycamore trees have been cut down, but we will replace them with cedars,"[2] they swore. "We will rebuild! We're going to come out of this stronger than before. . ."[3] "We remember, we rebuild, we come back stronger!"[4] "We will rebuild!" newspaper headlines echoed repeatedly. [5] They didn't know that they claimed a prophecy of judgement upon a nation who had broken her vows. They failed to understand the prophecy in context:

8 "The LORD has sent a plague against Jacob, and it will fall on Israel;
9 and all of the people were evil—Ephraim and the inhabitants of Samaria—saying proudly with arrogant hearts:
10 'The bricks have fallen, but we will build with dressed stones; the sycamore trees have been cut down, but we will replace them with ce-dars.'
11 But the LORD has raised adversaries from Rezin against him, and he stirs up his enemies—12 Arameans from the east and Philistines from the west—and they devour Israel with open mouths! "Yet for all

this, his anger has not turned away, and his hand is still stretched out, ready to strike."

13 "But the people have not returned to rely on him who struck them, nor have they sought the LORD of the Heavenly Armies. 14 So the LORD has cut off from Israel head and tail, palm branch and reed in a single day — 15 the elder and the dignitary is the head, and the prophet who teaches lies is the tail. 16 For those who guide this people have been leading them astray, and those who are guided by them are swallowed up.

17 Therefore the Lord does not have pity on their young men, and has no compassion on their orphans and widows, because each of them was godless and an evildoer, and every mouth spoke folly. "Yet for all this, his anger has not turned away, and his hand is still stretched out, ready to strike."

18 "For wickedness has burned like a blaze that consumes briers and thorns; it sets thickets of the forest on fire, and skyward they swirl in a column of smoke. 19 From the wrath of the LORD of the Heavenly Armies the land has been scorched, and the people have become like fuel for the fire; no one will spare his neighbor. 20 They cut meat on the right, but they're still hungry, and they devour also on the left, but they're not satisfied; each devours the flesh of his own children. 21 Manasseh devours Ephraim, and Ephraim devours Manasseh; together they are against Judah. "Yet for all this, his anger has not turned away, and his hand is still stretched out, ready to strike." (Isaiah 9:8-21 ISV)

True to her word, America proudly rebuilt. Part of her national makeover was the passing of more laws *disregarding the eternal rules of order and right which Heaven itself hath ordained.* And she boldly built a new *tower* to replace the World Trade Center. Spending 4 billion dollars, America constructed a monument to herself; it was the most expensive building in the world at the time. At 1,776 feet (signifying the year America signed her *Declaration of Independence*) this symbolic tower was also the tallest building in the Western Hemisphere; she named it the *One World* Trade Center. A symbolic cornerstone ("dressed stone" from the quarry) was brought in and called the "Freedom Stone." The sycamore that fell within the courtyard of St.

Paul's Chapel was replaced with the same *genus* of tree spoken of in the prophecy of Isaiah 9. The new tree was dedicated as "the Tree of Hope." Workers engraved the new One World tower with graffiti symbolizing "rebirth and resilience." America marched forward in the footsteps of ancient Israel, prior to her total destruction. But these actions also aligned with future prophecies of a rebellious *One World* government that arises in the end times.

Oh, little Christian, listen and take heed! These facts apply to us! It is within this context, this exact prophecy — this judgment upon a nation that has turned from her God — that God declares *"he will not show pity on any of the widows and orphans, because all the people are godless and wicked."*

Have the children of our age become so godless and wicked that God cannot tolerate them? Will the children that *I raise,* and that *you raise,* fail to receive His pity and protection, because we have not turned them from the sin and guilt of this society? May it never be! Please stand with me, saying, "Not on my watch!" Beloved brothers and sisters, regardless of what age we live in, God has called us to do more than just feed and clothe the orphans. It's not enough to lift them out of the ashes that they might become like America's rebel sons and daughters — sharing the pride, riches and ungodly lifestyle of our society, thereby sharing her guilt. The voice from heaven declares, *"Come out of her, my people, so that you may have no part in her sins and in her punishments."*

Our mission, if possible, is to turn orphans away from the wickedness within society — to encourage and enable them to be separate — so they will receive God's mercy. To do this, we must first *come out* and *turn away* ourselves.

"And so the Lord says, 'You must separate yourselves from them. Have nothing to do with what is unclean, and I will accept you. I will be your father, and you shall be my sons and daughters, says the Lord Almighty.'" (2 Corinthians 6:17-18 GNB)

"Put aside the deeds of darkness and put on the armor of light. . . . Clothe yourselves with the Lord Jesus Christ." (Romans 13:12b, 14a NIV)

1: Excerpts from George Washington's first inaugural speech, April 30, 1789
2. Senate Majority Leader Daschle, September 12, 2001; John Edwards, September 11, 2004; President Barack Obama, February 24, 2009
3. New York City mayor Rudy Giuliani, September 11, 2001
4. President Barack Obama, June 2012, writing on a steel beam of the One World Trade Center
5.CBS News, CNN, MSNBC, The Guardian, National Public Radio, Times Online, Fox News, Al Jazeera, Drudge Report, Associated Press, New York Times

What's Your Problem?

So what's your story? Most people do not adopt. They do not take in foster children, nor do they work with street children. Why are you different? What brought you here, to where you'd even consider doing this?

Think about that, pray about it. Write down your answers—call it your *List of Reasons*. Then put your list in a very safe place; never let it go. Look at it every time you get discouraged—even if what I'm about to write discourages you; especially if what I write discourages you, because that's not my goal. Take out your List of Reasons, hold it up to God who gave it to you (as often as necessary) and ask the Lord of Heaven and Earth to set your face like flint in the way He would have you to go.

FIRST, THE BAD NEWS

I met a pretty, young-looking grandmother the other day; she was sobbing and wanted prayer for her grown son, Will, and his wife, Becky—they had a tough decision to make. But she especially wanted prayer for her five-year-old granddaughter.

Will and his wife Becky were Christians, and they had just the one little girl. Because of their faith—in response to the sacrificial love that flowed from Jesus to them—and because the Lord had blessed them with extra room and plenty of good things to share, Will and Becky decided to help orphans. They began a long process, which eventually resulted in them adopting a very handsome nine-year-old boy, from South America, called Julio.

Will and Becky were prepared for the difficulties of new family-dynamics; they were patient and encouraging while Julio learned a new language, in a strange environment. Julio was a charming child and they were very proud of him for his accomplishments; his life had been harsh, but his resiliency was amazing. Granted, they were fairly surprised to find out that Julio's age had been miscalculated by the orphanage. Their own doctor believed Julio was closer to twelve-years-old, at least. Oh well, they'd heard it was a common mistake. But Will and Becky were bewildered, devastated and totally caught off-guard when, after Julio had been in their home six months, they walked in on him while he was raping their five-year-old daughter.

As the little girl's grandmother told me this story, I could only nod my head. I've heard similar stories so many times, I almost expect it. (American statistics say an estimated one in 20 boys or men sexually abuse children, while only one in 3,300 females molests children. Thirty-percent of molesters abuse a step, foster or adopted child, and forty-percent abuse the child of a friend or neighbor.)[1] I sometimes wish I could return to the days when I didn't know that these things happen. But for this dear grandmother and her family, it was all new; they almost couldn't believe it had actually happened. Now, on top of their grief and the task of helping their daughter to heal, they had to decide what to do with Julio. They were horrified, grieved and distraught on their daughter's behalf, but they also loved Julio. They felt honor-bound to take care of this little lost boy; *they had promised to be his forever family!* Because of their concern and the tremendous guilt they felt when they considered abandoning him, they were contemplating building a room for Julio *in their garage.* Against the grandmother's frantic wishes, Will and Becky were seriously considering running back and forth, from house to garage, parenting both children while keeping them separate. I prayed for the family. I wish I could tell you what they decided, but I don't know.

What would you do, if that were your story?

About those rose-colored glasses of ours: after years pondering, I've finally concluded that there is a way to have an experience with orphans, foster children, street children (and other groups of the neediest people) that's filled with joy (warm-fuzzies, happy little bunnies, etc.) and remains unblemished by sin and other unsightly rubbish. Can you guess what it is?

Don't adopt, don't do foster care, and (whatever you do) don't go near the street children!

By not engaging them, personally, long-term, we get to keep our idealized view of orphans. We can also keep our idealized view of ourselves, because we'll avoid putting ourselves into really difficult situations where we might discover that we're not nearly as clever, patient nor loving as we thought we were!

Orphans and abused children are so easy to love when they're just pictures on the Internet—or if we just visit them occasionally, bringing gifts. As we gaze at their cute faces, we experience overwhelming feelings of compassion. It feels so right to care! But it's quite another matter when they live in our homes; when we cannot even walk into our front yard without locking our office, bedroom and any other room that holds something we might want to keep. It's something else indeed when even that doesn't work because they've learned to pick locks. And it's a whole different story when we're afraid to close our eyes at night because we fear what might happen to the baby while we're sleeping.

If you don't want to know how hard it can be, then don't bring home wounded children. But if you can accept it, be bold, be brave, and prepare to be disappointed—in others and mostly in yourself—then take a step of faith.

(I really hope you can, but if your household isn't ready yet, I'll understand. There are many ways to help children; bringing them home is only one way. Orphan-advocates are always needed to support those who are raising the world's neediest children.)

BAD NEWS, CONTINUED

Just like ministry in any other form, (if you're really sharing the gospel) Christian adoption is a declaration of war in the spirit realm; you're challenging an unseen enemy who is stronger and smarter than you.

If you're going to succeed, you must realize the significance of your actions in light of eternity. By meddling in broken lives, in the name of Jesus and with the power of His love, you are storming the gates of hell. Lives don't get broken on accident—this is Satan's handiwork. Now you're attempting to undo his work, to rescue these lost souls and to bring them to safety, healing and the light of the truth. Your only weapons are prayer, the power of the Holy Spirit and the knowledge of God and His Word. (If this doesn't make sense to you, go to the back of the book and work through the Basics Bible Study first, praying that God will indwell you and explain it to you.)

If you've never thought much about "spiritual warfare," you're destined to learn the hard way. I'm not talking about the common myths and misconceptions called spiritual warfare, but the real thing as seen in the Bible—in the life of Jesus, the apostles and other believers.

Pray and ask God to help you see the unseen battles you're in!

Study the Scriptures as if your life depends upon knowing them! If you haven't been actively fighting a spiritual battle, then you've been losing. And if you haven't even noticed the battle, maybe you're no longer in a spiritual battle (prisoners-of-war do not engage in battle, nor do *dead* people).

Parents who've read what I'm about to tell you suggest that you stop and pray right now; ask God to help you make it past the diversions and finish reading this information. Similar to when they read their Bibles, each time they picked this book up to read, they were distracted. Just like clockwork: the phone rang, there was a knock at the door, their spouse suddenly needed to talk, the dogs started barking or the kids threw up. Some parents became suspicious and started reading just to see what would go wrong next!

Satan doesn't fight fairly and this battle is serious!

Your faith is powerful because the One you've placed your faith in is powerful. If you follow the Holy Spirit toward orphans, foster children or street kids, sowing the seeds of God's Word as you go, He'll make His seeds grow—He promises His Word won't return void, but it will accomplish His purposes (Isa. 55:11). There will be a harvest of souls! People will be saved, set free from their sins, delivered from the power of darkness and brought into His glorious light; they'll enter the kingdom of heaven and live forever in paradise, instead of burning in hell! *Just because you bothered!*

Think about that.

But when you go out to sow these seeds, there'll be someone waiting for you. He'll be disguised as an angel of light; he'll oppose you and try to destroy you. Therefore, you must be fully equipped. Read the gospel accounts in the Bible and you'll see that each time Jesus went in to a town or region, He did the same two things—regardless of where He was. Do you know what they were?

One: He healed sick people.
Two: He freed people from harassment, oppression, and possession by evil spirits.

Have you ever known anyone who was sick? That's a ridiculous question; we must realize that harassment, oppression and possession by evil spirits are just as common as physical sickness. And if Satan went after even Jesus, he won't leave *little old you* alone. Once you see this, you'll be ready for the attacks you and your family are already experiencing.

Regarding abused, neglected or otherwise needy children, understand that (usually) Satan has blinded and captured their biological parents. This is why these children ended up on the streets, in foster care or needing an adoptive family. Satan blinded these parents with lies and enslaved them to destructive sins, devastating what should have protected and nurtured helpless children: their families. Now he intends to destroy the children as well. Enter you! Joyful little you, wearing your cross, *Jesus-Loves-You* T-shirt and your rose-colored glasses, bringing gifts—with your smiling, idealistic family in tow. *What are you doing here? These children aren't your responsibility. Why have you come!?* (Remember your answer; hold on to it!)

You're in a dangerous spot, and you're meddling. Not only are you meddling in the physical realm, but in the spiritual. You're attempting to enter *Satan's territory* and walk away with (what he views as) his property—you're starting this fight, and *you didn't even know it.* Don't think he'll let you take them without a battle. You may be trying to help a child whose biological family has experienced centuries of darkness and possession. Satan will attack you individually, as a family or even as a church. Be prepared (put on the full armor of God) and you can stand; be caught off-guard and he'll damage your family, your church, your witness and your threat to his kingdom-of-destruction. (Hint: Jesus is the armor!) The rest of this chapter will supply you with practical tips before we get into the issues and challenges typical with orphans and otherwise neglected children.

Ready, Mom? Please take this seriously and beware of these things in your life!

These are some common ways he specifically attacks Moms:
Your enemy will make you sick and tired to cripple you as a mother.

Your enemy will try to isolate you from godly influences by keeping you away from church, Bible study and times of fellowship.

Your enemy will send worldly people to teach you lies, telling you they're the latest, greatest methods. (Many worldly people will claim to be "christians.")

Your enemy will tempt you to shift your focus away from the kingdom of God and onto your self, your career, your worthiness, your body image etc.

Mom, you must be on your guard. Your enemy has an ally inside of you—it's your own nature. Do you hear me? The natural thing for you to do is *lose this battle*. But for the sake of the children, and your own soul, you must win it. You're the nurturing force of the family and you're the gate-keeper.

Be on your guard or you'll stop looking to Jesus (your commander and life-force); you'll focus on your ill health, the children's bad behavior and an ever-increasing desire to learn new and improved methods of parenting. Instead of reading the Bible and seeking God, you'll look to people who have an ungodly world view for help and answers. Instead of spending time nurturing your relationship with your husband (this is the backbone of the family), your attention and energy will all go to the child or children.

Or you might forget you're the *bride of Christ* and elevate your mortal husband's worldly desires or bad example above the perfect desires and example of Christ.

Ready, Dad? Please take this seriously and beware of these things in your life!

Dad, Satan has an ally inside of you as well. And the Bible doesn't say that you're *supposed to be* the spiritual leader of the family. Whether you're falling or standing, *you already are the spiritual leader*. Where you let yourself go—even secretly—Satan will assume permission to try and take your family also. If you give yourself permission to be proud, your powerful nature will enslave you to lust and anger, destroying you and the lives around you.

These are some common ways Satan specifically attacks Dads: Your enemy will try to keep you away from your family so they're not protected, encouraged nor taught through you. This often comes in the guise of a "better job" offer, more hours at work or a job that makes you so tired you're hardly awake, let alone praying fervently for your family.

Your enemy will try to keep you away from church, Bible studies and other times of fellowship with godly men; he wants you isolated so you're easier to defeat and so you're not encouraging others. (Or he'll send you worldly-minded friends who claim to be "christians.")

Your enemy will feed you a false gospel through the preaching of proud, deluded men who condone sin in their lives, and in yours. They preach, "God understands that you're not perfect, He only wants to see that you're trying to follow Him." This is called "striving in the flesh." It's the same as trying to be justified by keeping the Law of Moses; it depends upon your human effort (which produces only filthy rags in God's sight). It leaves you floundering, controlled by your desires and on the road to destruction. Instead, the Bible teaches you to admit you need help, admit that a holy God requires obedience and purity, and then die to your flesh (deny your feelings) and surrender your will to God—asking Him to fill you with His Holy Spirit and to empower you to miraculously live the life He desires for you.

Your enemy may also tempt you with a me-centric false version of Christianity. Instead of living to know, obey, love and bring glory to Jesus, you ll do "Christian work" to feel good about yourself. Instead of denying yourself and humbly serving, you'll strive to be noticed and fight for positions of leadership. Beware: God is not mocked and He will not share His glory.

Your enemy will tempt you to let your guard down regarding morality: he'll say it's okay to expose yourself to ungodly TV shows, movies, magazines, games and conversations, etc.; it starts mild and then progresses as you become dull and desensitized. Yes, fiery darts come to all believers, but the Bible instructs us to take every thought captive to the obedience of Christ and to remove ourselves from tempting situations. Your enemy counts on you to ignore those commands and warnings. Once you allow Satan's flaming arrows to lodge in your mind and burn, he'll increase the strength of the temptations, pushing you toward sin. If you choose to sin, you'll either confess (and your family will be damaged or destroyed) or you'll begin to hide the truth. If you're lying and hiding your sin, you'll be separated from God and His power. Your trust and relationship with your wife will become diseased and eventually die. While the above is going on, Satan will whisper to your spouse, telling both truth (about your sin) and lies, driving a wedge between you.

Yes, these things happen to all believers, but the spiritual attack increases when you involve yourself in ministry—the battle for souls. Many believers publicly fall, others privately. Countless families have been destroyed and ministries dissolved.

But wait! *Isn't God all-powerful?* How can Satan do all of this damage to God's people? Isn't God in control of a believer's life?

Yes, He is. *But our God is a consuming fire.*

God is testing your faith to prove whether it's genuine, or not. If you don't prepare yourself and guard against these things, you'll fall into the trap of the faithless. Once you've fallen, unless you repent and confess your sins to God *and to the person you've wronged*, you'll remain trapped. The power of the Holy Spirit will leave you. You'll stop praying for your family, you'll become a poor example, or worse, and the children will no longer have a covering of spiritual protection.

"In the paths of the wicked lie thorns and snares, but he who guards his soul stays far from them." (Proverbs 22:5 NIV)

Think that's bad? In case that wasn't enough, Satan will attack your family through the children you try to help:

Just as in the Vietnam War, as American soldiers were unprepared when the enemy sent little children into their camps carrying grenades, Satan uses needy children to carry a bomb into the Christian family. The child is a victim, but so is the family, especially if they're unprepared.

Some of the common challenges needy children come with are:

Fetal alcohol effects: Learning disabled, with very little impulse control due to alcohol related brain damage.

Inability to bond: Extreme difficulty learning to return love or to consider others.

Sexually inappropriate behaviors: Sometimes learned through exposure and abuse, sometimes due to brain damage/lack of impulse control.

Learning disabilities: Possibly temporary if caused by neglect, but permanent if due to alcohol or drug exposure.

Violent tendencies: Often due to exposure to drugs inutero, neglect in infancy, emotional trauma or inherited mental illness.

Mental Illness, bizarre or self-destructive behavior: Difficult to diagnose; many temporary, emotional or spiritual conditions mimic or produce these.

Extreme manipulative skills: Previously neglected or abused children often "divide and conquer" as a means of getting their way. They may purposely try to turn family members against each other; many will use false accusations of abuse or molestation as a tool or means of revenge.

I pray that after reading this, you still want to foster, adopt or love the street kids. As a Christian on the offensive, you're marked by the enemy. There's a price on your head (a bulls-eye on your forehead, if you will). Yet I pray this information will not discourage you but will make you more determined to fight for the lives of the lost and lonely. This fight can be won! How do we win? By humbling ourselves and submitting to God!

"You adulterous people, don't you know that friendship with the world is hatred toward God? Anyone who chooses to be a friend of the world becomes an enemy of God. Or do you think Scripture says without reason that the spirit He caused to live in us envies intensely? But He gives us more grace. That is why Scripture says:
"God opposes the proud but gives grace to the humble."
Submit yourselves, then, to God. Resist the devil, and he will flee from you. Come near to God and He will come near to you. Wash your hands, you sinners, and purify your hearts, you double-minded. Grieve, mourn and wail. Change your laughter to mourning and your joy to gloom. Humble yourselves before the Lord, and He will lift you up."
(James 4:4-10 NIV)

We are the Champions

Jf you finished the last chapter with the *heebie-jeebies* and you're seeing demons shifting in the wallpaper, then hold on a minute. I need to clarify something: we are more than conquerors, when fighting back *in the Spirit*. The information from the previous chapter is biblical, but it only tells half of the story. Remember, God is omnipotent—He's all powerful and totally in control of what enters your life. Nothing comes your way unless your heavenly Father— who loved you enough to give His only begotten Son as a ransom for you— allows it. So, in light of that, *it's all good*. He'll take care of the boogie-man, and you don't need to give him a second thought.

Right?

Um, wrong. Scriptures warn us, time and again, that we must persevere in our trials, because God is using them to produce good things. Yes, the enemy, Satan, is trying to steal, kill and destroy our families. But our trials come directly from God; His purpose is to bring glory to Himself, to conform us into the likeness of Christ and test our faith—to prove whether it's real or not. (See Romans 8:29, James 1:2-3, 12, Jer. 17:10, 1 Peter 4:12.)

". . . it may now be necessary for you to be sad for a while because of the many kinds of trials you suffer. Their purpose is to prove that your faith is genuine. Even gold, which can be destroyed, is tested by fire; and so your faith, which is much more precious than gold, must also be tested, so that it may endure." (1 Peter 1:6b-7a)

Your loving heavenly Father is always available to give you wisdom, to help you pass your tests and to make you stand—so go to

Him. Ask Him to fill you with His Holy Spirit; ask Him to carry you victoriously through the trials; ask Him to gift you with a genuine faith that will persevere and pass the test; ask Him to help you yield to His glorious work within your heart and life.

A friend of ours wrote a song that I think really applies here. One line says this: "Lord, You never left me, but I fell behind." Nothing and no one can separate us from the love of God in Christ Jesus. But can we be separated from Jesus? Surely His love for us will always remain, but Scripture is clear that, yes, we can be defeated. We can turn back, fall away, or "fall behind" when walking with the Lord. We must make a constant effort to stay in step with the Spirit.

"Those who belong to Christ Jesus have crucified the sinful nature with its passions and desires. Since we live by the Spirit, let us keep in step with the Spirit." (Galatians 5:24-25)

Here are some practical things you can do to stand firmly and stay in step with the Spirit:

When you suddenly become sick or unexplainably tired, know that Satan sees you as a threat; he's trying to stop you. Determine to fight back: Pray! Ask God to fill you with the power of His Holy Spirit. Ask Him to reveal (to you) if there's rebellion or disobedience in your life and to forgive you. Then get up, work hard, smile, sing praises, pray for your family, and act like a nice parent even when you aren't feeling nice... especially when you aren't feeling nice! Expect your nature/flesh (how you *feel* about things) to take Satan's side. Determine to resist your traitorous sinful nature and to follow God's Spirit instead. Get suspicious. Why is Satan trying to slow you down and make you ineffective now? What is he planning that he doesn't want you awake, alert and involved in? Ask God to fill your home with His holy presence and to protect your family. Ask God for the strength to drag yourself around on your family's behalf if that's what it takes. When the illness tactic doesn't stop you, Satan often stops attacking there and moves on to something else.

Determine to guard your health and stay off mood or mind altering medicines whenever possible. Stay alert! Prescription drugs often cause depression and worse side effects; they interfere with your ability to think clearly and make wise choices. They have the same effect on children, and special needs children may have intensified reactions to even over the counter medications. Ask God to heal you and show you how to use prevention, nutrition and lifestyle adjustments to bring health and strength to your family.

Satan will try to keep you away from church, Bible studies, and other times of fellowship with godly believers or any actions of ministry. He wants you isolated so you're easier to defeat and not encouraging others. When you desire to let God live through you and use you to set people free from Satan's hold, the Holy Spirit will prompt you to get involved in a Bible teaching church and other fellowship groups or ministries. Do you remember in the previous chapter where I said Satan will feed you a false gospel through the preaching of proud, deluded men? Well, I'm sorry to say, you won't be able to recognize false teachers unless you know the Scriptures *and* allow God to purify your heart by faith (taking steps of faith in obedience). Bible-knowledge won't be enough; only the pure in heart will see God. (Matthew 5:8, 2 Tim. 2:22.) Sadly, a false message is the dominant doctrine in many American churches these days. But don't believe the enemy when he whispers to you, "The majority can't be wrong!" Hogwash. The majority is almost always wrong!

"Go in through the narrow gate, because the gate to hell is wide and the road that leads to it is easy, and there are many who travel it. But the gate to life is narrow and the way that leads to it is hard, and there are few people who find it. Be on your guard against false prophets; they come to you looking like sheep on the outside, but on the inside they are really like wild wolves." (Matthew 7:13-15)

Prayerfully examine the theme of the messages at your church. If it's predominantly the false message of striving in the power of your flesh (doing your best, struggling, sinning, feeling condemned and enslaved to your sinful habits, needing to be encouraged to rest on "grace" because God knows you're just a sinner), and if they cannot tell you how to break free of your old nature (or even that you're supposed to crucify it), but instead they try to cheer you up by telling you that you're *saved and special* to God, then prayerfully consider moving on. In most fellowships there are new-believers who speak this way; that's unavoidable—they're spiritual-babies and their ignorance of God produces an inadequate understanding, even if they can *parrot the Scriptures.* However, your elders and pastor should be spiritually mature men whose intimacy with God produces the *fruits of the Spirit,* which include humility and pure lives (see Galatians 5:13-26). Their doctrine will align with all of Scripture, not just certain passages; their messages will have the power to change their lives and yours. If they do not, you may be following blind guides.

[Jesus said to his disciples] "'Take care; be on your guard against the yeast of the Pharisees and Sadducees.'" . . . . "'Guard yourselves from the yeast of the Pharisees and Sadducees!'
Then the disciples understood that he was not warning them to guard themselves from the yeast used in bread but from the teaching of the Pharisees and Sadducees." (Matthew 16:6, 11b-12)

Just as we cannot be justified by keeping the Law of Moses, (not even if we're as good as the Pharisees) we cannot follow Jesus through human effort. Only pride makes us think we can. The Christian life is a supernatural miracle, and true grace is God's offer to live inside us and change us. A preacher of biblical truth will encourage you to humble yourself, crucify your sinful nature's desires and fully surrender yourself to God—asking Him to fill you with His Holy Spirit and empower you to miraculously live the life He desires for you.

If you cannot find a sound Bible teacher in your area, here's a small list of teachers that I highly recommend reading and listening to. (The first three have sermons available online—for free.) With this list you can always have church with your family and be fed spiritually, regardless of where you live:

Chuck Smith, pastor, author, founder of Calvary Chapel
Eric Ludy, pastor, author, founder of Ellerslie
Francis Chan, pastor and author of Crazy Love, etc.
A. W. Tozer, pastor and author

Although this list will help you to be fed spiritually and equipped for ministry, God instructs us to also fellowship with other believers—for their sakes. We're part of His body, meant to love and serve one another. I trust you'll continue to look for opportunities to be faithful in that matter. Pray, asking God to help you make every appointment He sets for you.

In my experience, it seems very easy to *get in a rut* and attend *the wrong church.* But when we fervently pray, asking God to show us the exact fellowship He wants us to attend and serve at, things start to get a little crazy. You can expect to meet fierce spiritual opposition from your enemy (and plenty of distractions) when you try to attend *the right church.*

Once you've made up your mind and pushed past the distractions a few times, you'll see how predictable they are and their intensity might decrease. The enemy will leave . . . and look for *a more opportune time.*

Here are some things he might try next:

Are you suddenly having lustful, hateful, or otherwise sinful thoughts about someone? I see these probable "fiery darts" as a warning bell or the sounds of a snarling guard dog; I've just come too close to someone whom Satan was attacking or guarding fiercely—or he's trying to distract me from some area of ministry. Because the spirit of God lives in me, I'm a powerful threat. Satan wants to push me away from that person as far and fast as he can. I suspect he's flooding my mind, hoping I'll let it catch fire (and then be guilty) or that I'll just feel guilty and run away.

If this happens, ask God to forgive you for the thoughts in your head (maybe they came from your own sinful nature) and to clean your mind and heart. Then, go on the offensive! (Ask God to fill you with the power of His Holy Spirit.) Begin to fervently pray for the person that Jesus will set them free from Satan's grasp. Pray they'll be lifted out of the pit they're in. If unbelievers, pray their eyes will be opened to the Good News of Christ's redeeming work to save them. Anytime the thoughts return, pray for the person again; pray and ask God what He wants you to do. Put this person on a prayer list and if God opens a door, share the hope that's inside you, but never put

85

yourself in a position that could be misinterpreted or lead to sin. One example: Don't spend time alone with someone of the opposite sex nor enter into a friendship of this type; even if it doesn't turn into something ugly, it looks bad and may be misinterpreted or used to hurt people. Refer them to a godly person of their own gender for friendship and counsel.

"Watch and pray so that you will not fall into temptation. The spirit is willing, but the body is weak." (Mark 14: 38)

"The weapons we fight with are not the weapons of the world. On the contrary, they have divine power to demolish strongholds. We demolish arguments and every pretension that sets itself up against the knowledge of God, and we take captive every thought to make it obedient to Christ." (2 Corinthians 10:4-5)

"In addition to all this, take up the shield of faith, with which you can extinguish all the flaming arrows of the evil one." (Ephesians 6:16)

Satan will try to separate you from your spouse and children (by too many hours at work, too many extracurricular activities, etc). Know that Satan sees your family unit as a threat; he's trying to separate you. Fight back! Refuse to conform to how many people live: with bigger houses, shinier cars and more extracurricular activities. Don't love money and become a slave to your job. Don't remain trapped in debt because you're greedy for more stuff. Don't waste valuable family time entranced by television, movies, computer games and other entertainment. Protect your family from the influences of these things, which are usually pretty packaging on an ugly and ungodly, false message. Spend time with your family, getting to know them. Listen to your spouse and children and share your heart with them daily.

"For the love of money is a root of all kinds of evil. Some people, eager for money, have wandered from the faith and pierced themselves with many griefs." (1 Timothy 6:10)

Satan will send people to teach you lies, telling you they're the latest, greatest methods by which to raise children (or otherwise live). Every time I believe the Holy Spirit is leading me to do something, I'm suddenly surrounded by people who warn me not to do it! They're so convincing with their horror stories and worldly wisdom. They're often beloved relatives or accomplished colleagues (whose own walk with Jesus doesn't appear to be thriving). Isn't it suspicious that they always rush to the scene and care so much about what I'm doing only when I've decided to follow God's lead? Likewise, when you decide to allow the Holy Spirit to lead you, Satan will send people to insist you take another path. Expect it, and beware of ungodly counsel. How can you tell the difference between godly counsel, wisdom borne from experience and ungodly counsel? Prayerfully consider the lifestyle of the messenger and the foundation of the message. Ask yourself: Is this messenger led by the Spirit? Are they well-grounded in their knowledge of the Word of God, and does their advice stem directly from God's Word and prayer for me? If their advice isn't founded on Biblical truth and they are not led by the Holy Spirit, know that they are extremely vulnerable to spreading lies and being used and led by a darker spirit.

Examine the underlying beliefs they live by; these will be the origins of their counsel. If their underlying beliefs, as illustrated by how they live, are contrary to Scripture, their counsel will be ungodly—even if it sounds good. Godly counsel comes through a humble, wise, spiritually mature (servant-hearted) person who doesn't try to draw attention to themselves but rather points people to Jesus. They live what they preach and pray for you. Godly counsel will always line up with the entirety of Scripture, not just with a few twisted Scriptures. Here's an example: If Uncle Fred, an unbeliever who builds homes, teaches you to use a level when framing a house, this is probably harmless knowledge borne from experience. The rules of straight and crooked walls remain the same regardless of morality or spiritual beliefs. However, if Uncle Fred, as an unbeliever, encourages you to build a new house because he knows you'd like one, he thinks you can afford it, and he assumes you deserve it, you'd best use caution—a lot of caution. Only the Lord can tell you if He's given you the current funds to build yourself a nicer house, or to build an orphanage in Kathmandu.

"You, dear children, are from God and have overcome them, because the One who is in you is greater than the one who is in the world. They are from the world and therefore speak from the viewpoint of the world, and the world listens to them. We are from God, and whoever knows God listens to us; but whoever is not from God does not listen to us. This is how we recognize the Spirit of truth and the spirit of falsehood." (1 John 4:4-6)

Test everything with the Bible as your, well, *Bible!* The Sanballats and Tobiahs are very convincing and discouraging (read the book of Nehemiah for a refresher on these characters), but if we're led by the Holy Spirit, statistics don't apply to us. The Bible is filled with illustrations of God leading His people in one miraculous victory after another, when they remained faithful and allowed Him to lead. God is in control. Therefore, victory doesn't come from our own strength, clever choices or schemes. We're not defeated by outward influences or circumstances. We're defeated when we follow the ways of the nations and ungodly cultures around us. If we condone sin within our lives or put our hope in something or someone other than our Lord, He will allow us to be defeated. In fact, He'll *arrange our defeat.*

"At that time Hanani the seer came to Asa king of Judah and said to him: 'Because you relied on the king of Aram and not on the LORD your God, the army of the king of Aram has escaped from your hand. Were not the Cushites and Libyans a mighty army with great numbers of chariots and horsemen? Yet when you relied on the LORD, he delivered them into your hand. For the eyes of the LORD range throughout the earth to strengthen those whose hearts are fully committed to him. You have done a foolish thing, and from now on you will be at war.'" (2 Chronicles 16:7-9)

"But the Israelites acted unfaithfully in regard to the devoted things; Achan son of Carmi, the son of Zimri, the son of Zerah, of the tribe of Judah, took some of them. So the LORD's anger burned against Israel. Now Joshua sent men from Jericho to Ai, which is near Beth Aven to the east of Bethel, and told them, 'Go up and spy out the region.' So the men went up and spied out Ai.
"When they returned to Joshua, they said, 'Not all the people will have to go up against Ai. Send two or three thousand men to take it and do not weary all the people, for only a few men are there.' So about three thousand men went up; but they were routed by the men of Ai, who killed about thirty-six of them. They chased the Israelites from the city gate as far as the stone quarries and struck them down on the slopes. At this the hearts of the people melted and became like water.
"Then Joshua tore his clothes and fell facedown to the ground before the ark of the LORD, remaining there till evening. The elders of Israel did the same, and sprinkled dust on their heads. And Joshua said, 'Ah, Sovereign LORD, why did you ever bring this people across the Jordan to deliver us into the hands of the Amorites to destroy us? If only we had been content to stay on the other side of the Jordan! O Lord, what can I say, now that Israel has been routed by its enemies? The Canaanites and the other people of the country will hear about this and they will surround us and wipe out our name from the earth. What then will you do for your own great name?'
"The LORD said to Joshua, 'Stand up! What are you doing down on your face? Israel has sinned; they have violated my covenant, which I

commanded them to keep. They have taken some of the devoted things;
they have stolen, they have lied, they have put them with their own pos-
sessions. That is why the Israelites cannot stand against their enemies;
they turn their backs and run because they have been made liable to de-
struction. I will not be with you anymore unless you destroy whatever
among you is devoted to destruction.
"Go, consecrate the people. Tell them, 'Consecrate yourselves in prepa-
ration for tomorrow; for this is what the LORD, the God of Israel, says:
That which is devoted is among you, O Israel. You cannot stand
against your enemies until you remove it.'" (Joshua 7:1-13)

(Read also 2 Kings, Chapter One.)

For Better or Worse

$\mathcal{I}$ hope you understand that your story matters. Most people do not adopt, they do not take in foster children, nor do they work with street kids. Will you be different? Will you let what brought you here, keep you here? Will you stay, even if it gets difficult? Really difficult?

In the previous chapters we discussed your need to put on the armor of God—to be prepared for your spiritual battles. We discussed some common pitfalls and temptations that moms and dads encounter as Satan tries to destroy their families.

Now I'd like to tell you to prepare your marriage, because (if you're married) that relationship is the backbone of your family. But I can't tell you that. It's impossible for you to prepare your marriage, because a marriage is made of two people. You're only one person. You cannot prepare your marriage; you can only prepare *yourself.* However, if you will be the type of spouse God desires you to be, your marriage will be strengthened.

There's something else I want to tell you. I hope you won't be surprised, but wholeheartedly following Jesus can be a lonely road. Even if you are in church 24/7, you might be seeking Jesus all by your lonesome, while the others are just playing church. It happens; in these Last Days, it'll become even more common.

That hurts, but it's not what will hurt you most. If you're married, there's a good chance that you'll wake up some day and realize that you and your spouse are not on the same path, spiritually, emotionally . . . maybe not even physically. I hope this will never be your story, but it's more common than you may realize. If this doesn't apply to you at all, bear with me for the sake of those who need to talk about it.

If your spouse stops following Jesus, will you stop too? Will you put your List of Reasons (that you should love orphans) into the trash, assuming that God will now excuse you from your calling, because your spouse is making it too difficult, or you've got a broken heart?

It's not easy to take care of damaged, bewildered and often unruly children who started out as someone else's responsibility. But if you think that's hard, try doing it in the midst of a marriage-crisis — when you're at least as wounded and confused as the children are. Try doing it when you've just found out that the beautiful, happy family you planned to bless children with was just your own fantasy.

Think about that.

Will you quit? Or will you throw yourself more thoroughly into Jesus' arms, praying that the Holy Spirit will fill you with the love and power of God, so that you can continue to be the sun and moon to little children who (without you) might have no light? I hope you won't quit; I hope you'll remember that your story matters. I hope you'll remember that God commands us to care.

I'm not advocating marital-rebellion — not at all. If your spouse vetoes your decision to work with needy children, I beg you to cease. Wives are to respect and submit to their husbands, and husbands are to give up their lives for their wives and treat them with respect. Husbands and wives both are to submit to everyone, out of reverence to Christ. (Please take time to study Ephesians 5:21-33, Col. 3:18-19, 1 Peter 3:1 etc.)

"Submit yourselves to one another because of your reverence for Christ." (Eph. 5:21 GNB)

"Yea, all of you be subject one to another, and be clothed with humility: for God resisteth the proud, and giveth grace to the humble." (1 Peter 5:5 KJV)

"Humble yourselves, then, under God's mighty hand, so that he will lift you up in his own good time. Leave all your worries with him, because he cares for you." (1 Peter 5:6-7 GNB)

If your spouse disagrees with your decision to adopt or do foster care, then stop it. You can always find some other way to help, such as praying for orphans and financially supporting ministry to needy children. Submit to your spouse in love. You can silently pray that if it's God's will for you to do more, He'll soften their heart and change their mind.

But if your spouse doesn't oppose your passion for needy children, but instead your spouse is just somehow incapable of being a source of love and inspiration for you, I'm asking you to disrespect *yourself*. Don't let pride or hurt feelings control how you spend your life. If a sad marriage is your reality, don't let it steal your joy, make you bitter or cripple you and stop you from doing good. When you're looking for love, so you can turn around and pour it onto the children in your midst, look to Jesus; His love is enough.

I pray that when you feel unloved, or you meet a crisis—and you definitely will meet some—you'll take out your List of Reasons, hold it up to God who gave it to you and cry out, in a loud voice if need be, "Lord of Heaven and Earth, I beg you to set my face like flint in the way You would have me to go . . . no matter how I'm feeling right now."

Read the following section of Scripture with me, and then let's discuss it:

". . . there is not much time left, and from now on married people should live as though they were not married; those who weep, as though they were not sad; those who laugh, as though they were not happy; those who buy, as though they did not own what they bought; those who deal in material goods, as though they were not fully occupied with them. For this world, as it is now, will not last much longer. I would like you to be free from worry. An unmarried man concerns himself with the Lord's work, because he is trying to please the Lord. But a married man concerns himself with the worldly matters, because he wants to please his wife; and so he is pulled in two directions. An unmarried woman or a young virgin concerns herself with the Lord's work, because she wants to be dedicated both in body and spirit; but a* *married woman concerns herself with worldly matters, because she wants to please her husband.*

I am saying this because I want to help you. I am not trying to put restrictions on you. Instead, I want you to do what is right and proper, and to give yourselves completely to the Lord's service without any reservation."

(1 Corinthians 7:29-35 GNB)

I'd like you to read through these verses a number of times, praying for understanding. Then look at the very last sentence again.

"Instead, I want you to do what is right and proper, and to give yourselves completely to the Lord's service without any reservation."

He's saying that it IS possible to be completely devoted to Jesus and to serve him wholeheartedly—even if you're married. But it won't come naturally, or easily. You need to be filled with the Holy Spirit, asking God to give you the power and the desire to continue on, seeking first His kingdom, regardless of what your mortal spouse does. Of course, don't miss this, the first thing God will ask you to do is love, serve and cherish your spouse—*that's what being completely devoted to Jesus looks like.*

DANGERS of DIVORCE

Preparation requires education. By discussing marital problems, I don't mean to insult *your* marriage. I hope and pray that you and your spouse are both wholeheartedly serving Jesus. Regardless, a little education about the dangers of divorce won't hurt you.

Each year about one million American kids become the newest casualties of divorce. [1] Their parents divorce to escape the stress of a loveless marriage, the strife of having irreconcilable differences, or to ease the heartache of betrayal. They might divorce for the sake of the children. Many parents who divorce assume that living within the confines of a miserable marriage is more harmful to their children, but statistics say they're wrong.

What was once a forbidden practice in America, is now very common. The biggest change to divorce law came with "no fault divorces" in the 1970's. Previously there had to be a party at fault; an adulterer (or such) had to be identified in family court. But with the new law, couples could now divorce without admitting or proving any fault. [1] Divorce is toxic for children, as well as for society. American lawmakers used to know this. But when the enemy succeeds in corrupting the gate-keepers, the city is soon ravaged.

The medium length for a marriage in America is now between 8 and 11 years (variables and opinions differ). Divorce rates have risen steadily throughout the 20th century. The current divorce rate for first marriages is about 42 percent. Meanwhile, 60 percent of second marriages and 73 percent of third marriages will end in divorce. Oklahoma has the highest overall divorce rate, with Arkansas and Alaska second and third. As a region, the southern states (the *Bible Belt*) take first place for the most divorces. [1] As the divorce rates rise, the damage increases. Consider these statistics: Forty-three percent of children growing up in America today are being raised without their fathers; fatherless homes account for 90% of homeless/runaway children, 85% of children with behavior problems, 71% of high school dropouts, 85% of youths in prison, well over 50% of teen mothers and 63% of youth suicides. Divorce also weakens the health of children; even their life-spans will be shortened. [8] People whose parents are divorced are 50% more likely to get divorced than their counterparts from intact families. Additionally, sexual abuse by stepfathers is five times higher than among natural fathers. [2]

Seventy-five percent of children with divorced parents live with their mother, and twenty-eight percent of children living with a divorced parent live in a household with an income below the poverty line. However, research says children are less likely to be abused or neglected in families with incomes above $30,000 per year. (The overall rate of abuse and neglect is twenty-two times higher for families with incomes below $15,000 per year.) [4] Since about forty-five percent of women experience a drop in their standard of living after divorce, this puts them statistically at a higher risk. [3] Other strongly implicated family characteristics that contribute to abuse risk were single parent status, substance abusing parents and large family size. [5] In addition, cohabitation is a major factor in child abuse. The evidence suggests that a lack of commitment between biological parents is dangerous for children and that a lack of commitment between mother and boyfriend is exceedingly dangerous. The risk of child abuse is twenty times higher than in traditional married families if unmarried biological parents are living-together (as in "common law" marriages) and thirty-three times higher if the single mother is cohabiting with a boyfriend (not related to her children). [2]

How rampant a problem is child abuse and neglect? Compare it with another known danger and you'll see:

* In one five year period 67 children died in automobile crashes involving air bags; the result was mass awareness of this danger.

However, during this same five-year period, nearly five-thousand children (in our country alone) died from abuse or neglect at the hands of the parent or guardian responsible for their care. Approximately fifteen million American children were victims of abuse or serious neglect during this time. Child abuse and neglect is definitely a serious danger. A home life with two married biological parents is by far the safest environment for a child. [6]

Of course not every divorce will result in the children being abused and molested by a step-parent, running away from home, doing drugs, getting pregnant, going to jail and then committing suicide. However, the effects of divorce are negative, and research hasn't yet found the limits of these effects. Unlike the experience of their parents, the child's suffering does not reach its peak at the divorce and then level off. Rather, the effect of the parents' divorce impacts the children's lives indefinitely. One longitudinal study tracked children whose parents divorced, testing them two and three decades later. Even thirty years after the divorce negative long-term effects were clearly present in their income, health and behavior. [8] The divorce permanently weakened the relationship between children and parents, led to destructive ways of handling conflict, diminished social competence, led to early loss of virginity and a diminished sense of masculinity or femininity. They had more trouble in dating, more cohabitation, higher divorce rates, higher expectations of divorce and less desire for children. In religious life, divorce diminished the frequency of prayer and worship of God. In education, they had diminished learning capacities and lower high school and college attainment

But if you're wholeheartedly following Jesus, the statistics above are not what guides you. Your family depends upon the loving care of your Heavenly Father; if you want to stay safely "in His will," and thus continue to experience His blessing and protection, you must *know His will*, by knowing what the Bible teaches about marriage, divorce and remarriage. We'll talk about that in the next chapter.

1.   The History Of Divorce Law In The USA, History Cooperative, 2014 & USA.gov Centers for Disease Control and Prevention, Robert Schoen and Vladimir Canudas-Romo (2006), & sociologist Paul Amato
2.   www.childabuse.com/perp.htm, "Why Child Abuse Occurs & The Common Criminal Background of the Abuser"
3.   http://www.divorcemag.com/, U.S.A Divorce Statistics, 1997
4.   Sedlak and Broadhurst, Third National Incidence Study of Child Abuse and Neglect, p. 53
5.   www.childabuse.com/ taken from National Center on Child Abuse and Neglect's National Incidence Study, 1993 by Westat Associates.
6.   Whelan, Broken Homes & Battered Children.
7.   Patrick Fagan, Ph.D., Remarks to The World Congress of Families II, November 8, 1999
8.   Parliament of the Commonwealth of Australia, House of Representatives, Standing Committee on Legal and Constitutional Affairs, To Have and To Hold, (Canberra, Australia, Parliament of Australia:1998)

God's Will for Your Marriage

". . . You drown the Lord's altar with tears, weeping and wailing because he no longer accepts the offerings you bring him. You ask why he no longer accepts them. It is because he knows you have broken your promise to the wife you married when you were young. She was your partner, and you have broken your promise to her, although you promised before God that you would be faithful to her.
Didn't God make you one body and spirit with her? What was his purpose in this? It was that you should have children who are truly God's people. So make sure that none of you breaks his promise to his wife. 'I hate divorce,' says the Lord God of Israel. 'I hate it when one of you does such a cruel thing to his wife. Make sure that you do not break your promise to be faithful to your wife." (Malachi 2:13-16 GNB)

Your enemy is trying to destroy your children and their faith, by destroying their family. God created the family around a living, growing, life-giving core; it's called marriage—a covenant between one man and one woman. If Satan succeeds in destroying your marriage, it won't be because you forgot to pick up your socks and close the toilet seat—or you didn't have enough *date-nights*. Your enemy simply has to *destroy the covenant.*

He's a wily fellow, this enemy. He understands the lusts of your flesh (your nature); they too are enemies of your covenant with your spouse. Satan has an ally inside you, one that enjoys the evil darts his snipers shoot into your mind. Once you allow your lusts to rule your mind, the gate is wide open. When you're in that position, he'll send in real temptations, and you'll break your covenant: mission accomplished. Without a miracle, your marriage is sunk.

You'll either confess (and the family will be damaged or destroyed) or you'll try to hide your sin. If you're lying and hiding your sin, this will poison your relationships, and you'll be separated from God and His power. Satan will whisper things to your spouse, telling both truths (about the things you're doing wrong) and lies, driving a wedge between you. Also, because you opened the gate, Satan and the demons will be playing deadly games with your children.

I'm painting a dreary picture, but it's biblical. If your marriage has even small cracks, it may begin to crumble when you attempt to adopt or foster troubled children. Therefore, I'm devoting a second chapter to your marriage, in hopes that more preparation will mean less casualties.

God created marriage. He intends it for good, not harm. He uses it to illustrate Christ's love for His bride, the church. God is the one who governs and sustains marriages. Therefore, we need to know His mind about these matters.

Let's start at the beginning. Many people remember repeating this poem on their wedding day:

"I, _____, take you, _____, to be my husband (or wife), to have and to hold from this day forward, for better, for worse, for richer, for poorer, in sickness and in health, to love, cherish and obey, till death do us part, according to God's holy law, and this is my solemn vow."

They also answered questions, such as this, which the officiating minister asked them:

"Do you take this woman as your wedded wife, to live together after God's ordinance in the holy estate of matrimony? Will you love her, comfort her, honor, and keep her, in sickness and in health; and, forsaking all others, keep yourself only unto her, so long as you both shall live?"

If you're married, you repeated the first and said "I do" to the second. But hopefully you caught my mistake above. This was not a cute little poem; it was a solemn vow, binding until death!

God's will for marriage is an unselfish, pure, exclusive, covenant relationship between one man and one woman. It's binding until death; you're to sustain and cherish one another, cleaving only to each other, in sickness and health, as long as you both live.

However, if you've broken your solemn vow, you have a huge problem.

"He that troubleth his own house shall inherit the wind. . ." "For they have sown the wind, and they shall reap the whirlwind . . . " (Pro. 11:29a, Hosea 8:7 KJV)

Despite His great love, if we're rebelling, we are objects of God's wrath. But there's hope, if we're willing to repent. Full repentance is the necessary first step to restore our relationship with our Heavenly Father. After that, we can beg him to have mercy on our poor troubled family. Perhaps he'll restore the years the locust has devoured.

"But if we confess our sins to God, he will keep his promise and do what is right; he will forgive us our sins and purify us from all our wrongdoing." (1 John 1:9 GNB)

". . . if you are about to offer your gift to God at the altar and there you remember that your brother has something against you, leave your gift there in front of the altar, go at once and make peace with your brother, and then come back and offer your gift to God." (Matthew 5:23 GNB)

We're in a stalemate with God until we fully repent. After we've repented, He will move on our behalf and give us victory over our sin. But read the second verse above again. Read it a few times if it isn't soaking in. If your brother, or sister, has something against you—in other words, you've sinned against them—get up off your knees. Go and confess to your brother/sister first. Make things right there, and then return to the altar. God will be waiting.

Yes, when possible, this means confessing our secret sin to the person we've wronged, even though it will make them sad. Many people try confessing privately, only to God (or to friends who are also guilty and hiding their own sin). They're mistaken because they do not know the Scriptures. God will not accept their gift until they make things right with the brother or sister whom they've hurt. Until they obey, they'll remain trapped in their sin (this is why they keep repeating it).

"So then, confess your sins to one another and pray for one another, so that you will be healed . . . " (James 5:16a GNB)

Remember, if our sin hasn't been confessed to the person we've hurt, it's not *in the past*. It's here and now, like an invisible creature devouring our family. The only way to kill it is to lay it on God's altar—after confessing it to the person we've sinned against.

(I know I'm repeating myself, but this is the key to your family's deliverance!)

When interpreting their own moral failures, and especially their sexual immorality, people often use Old Testament saints to excuse themselves. They're mistaken; there are zero Christians in the Old Testament. Yes the God of the Old Testament is the same God of the New Testament, however, the people are not the same. There were no Christians until after the day of Pentecost.

Peter denied Christ, the other disciples trembled in fear, hiding themselves in the upper room; they were *natural men*—prior to being filled with the Holy Spirit. After Pentecost they lived bold, victorious, miraculous lives in service to God. In fact, when Paul encountered believers who hadn't been filled with the Holy Spirit, he concluded they hadn't yet heard the gospel.

[John the Baptist said,] "I baptize you with water to show that you have repented, but the one who will come after me will baptize you with the Holy Spirit and fire." (Matthew 3:11a GNB)

"There he [Paul] found some disciples and asked them, 'Did you receive the Holy Spirit when you became believers?'
'We have not even heard that there is a Holy Spirit,' they answered.
'Well, then, what kind of baptism did you receive?' Paul asked.
'The baptism of John,' they answered.

Paul said, 'The baptism of John was for those who had turned from their sins; and he told the people of Israel to believe in the one who was coming after him — that is, in Jesus.'

When they heard this, they were baptized in the name of Jesus. Paul placed his hands on them, and the Holy Spirit came upon them..." (Acts 19:2-5a GNB)

Besides total honesty, the second thing our marriage needs is the Holy Spirit. The old covenant could only point out our sin and then kill us for it. But Jesus came and established a glorious new covenant. The miraculous lives of the New Testament Christians are our example; theirs is what life lived under God's glorious new covenant looks like. (If you don't understand this, prayerfully study the book of Hebrews.)

Do not be deceived or led astray by weak teachers; we have the ability, through God's Spirit, to stay firmly within His will. If we've strayed, or we were ignorant of this fact, we must repent, be filled with His Spirit and get into step with Him.

"Marriage is to be honored by all, and husbands and wives must be faithful to each other. God will judge those who are immoral and those who commit adultery." (Hebrews 13:4 GNB)

God's will for marriage is clearly spelled out in many places in the New Testament; study them. Not only must our sexual relationship be physically exclusive (between you and your spouse ONLY), but also exclusive in our cravings and imaginations.

"You have heard it is said, you shall not commit adultery. But I say to you that whoever looks at a woman with lust, has already committed adultery with her in his heart." (Matthew 5:27-28 LMSA).

Take even your thoughts captive and make them obey Christ (2 Cor. 10:5). If your marriage has been defiled or is impure, ask and allow God to purify it. If you try to continue on with a defiled marriage, it will groan more loudly beneath the strain of adopting or fostering troubled children.

DOES GOD ALLOW DIVORCE and REMARRIAGE?

Yes, God allows a person to divorce and remarry another person, but only if their spouse has committed adultery.

"I tell you then, that any man who divorces his wife for any cause other than her unfaithfulness, commits adultery if he marries some other woman." (Matthew 19:9 GNB)

If your spouse was unfaithful, you're not required to divorce, but you're allowed to. You have a choice to make. God has healed many marriages, but only after the offending partner experienced a true change of heart and actions. Ask God to show you what's best for the children. Every situation is different.

On the other hand, if you're the person who committed adultery, God can forgive you if you'll ask Him, with willingness to forsake your sin. But remember, when you broke your vows, God released your spouse from the covenant. A broken covenant has been voided; it's no longer binding. It's impossible to hijack your way into a happy marriage with a hostage spouse. God will not be mocked, and He will defend your spouse. He will leave you in ever-tightening chains of bondage to your impure lusts, until you free your spouse by confessing your sin.

By being honest, you may lose your marriage, but you'll be set free from your sin and save your soul.

"No more lying, then! Each of you must tell the truth to the other believer, because we are all members together in the body of Christ." (Ephesians 4:25 GNB)

I have no clear remarriage advice for a person whose divorce was due to their own adultery; the Lord must reveal His will to you.

To study more on this subject, read the following Scriptures: (the two mentioned above—Malachi 2:13-16, Matthew 19:9 plus) Matthew 5:32, 1 Cor. 7:10-11, 15, Mark 10:11-12, Luke 16:18, Lev. 21:7, Num. 30:9, Deut. 24:1-4) Not all Bible translations are as accurate as others. Look in many translations to get a wider view of the original meaning.

A biblically allowed divorce is one caused by adultery. In this case, remarriage is allowed. In cases where there has been no adultery, the Bible instructs the couple not to divorce, but to be reunited.

"Yet to those who have wives, I command (yet not I but my Lord), let not the wife be separated from her husband; but if she separate, let her remain single, or be reconciled to her husband; and let not the husband desert his wife." (1 Cor. 7:10-11 LMSA)

However, if there's been no unfaithfulness, but your spouse will not return, 1 Cor. 7:15 tells you to live at peace with their decision; continue on without them. You cannot force them to return to you.

"But if the one who is not a convert wishes to separate, let him separate. In such cases, a convert man or woman is free; for God has called us to live in peace." (1 Cor. 7:15 LMSA)

Some people add the words "to remarry" after the word "free"— but those words don't exist here. They're not in the original texts, nor in any accurate translation. To add those words, we must disregard four of the other Scriptures (listed above) which clearly state that this person is *not* free to remarry, unless adultery becomes evident. (Note: most translations don't even have the word "free" in this verse. They say, "you are not enslaved," or "you are not in bondage" etc.)

"But now I tell you: if a man divorces his wife for any cause other than her unfaithfulness, then he is guilty of making her commit adultery if she marries again; and the man who marries her commits adultery also." (Matthew 5:32 GNB)

Even the innocent party, such as this poor woman whose husband wants to divorce her without cause, cannot remarry when the divorce isn't biblically allowed; this couple is still bound by a solemn vow—a covenant. They are supposed to reunite, or remain single and pure.

You might wonder if there's ever a case where a spouse separates and doesn't commit adultery. You're right to wonder, but it happens occasionally. I know of a gentleman who was a police officer; during a high-speed chase he was in a car accident and became moderately brain-damaged. He could no longer take care of himself, and his personality was drastically changed; after his accident, sometimes he was a scary guy. But has he committed adultery? No. His wife divorced him and remarried. He currently lives in a group-home with caretakers. I understand this was difficult for his wife, but she'd taken a vow to love him in sickness and health. The Bible did not give her permission to divorce her husband and remarry.

Another woman I know divorced and remarried because her first husband was depressed and she grew weary of living with his anger and moods. A third divorced and remarried because her husband got involved in a cult and became deluded and controlling. These men weren't easy to live with. But these are not instances where divorce and remarriage are allowed. God will not bless our disobedience, but He very faithfully answers prayers and blesses our obedience if we will *trust Him.*

"A man should fulfill his duty as a husband, and a woman should fulfill her duty as a wife, and each should satisfy the other's needs. A wife is not the master of her own body, but her husband is; in the same way a husband is not the master of his own body, but his wife is. Do not deny yourselves to each other, unless you first agree to do so for a while in order to spend your time in prayer; but then resume normal marital relations. In this way you will be kept from giving in to Satan's temptation because of your lack of self-control." (1 Cor. 7:3-5 GNB)

WHAT ABOUT DOMESTIC VIOLENCE?

As a parent, it's your responsibility to provide a safe, peaceful home for your children—to the best of your ability. If your home is a place of violence, it's my belief that you should remove the children from danger and separate from your spouse, for a time of prayer—as in the Scripture above. You might conclude that your spouse agreed to this plan when he/she chose to threaten you or the children. There's no clear command in the Bible on this subject, but this is not a biblical excuse for divorce, nor for remarriage. (However, you should pray and ask God to show you the root of the problem. When men are aggressive toward their families, they're usually fully given over to their lusts and evil desires in other areas as well. Ask God to expose your husband's adultery, if it exists.) Remember, if you separate, be sure you really do spend your time *praying* that God will intervene and bring peace. God answers prayer; Jesus is the Prince of Peace.

What if you're divorced and remarried, and you've read these Scriptures, and this chapter, and concluded that your divorce and remarriage were not biblically allowed? You and your current spouse should seek God's forgiveness, which He will give, and from here on out walk in obedience to what you know. Begin to study the Scriptures diligently, because ignorance is no excuse for disobedience. We have been commanded to learn what pleases the Lord.

"You yourselves used to be in the darkness, but since you have become the Lord's people, you are in the light. So you must live like people who belong to the light, for it is the light that brings a rich harvest of every kind of goodness, righteousness, and truth. Try to learn what pleases the Lord. Have nothing to do with the worthless things that people do, things that belong to the darkness. Instead, bring them out to the light."
(Ephesians 5:8-11 GNB)

Maybe you've been divorced and remarried many times. Regardless of your past mistakes, once you realize your sin and confess it, God will forgive you. God desires that you walk in obedience *today*, within your current situation. Are you currently married? Stay with your current spouse; love, cherish and cleave only unto her/him until death.

Yes, divorce hurts children—but remember that God is the healer. Even if your marriage has been destroyed, if you will firmly and obediently plant yourself *in Christ*, praying that He'll protect and guide you and your children, you'll weather your storms.

Remember, above all else, you are the *bride of Christ*; be faithful to Him; He is always faithful to you.

Lost Boys and Girls

Introduction to Part Three:

If I overwhelmed you in the last section, I'm sorry. Before we talk about more challenges, you need to hear a praise report.

Years ago, a fearless preschooler waltzed into my home (ahead of her case-worker) and plunked down the bag that held her things. Not yet four-years-old, she'd already been moved many times. She took one look at my nine-year-old daughter and declared, "Hi, I'm your new sister. Let's go play!" But this petite, blonde cutie wasn't coming to stay—we were a temporary (respite) foster home then. Children came to us when they first entered CPS custody, or when long-term homes were all full, or if a foster or fost-adopt family had a crisis (which is how she'd arrived; *she was their crisis*). She'd likely be with us a few days or weeks and then be moved again. But my daughter smiled, linked arms with the little charmer and off they went. When my husband came home and entered the back yard, our adorable new guest looked up and saw him. Grinning broadly, she waved and cried out, "Daddy! Daddy! I'm home, Daddy! Will you push me on the swing?" My very bewildered husband smiled, waved back and replied, "Um, sure." As he walked past me, he whispered into my ear, "Who is this?"

To make a long story short, she stayed—forever. She wasn't easy to raise; she frustrated me beyond belief, occasionally. But she formed a deep bond with our other children and brought our family much joy. Not long ago, as I sat writing this book, that same little girl (all grown up, married and a mother herself) traveled across the country to meet the biological mother whom she lost as an infant. Some months later, she took her bio mother into her own home to give her a change of scenery and help escape her old habits. Despite Mom's problems and history, this girl loves her. She desires to see Jesus do miracles in Mom's life, and she *knows* He can. This little blonde cutie, who took my family by storm, has grown up with a *missionary's heart*—for her *other* family. Yes, I felt like a failure with her on many occasions. But God works miracles despite my inadequacy. You too will have challenges, but it's all worth it in the end.

You and Your Big Heart

If you've read this far, congratulations; I assume you understand you're in a spiritual battle for souls, or you're at least humoring me and my opinions. I also assume other things about you: You have a very big heart. You love kids. You're willing to let God lead and reveal His will to you. You trust in Jesus and you're praying to be used to enrich the lives of others, saving those who can be saved and so forth. But if you're new to fostering or adopting, please take a moment to realize that however mature you might be in your faith (it might be a healthy, large faith; if so, good for you!) you're still new to fostering or adopting.

One of the first things to learn is that the vast majority of foster and/or adoptable children have lasting developmental, psychological, or emotional disabilities and challenges. Yes, even the *healthy ones.*

Whether abused, neglected, or even if you adopt an infant, most children adopted through foster care have permanent damage because their birth mothers drank alcohol or used drugs during pregnancy. Likewise, children adopted internationally will have damage directly related to the social ills specific to their culture. It's quite natural for a parent to love and protect their children—even animals are born with these instincts. So when that doesn't happen, substance abuse is usually involved. While extreme poverty, social or domestic violence, inherited mental illness or learning disabilities sometimes play a big role in a parent's inability to care for children, in many of those cases you'll also see alcohol and drug abuse. Therefore, all parents considering adoption or foster care should understand what maternal alcohol and drug usage do to a developing infant.

Much of the information in this book applies to the children labeled as "healthy" by adoption agencies. If a child has already been labeled with a disability, they're exhibiting obvious, more pronounced symptoms. Many children in the American foster and adoption system are either too young or too transient (haven't been with one caregiver long enough) to be accurately evaluated. Additionally, sometimes professionals choose to hide the facts because the truth would make it harder to find an adoptive family for the child. (This appears to be more prevalent in some cultures than in others.) A majority of these *healthy* children will manifest disabilities and extreme challenges (discussed in further chapters) as you live with them. For this reason, go slowly. Don't jump in the deep end before you can swim; don't bite off more than you can chew and any other clichés that might apply.

During my early years as a foster parent, I had a strong desire to adopt a six-year-old girl who was diagnosed with many things, including RAD (Reactive Attachment Disorder). She lived in a shelter because she was too troubled and disruptive to be in a foster home. She spent a long time in the shelter before they even classified her as "ready to adopt." She was a damaged child with many serious emotional and behavioral issues.

This information didn't scare me; it increased my desire to save her. However, at this time our oldest biological daughter was about seven-years-old and our younger kids were all younger than six-years-old. Thank God, I had a seasoned and wise licensing worker. She told me that I wasn't ready to take home such a challenging girl. I argued; she argued back. She cautioned that bringing in a difficult child of that age would upset the whole order of things in my family. The girl was older than my youngest children, so she would become the leader. Instead of my loving children being the examples, the troubled child would exert the peer pressure. Because my children were younger, they'd be vulnerable to abuse; they would look up to her and follow her example.

In the end, after much prayer I conceded that perhaps my licensing worker was right. Now, years later, I could kiss her for that advice. I know, without a doubt, that it would have been a damaging mistake.

Mistakes happen, but once you adopt, what do you do if you suspect you've created an impossible situation, and your family is failing, or worse? Many adoptions disrupt each year (the children are given back to the child welfare system or a private agency), but as a big-hearted person with more faith than experience, you wouldn't want to quit on this child, even if you were losing your sanity and your family were falling apart. So slow down, read on and let's be sure you're prepared before you commit. Why do dogs bark? Why do cats meow? Isn't it because it's part of their nature? Now read the following and then consider what behaviors originate from the sinful nature (with which all people are born):

"So I say, live by the Spirit, and you will not gratify the desires of the sinful nature. For the sinful nature desires what is contrary to the Spirit, and the Spirit what is contrary to the sinful nature. They are in conflict with each other, so that you do not do what you want. But if you are led by the Spirit, you are not under law.
"The acts of the sinful nature are obvious: sexual immorality, impurity and debauchery; idolatry and witchcraft; hatred, discord, jealousy, fits of rage, selfish ambition, dissensions, factions and envy; drunkenness, orgies, and the like. I warn you, as I did before, that those who live like this will not inherit the kingdom of God.
"But the fruit of the Spirit is love, joy, peace, patience, kindness, goodness, faithfulness, gentleness and self-control. Against such things there is no law. Those who belong to Christ Jesus have crucified the sinful nature with its passions and desires. Since we live by the Spirit, let us keep in step with the Spirit. Let us not become conceited, provoking and envying each other." (Galatians 5:16-26)

When you plan to adopt you'll be given a checklist of behaviors and disabilities. You'll mark this paper up like a Christmas wish list, naming the disabilities and behaviors that you'll accept in a child and those you absolutely will not consider.

Defiant? *Okay, I guess.*
Fire-starter? *No way.*
Needs medication? *Sure, that's fine.*
Sexually abuses other children? *Absolutely not!*

There's nothing wrong with being selective; this is your family and your home. You're responsible for controlling the environment. You know there are some things just too difficult for you to handle. But guess what? If you adopt any child who hasn't been born again, who is not indwelt by and led by the Holy Spirit of God, that child is still only natural; he is, as all unbelievers, blind to spiritual things and ruled by his sinful nature. So even if he's never been abused, never been exposed to uncommonly evil things, if he lacks normal inhibitions and has poor impulse control (as most needy children do), what behaviors will you likely see? (Hint: read Gal. 5:16-26 again.)

Sexual immorality, impurity and debauchery; idolatry and witchcraft; hatred, discord, jealousy, fits of rage, selfish ambition, dissensions, factions and envy; drunkenness, orgies, and the like.

Are you prepared to deal with these behaviors in your home? Even if you were promised a healthy child, without negative labels, this is the natural (sinful) core of each human. Every child has the potential to act upon their sinful desires. Every child or adult, due to a sinful nature, has the potential to become violent, lie, steal, start fires, or molest others, etc. But a child who lacks normal inhibitions and impulse control (from drug or alcohol induced brain damage prior to birth and/or neglect and abuse after, etc.) will almost definitely act out rather than control their urges. Do you understand what I'm saying? I'm trying to be gentle, but countless adoptions are dissolved (or disrupted) each year because the adopted child has behaviors that are so disturbing or harmful that the family believes they cannot survive, or the child cannot survive, unless they're removed—un-adopted. Other adoptive families are still trying to make it work, but paying "therapeutic" ranches and other facilities to care for their most troubled child. This can easily cost $3,000 to $10,000 monthly, but they see no other option; they don't believe it's possible to safely raise this child inside their home.

Enter every single case of adoption or foster care prepared, expecting and guarding against extreme negative behaviors so they'll not injure the child or anyone else. For instance: It's usually extremely unwise to bring a child into your home that's older than (or the same age as) your youngest child. Guard the children you've already been given to protect! Remember, not every child is intended for your home, and there are many different ways to help children. If you're the one God has called to do this particular job, it will work without damaging your family or your loved ones.

(Note: We sometimes view "damage" differently than God does. There are times that (what I would call) damage has occurred, but in the end (as people prayed and persevered) God used that trial to save souls, heal broken people and bring new life to dead situations.)

Also remember that there's no such thing as a truly "well adjusted" non-believer. Yes, some repress their destructive urges and some are really good at hiding their bad behaviors. Some are so good at repressing destructive urges or hiding bad behaviors that they're quite successful in this life. So what? What does it profit a man if he gains the whole world, yet loses his soul?

Our main goal is not to raise well-adjusted children, but rather to bring the life-changing message of the gospel to lost souls. If you work with a troubled, damaged child and he never becomes a successful or productive citizen, but he believes the gospel and has a saving faith in Jesus Christ, you have succeeded. Foster care or adoption (as every other activity we involve ourselves in) should be ministry to unsaved souls. Only then will the results be eternal.

Be in prayer and read the Scriptures daily. Ask God to guide you; be filled and led by the Holy Spirit, not by your feelings or your big heart.

God's Children

Happy, successful adoptions of healthy, emotionally stable children definitely are a reality. In these adoptions, both child and adoptive parents will sprout a deep and abiding bond for the other; their parenting challenges will be similar to those of any biological parent. My writing often focuses more on raising the difficult (or troubled) child; however, it also gives you a *better chance* of choosing the less difficult, if that's what you wish. By knowing circumstances to avoid before you adopt, you're prepared to make informed choices. The following could be considered *green flags:*

*   The child is adopted young (an infant or toddler).
*   If not an infant, the child has been lovingly nurtured from the moment of birth and has a bond to their caregiver. (This child was not in an institution with rotating employees and wasn't transient with multiple, temporary caregivers.)
*   Their needs were always met; they never felt the need to protect themselves or fight to survive.
*   Their biological parents didn't have inherited mental illness, mental deficit or severe emotional instability.
*   This child didn't suffer any prenatal exposure to alcohol or drugs.

If the child fits *all of the above* green flags, the outlook is very positive. For example: If a young but stable/intelligent, healthy mother (non-drinker, avoids drugs, etc.) gives up a child at birth simply because she doesn't feel ready to raise a baby, and if the baby goes directly to a nurturing caregiver, the child's outlook is very good.

Or if you adopt from a country that has little to no substance abuse problem, and if the baby has one-on-one love and nurturing from the moment of birth until they're put in your arms, problems will likely be minimal. But for children born into other situations, they and their parents should prepare for challenges above and beyond those of typical parenting. Armed with that information, prayerfully consider where you fit into foster care or adoption. Each person has his gift. Jesus is the savior of the world—not me; not you. We're each pieces of Christ's body, and when working together, we form a whole.

For those who adopt disturbed or disabled children (whether by choice or through ignorance), we know we need help raising them and that God will give the Holy Spirit to all who ask. When faced with extremely troubling behaviors, remember that God adopted you also, and you were probably not the *cream of the crop*.

"For the foolishness of God is wiser than man's wisdom, and the weakness of God is stronger than man's strength.
"Brothers, think of what you were when you were called. Not many of you were wise by human standards; not many were influential; not many were of noble birth. But God chose the foolish things of the world to shame the wise; God chose the weak things of the world to shame the strong. He chose the lowly things of this world and the despised things—and the things that are not—to nullify the things that are, so that no one may boast before him. It is because of him that you are in Christ Jesus, who has become for us wisdom from God—that is, our righteousness, holiness and redemption. Therefore, as it is written: 'Let him who boasts boast in the Lord.'" (1 Corinthians 1:25-31 NIV)

Learn to see adoption as spiritual or *evangelism:* The Bible teaches that we are to live for the glory of God, sharing His love and advancing His kingdom through our interactions with others—especially with the vulnerable and needy.

Regarding children and faith, I'm always amazed at how many of the believers I know were first exposed to the gospel (and believed wholeheartedly) as children. For most of us, our faith didn't become life-changing until we were adults. We forgot Jesus for awhile, but He remembered us. God remained faithful, kept us *set apart* and *called us back* to Himself. This is my prayer for the children that God lets me hold in my arms.

How much impact do you have on the people around you?

In the Bible we read of Joseph, who was sold into slavery and bought by an Egyptian named Potiphar. Because the Lord was with Joseph and gave him success in everything he did, once Potiphar put Joseph in charge, the blessings of the Lord were soon upon Potiphar's entire household. The same thing happened in other places when Joseph was put in charge—because *the Lord was with him*. There are other similar stories throughout the Bible. Now please read the entire story of Paul's shipwreck in Acts, Chapter 27. Take special notice of this:

"Last night an angel of the God whose I am and whom I serve stood beside me and said, 'Do not be afraid, Paul. You must stand trial before Caesar; and God has graciously given you the lives of all who sail with you.'" (Acts 27:23-24 NIV)

Paul describes himself as one who both *serves* and *belongs* to God; if this also describes you, then ask God to give you the lives of those who "sail with you." We live in a world of storms that are driving the lives of many toward shipwreck; countless souls are lost in the sea of sin. Yet this isn't God's desire. All are born with a sin nature, thereby separated from their creator, but God longs to see us forgiven through the finished work of Christ on the cross, restored to fellowship with Him and free from the power of sin. He longs to see us rescued. Therefore, my goal as an adoptive mother is to bring the children into a relationship with the Lord Jesus through the glorious new covenant, so they'll be *saved*—adopted by Him and clothed in Christ's righteousness.

"Praise be to the God and Father of our Lord Jesus Christ, who has blessed us in the heavenly realms with every spiritual blessing in Christ. For he chose us in him before the creation of the world to be holy and blameless in his sight. In love he predestined us to be adopted as his sons through Jesus Christ, in accordance with his pleasure and will—to

the praise of his glorious grace, which he has freely given us in the One he loves. In him we have redemption through his blood, the forgiveness of sins, in accordance with the riches of God's grace that he lavished on us with all wisdom and understanding." (Ephesians 1:3-8 NIV)

However, I'm convinced that (even before believing the gospel) children come under sanctification simply because we've held them in our arms as our children and prayed for them. Yes, everyone is responsible for his or her own sins, but God "sets apart" those who live as family with a believer—for example: In 1 Corinthians, Chapter Seven, we see that an unbelieving spouse is set apart, or sanctified, in God's eyes simply by remaining with his believing spouse. The result, it says, is that the *children are holy* (set apart). Or, as we saw earlier, 275 people were saved despite a shipwreck simply because they sailed with Paul!

Your faithfulness and trust in God very powerfully affects those around you. Remember that Abraham's children automatically received the covenant when *Abraham* believed God and was counted as righteous. And when God destroyed the cities of Sodom and Gomorrah, he saved Lot because He "remembered Abraham." (In Genesis, Chapters 11 and 12, we learn that Lot was orphaned, or at least fatherless, and was taken in first by his grandfather and then later by his uncle Abraham.)

"Therefore, the promise comes by faith, so that it may be by grace and may be guaranteed to all Abraham's offspring—not only to those who are of the law but also to those who are of the faith of Abraham. He is the father of us all. As it is written: "I have made you a father of many nations." He is our father in the sight of God, in whom he believed—the God who gives life to the dead and calls things that are not as though they were." (Romans 4:16-17 NIV)

"So when God destroyed the cities of the plain, he remembered Abraham, and he brought Lot out of the catastrophe that overthrew the cities where Lot had lived." (Genesis 19:29 NIV)

Open adoption verses closed adoption?

If you don't know the basics of open adoption and closed adoption, please review an adoption glossary. When comparing the two, it's impossible to say one is better than the other; there are positives and negatives to both and so many variables.

Whichever you choose, determine to put no stumbling block before these little ones. A stumbling block can be offering too much information before they can comprehend, or too little when they can. I see parents operating in both extremes; I caution you to pray over this area and be sensitive to God's direction.

Regarding "too much information too early," children can lose all sense of security and hope of having a happy, peaceful childhood because parents want to discuss everything *now*. But there are many subjects a child isn't capable of understanding; to force it confuses and worries her. For a child, the love and security of being part of a family (God's ideal design) are vital to her emotional health as she grows. Be sensitive and patient; give your child the most ideal childhood possible under the circumstances. Don't help Satan erode your child's sense of security by baffling her.

On the other hand are those who simply cannot tell the truth, ever; avoid this as well. When your child is mentally and emotionally ready to talk about biological matters, be honest. Don't promise him that his biological parents were wonderful people who loved him and had his best interests at heart when placing him up for adoption. Sure, that may have been their calculated motive, but (usually) if they'd been living the pure and circumspect, unselfish lives God intended for them, and which He promises to *enable us to live* if we'll stop fighting Him, they could've given their child a stable family environment in which to grow up.

But won't those facts make your child feel badly about himself? Maybe, but we shouldn't fear seeing our faults. We shouldn't teach our children to hide from, or deny, their inadequacies and deep needs. The heart of the gospel is man coming to terms with his inner depravity (his fallen nature), his lost state and lack of redeemable natural qualities. Yes. God created him wonderfully, but it's all been tainted by sin. Now he needs forgiveness, he needs to be born-again as a new creation, he needs to be clothed with Christ's righteousness, and he needs to be filled with God's Holy Spirit—but he won't ask if he doesn't understand his need! When a child is mature enough, give him the truth: His biological parents were sinners, just as we all are.

"But God demonstrates his own love for us in this: While we were still sinners, Christ died for us." (Romans 5:8 NIV)

If the sin of his biological parents rendered them incapable, or unwilling to spend their lives nurturing a child, be honest. If you don't allow your child to accept this fact, how will he face his own sinful nature and necessity to "die to himself" (deny his natural tendencies) and let Christ *live through him?*

But also be honest about the fact that his biological parents can be totally forgiven and become new creations if they put their hope in the Savior. Instill love and forgiveness into this child's heart; when he's old enough to understand, he should be taught to love and pray for his biological parents, even if they haven't yet become new creations in Christ.

Your child needs to understand that you chose to put aside your natural tendencies and selfish ambitions to nurture him. When he was without love in the world, you brought him into your heart and arms; you gave him your life, your family, and your name to call his own—regardless of whether he ever gave anything back. When your child understands this truth, it may help him to see God's heart toward him; it will give him an example of true love that he can follow.

What about preserving cultural roots?

It's often been popular to raise adopted children with constant reminders of their biological past. It's natural to desire these roots; we want to know where we came from; we long to understand who we are. Adoptive parents incorporate cultural or ethnic traditions into the family and sometimes even create "life books" chronicling the child's pre-adoption history. I believe these practices should be done carefully because they can be harmful in many instances. I'll explain—but first, read these Scriptures and consider where each child really came from:

"For you created my inmost being; you knit me together in my mother's womb. I praise you because I am fearfully and wonderfully made; your works are wonderful, I know that full well." (Psalm 139:13-14 NIV)

"'For in him we live and move and have our being.' As some of your own poets have said, 'We are his offspring.' Therefore since we are God's offspring, we should not think that the divine being is like gold or silver or stone—an image made by man's design and skill." (Acts 17:28-29 NIV)

"Do you not know that your bodies are members of Christ himself?" "Do you not know that your body is a temple of the Holy Spirit, who is in you, whom you have received from God? You are not your own; you were bought at a price. Therefore honor God with your body." (1 Corinthians 6:15, 19-20 NIV)

God carefully created our bodies (and our children's bodies!) and they were made *for Him*. Our bodies are called "tents" in Scripture; they're only temporary dwellings, but the implication isn't that of an old, tattered camping tent. The original wording suggests something more dignified, similar to the *"Tent of Meeting"* you find in Israel's history. Scripture suggests that the Tent of Meeting (a place where God met with man) was a reflection of the Temple (later built by Solomon) and that temple was a reflection of what we'll find in heaven. Our bodies were created to be filled with God's Holy Spirit; a place where we commune with God. They're a shadow of the bodies we'll have when we're fully in the presence of God in heaven and they are, in God's eyes, *His temple*. Regardless of where your child was born, or into which situation, the reason God created her was to be His child, walking in friendship with Him and being filled with His Holy Spirit and love.

This is my first concern with any "life books" which remind the child of a painful history or emphasize their biologically cultural ties; *we are not of this world!* In fact, we are warned in the Bible not to love this world and that friendship with the world is enmity with God.

"I have given them your word and the world has hated them, for they are not of the world any more than I am of the world." (John 17:14 NIV)

Our children shouldn't find their identities in their physical bodies or biological, earthly roots. If we are only a physical being, we have no hope of resurrection and no hope of being anyone apart from this temporary body. When this body died, we would cease to exist. In addition, much of the history, cultures or ethnic traditions your adopted child might be *biologically tied to,* stem from sin or idolatrous religions. Will God be pleased if He redeems a child from this evil and bondage and then her adoptive parents try to put her back in to it?

No, your child is not just a physical body whose origins began with two humans or a race of people. She has history prior to birth or even conception—when she was inside God's imagination and then in His hands as He decided to *fearfully and wonderfully* knit her together; teach your child *this heritage.* Give your child a "life book" that ties her to her Creator, not to a love of the world or to the sins of biological ancestors.

"Sing to God, sing praise to his name, extol him who rides on the clouds—his name is the LORD—and rejoice before him. A father to the fatherless, a defender of widows, is God in his holy dwelling. God sets the lonely in families, he leads forth the prisoners with singing; but the rebellious live in a sun-scorched land." (Psalm 68:4-6 NIV)

"Religion that God our Father accepts as pure and faultless is this: to look after orphans and widows in their distress and to keep oneself from being polluted by the world." (James 1:27 NIV)

"For the LORD your God is God of gods and Lord of lords, the great God, mighty and awesome, who shows no partiality and accepts no bribes. He defends the cause of the fatherless and the widow, and loves the alien, giving him food and clothing." (Deuteronomy 10:17-18 NIV)

Invisible, Physical Wounds

(Author's Note: Some of the disabilities common in children, and adopted children, are: Attention Deficit, Hyperactive Disorder (ADHD), Autism/Pervasive Development Disorders, Cerebral Palsy, Cleft Lip & Palate, Cystic Fibrosis, Down Syndrome, Fetal Alcohol Syndrome/Drug Babies, Epilepsy, Hearing Impairment, Learning Disorders, Mental Disorders, Reactive Attachment Disorder (RAD), Speech/Language Disorders, Spina Bifida, etc. Please research these; many books on each exist already.)

Chapters Eighteen, Nineteen and Twenty detail what I consider the *unexpected disabilities*. I believe these invisible wounds are the problems most often undiagnosed until after adoption, or improperly diagnosed as something else. I also believe they're some that present parents with the most frustrating challenges. The following small article, "Prenatal Violence," is something I put together many years ago. It isn't comprehensive; consider it a brief introduction to Fetal Alcohol Syndrome (FAS). You'll benefit from doing further research into this very real problem.

PRENATAL VIOLENCE: Basics of Fetal Alcohol Spectrum

Not long ago, a pregnant woman thought nothing of having a drink to relax. *"Better for the baby if I'm calm instead of stressed,"* she said. Today, the facts are too clear to deny: Alcohol and pregnancy don't mix. According to the U.S. Department of Health and Human Services, alcohol consumption during pregnancy is the number one cause of mental retardation. Damage varies depending on the amount consumed during pregnancy, but the results are always devastating. Research from the Centers for Disease Control and Prevention reports the following effects from inutero alcohol exposure:

94% experience mental health problems.

43% have a disrupted school experience (suspension, expulsion or drop out).

60% have trouble with the law.

60% experience confinement (incarceration for crimes or inpatient treatment for mental health, alcohol/drug problems).

30% struggle with drug/alcohol problems.

45% are reported to have inappropriate sexual behaviors.

80% are not capable of living independently when they mature. [1]

Although alarming statistics, the terrifying news is that doctors don't know how much alcohol during pregnancy is too much. In other words, no amount of drinking is safe for a developing infant. The idea that alcohol permanently damages babies is not a new one. Nevertheless, this knowledge has not spread quickly enough. Studies estimate that one out of every 1000 babies is born alcohol affected and that our economy is burdened by an annual 2.1 billion-dollar expense incurred by these children (and adults). At least as far back as 1750, letters circulated in English Parliament making these same claims. One such letter referred to the *gin epidemic:* ". . . too often the cause of weak, feeble, and distempered children, who must be, instead of an advantage and strength, a charge to their country." Nineteenth Century French physician, Dr. E. Lanceraux also described some significant characteristics of Fetal Alcohol Syndrome: "As an infant he dies of convulsions or other nervous disorders; if he lives, he becomes idiotic or imbecile, and in adult life bears the special characteristics: the head is small . . ., his physiognomy vacant [peculiar facial features], a nervous susceptibility more or less accentuated, a state of nervousness bordering on hysteria, convulsions, epilepsy... are the sorrowful inheritance,... a great number of individuals given to drink bequeath their children."[2] Nevertheless, issues of prenatal alcohol exposure were ignored then and still are by many today.

During the 1960s, the medical profession condoned moderate alcohol use during pregnancy. Many leading physicians expressed doubt that any relationship between birth defects and alcohol existed. Today, through breakthroughs in technology, the existence of Fetal Alcohol Syndrome is indisputable. Completely acknowledged now, we know it as "FAS," or in its milder form, Fetal Alcohol Effects,

"FAE." (When referring to both: *Fetal Alcohol Spectrum.*) Technology has gone so far as to expose why and how FAS children suffer. X-rays of a healthy infant's brain and one of an FAS effected infant are dramatically different. The FAS child's brain is small and shrunken and lacks an intact corpus callosum, the middle section—which processes information between the right brain and left brain. It is discernible that this brain has sustained damage to other areas as well:

> *The Cerebellum: which affects motor control.*
> *The Basal Ganglia: impairing the processing of memory.*
> *The Hippocampus: suppressing learning and memory.*
> *Frontal Lobes: which are vital to impulse control.*

The workings of an FAE or FAS person's brain are vastly different from a healthy one. According to studies done by Dr. Edward Riley in San Diego, teachers and parents of these affected children are correct: FAS/FAE children cannot "act their age." Dr. Riley says, "Children with FAS appear to plateau in social abilities at about the 4- to 6-year-old level. which suggests arrested development. This interpretation is further supported by Streissguth et al., who found that adolescents and adults with FAS had social abilities age-appropriate for a 6-year old child, and by Steinhausen, et al., who showed that children with the social abilities of FAS did not improve with age." Even if their IQ is normal, FAS individuals just never seem to get it together. As children, they want to do right, but seldom can. As teenagers and adults they cannot see cause and effect. Controlling their impulses may seem an impossible task—even speaking the truth is a challenge. They often say whatever comes to mind, unaware that they are lying. People with bad character prey on FAS individuals because they are so easily influenced and exploited. Seldom are they the masterminds of a crime, but they are *usually the ones who get caught.*

To many of us, FAS/FAE individuals are more than just statistics. They are our loved ones—an adopted child who throws unbelievable tantrums, an adored teen who keeps following the wrong crowds, or a relative whose mistakes are bigger than other people's. They are our beloved family members, no matter how often they break our hearts. As much as we would love to, we cannot erase the damage that's been done. So for their sakes, we look toward the future. We can protect the children who will be born. Some day, those future children will become the world's adults. They'll live and love, and they'll write books about us—about our times, our society and about FAS. They'll recognize that we knew enough to prevent Fetal Alcohol Syndrome. They'll say that all we needed to do was to spread that knowledge and to hold each other accountable. What they conclude then will depend on what we do today. Will we promote awareness of the dangers of drinking while pregnant? Will we protect unborn children by monitoring *and helping* pregnant women who are at risk? Will we end this tragic form of child abuse?

W hat about drug babies?

It won't hurt you to research the effects that prenatal exposure to specific drugs have on children. However, despite the media frenzy over "drug babies" (which is now waning in light of the facts), alcohol is proven to be far more damaging to an unborn infant than most drugs commonly used by pregnant women. Drugs are harmful, but remember, however, expectant mothers who use drugs also usually drink alcohol while pregnant. As a group, "drug using mothers" drink alcohol, use more than one drug, have inadequate nutrition, suffer poor health themselves and live in polluted environments filled with violence. Drugs or no drugs, these babies are likely to have problems. Although alcohol (readily available, widely consumed) is proven to cause specific and serious birth defects, common drugs such as cocaine are not proven to produce any pattern of serious defects. Why haven't you heard this? Perhaps because alcohol is legal, and the alcohol industry is extremely lucrative. But the effects of alcohol on a fetus are far reaching and last a lifetime.

Fetal alcohol effects are often misdiagnosed. They mimic abandonment issues, post-traumatic stress, attachment disorders, bi-polar, autism, and ADD/ADHD, etc. If you're adopting, the chances of your baby having fetal alcohol effects depend upon the country of his/her birth. The World Health Organization offers alcohol abuse statistics by country. This page even has a color-coded map:

http://www.who.int/gho/substance_abuse/burden/alcohol/en
and
http://www.who.int/gho/substance_abuse/burden/drug_prevalence/en

For more detailed statistics, country by country, I recommend purchasing the "Global Status Report on Alcohol" from the World Health Organization Press or downloading it in .pdf format from their website. To learn much more about Fetal Alcohol Spectrum (FAS, FAE), I recommend this website as a starting point:

http://www.come-over.to/FAS/

Lastly, the *Center for the Evaluation of Risks to Human Reproduction* (CERHR) maintains a comprehensive database of the latest information about potentially hazardous effects of chemicals on human reproduction and development. You can utilize their website to study the various effects of drugs on babies. Please study more about Fetal Alcohol Spectrum and also the effects of chemicals (drugs) on babies. Your time with these children will be less confusing once you understand their invisible wounds.

1. (Ann Streissguthl, 1996)
2. (Lanceraux, 1865; quoted by Gustafson, 1885).

Nature, Nurture and Nightmares

"...they realized they were naked; so they sewed fig leaves together and made coverings for themselves. Then the man and his wife heard the sound of the LORD God as he was walking in the garden in the cool of the day, and they hid from the LORD God among the trees of the garden.

"But the LORD God called to the man, 'Where are you?' He answered, 'I heard you in the garden, and I was afraid because I was naked; so I hid.'

"And he said, 'Who told you that you were naked? Have you eaten from the tree that I commanded you not to eat from?'" (Genesis 3:7b, 8-11)

Have you ever done something God commanded you not to do? Have you ever been dreaming and suddenly realized you were naked? Did you think this was mere coincidence?

I have a homework assignment for you: Ask your friends and relatives if they've had this same dream. Be careful who you ask, of course. If you walk up to a stranger and say, "Have you ever dreamed you were naked?" it could cause problems. I'm not making a dogmatic point, but I'm curious about what you'll learn. In all my asking, 100% of the people claim they've had this same dream. You know how it goes: You realize you're naked, you panic and spend the rest of the dream trying to get back home to get dressed, or otherwise trying to find something to cover yourself. In my dreams, prior to giving my life to Jesus, I never reached home, I never stopped worrying; I never found a covering.

I find it fascinating that people have such similar pre-conversion dreams. We know that all have sinned. Likewise, at some point we all realize we're naked; apart from Christ, we try to cover ourselves and hide from God.

Next, I asked born-again Christians (whose lives reflect Christ's nature), "When was the last time you had this dream?" So far every believer remembers having the dream only before they surrendered their lives to Christ; before they were clothed with Jesus' righteousness. (Since giving my heart to Jesus, I've dreamed that I was somewhat exposed, but I wasn't worried about it, and I quickly found a way to remedy the problem.)

[Jesus speaking] "You say, 'I am rich; I have acquired wealth and do not need a thing.' But you do not realize that you are wretched, pitiful, poor, blind and naked.
"I counsel you to buy from me gold refined in the fire, so you can become rich; and white clothes to wear, so you can cover your shameful nakedness; and salve to put on your eyes, so you can see.
Those whom I love I rebuke and discipline. So be earnest, and repent."
(Revelation 3:17-19 NIV)

I'm not saying a born-again believer will never worry and feel panicked about being exposed (even in a dream), but if that happens to me, I'll be asking God about it.

In the world of psychology, intelligent people often spend their lives seeking answers (in the most complicated ways) to the simplest questions. If they refuse to ask God, or accept His answers, they must take the long way around to finding the facts. Such was the long and bumpy road to discovery of how a child develops emotionally, mentally and in respect to his talents or inclinations, etc. At last, the argument over nature verses nurture has quieted. The truth that both impact the child is almost unanimously accepted now. "Nativism" went up for discussion next. In the field of psychology, nativism is the view that certain skills or abilities are "native" or "hard-wired" into the brain at birth.

People can save themselves a lot of time and energy if they'll believe the Bible; as you read through history as recorded in Scripture, you see that God creates each of us with certain talents and purposes.

"For we are God's workmanship, created in Christ Jesus to do good works, which God prepared in advance for us to do." (Ephesians 2:10 NIV)

We are God's masterpiece, created to do good—and both nature and nurture are instrumental in a child's development. Therefore, many people wonder, when a person exhibits neurotic behaviors, is it because of defective genes, or is this the result of a dysfunctional childhood? They wrongly assume that the natural state of man, without negative influence or defective genetic material, is an ideal person. In the beginning—in the Garden of Eden—this was probably true. We're not in the Garden anymore.

Consider our discussion in a previous chapter: Aside from any good effects from nurturing or any negative from abuse and neglect, what is the natural state of a person at birth, prior to a spiritual rebirth? All people are slaves to their fallen or sin nature. Any "likeness of God" (as we were created in God's likeness) is overshadowed and corrupted by the fallen nature. We're naked, sewing leaves together and trying to hide from God.

"So I say, live by the Spirit, and you will not gratify the desires of the sinful nature. For the sinful nature desires what is contrary to the Spirit, and the Spirit what is contrary to the sinful nature. They are in conflict with each other, so that you do not do what you want. But if you are led by the Spirit, you are not under law.

"The acts of the sinful nature are obvious: sexual immorality, impurity and debauchery; idolatry and witchcraft; hatred, discord, jealousy, fits of rage, selfish ambition, dissensions, factions and envy; drunkenness, orgies, and the like. I warn you, as I did before, that those who live like this will not inherit the kingdom of God.

"But the fruit of the Spirit is love, joy, peace, patience, kindness, goodness, faithfulness, gentleness and self-control. Against such things there is no law. Those who belong to Christ Jesus have crucified the sinful nature with its passions and desires. Since we live by the Spirit, let us keep in step with the Spirit. Let us not become conceited, provoking and envying each other." (Galatians 5:16-26 NIV)

The acts of the sinful nature are... *sinful*. We know from Scripture (and life experience) that engaging in and practicing sinful behavior has a devastating and destructive effect on a person's mental and emotional state. Neuroticism and other negative traits are enhanced and encouraged through our exposure and surrender to sinful behavior and urges. A complete *giving over* of ourselves to evil behavior can even result in psychosis—being unable to discern reality from hallucinations. (Some might say a person is demon-possessed at that point. I won't speculate here, but if you want to visit over a cup of tea, let me know.)

"Instead, their thoughts have become complete nonsense, and their empty minds are filled with darkness. . . . . And so God has given those people over to do the filthy things their hearts desire . . . . Because those people refuse to keep in mind the true knowledge about God, he has given them over to corrupted minds . . ." (Rom. 1:21b, 24a, 28a GNB)

". . . do not continue to live like the heathen, whose thoughts are worthless and whose minds are in the dark. They have no part in the life that God gives, for they are completely ignorant and stubborn. They have lost all feeling of shame; they give themselves over to vice and do all sorts of indecent things without restraint." (Ephesians 4:18-19 GNB)

All people are hard-wired with two opposite potentials: If living by the Spirit of God, His beauty and goodness can flow from our lives. If living ruled by the sinful nature, horrible and hurtful things will rot our minds and emotions and dominate our actions.

In light of the opposite potentials that war within each person, what part does nurture play? Never having experienced spiritual rebirth or life by the Spirit of God, children are born carnal; they're merely physical beings, led by their natural desires and conforming to social influences around them. They're spiritually asleep, stuck in Romans, Chapter Seven—waiting for Chapter Eight. In this realm the effects of nurture (or neglect and abuse) are *profound!*

Kings and Monkeys

In the 13th Century AD, Frederick II, King of Germany, conducted an experiment to determine what language a child would speak if he/she were not spoken to in infancy or the early years. The King placed a number of babies with foster mothers or nurses. He gave strict orders that no one speak to or play with the babies. His orders were followed, but his experiment failed. All of the babies died due to a lack of attention. Later, the Mogul Emperor Akbar tried to determine what religion children would adopt if raised in isolation. His experiment also failed. All of the children turned out deaf and mute. To those who know God's pure, loving nature, these experiments are not only unbelievably cruel, but also absurd; even a monkey could have told them they'd fail. In the end, it was a monkey—or a group of monkeys—who gave the hard-hearted world "scientific proof" that babies need love.

During the 1950s and 60s, an American psychologist named Harry Frederick Harlow caused quite a stir with his maternal-separation and social isolation experiments on Rhesus monkeys. Despite serious ethical concerns regarding his cruel experiments, he did demonstrate the importance of tangible affection in social and cognitive development of baby monkeys. In Mr. Harlow's beginning research, his interest was sparked when the baby monkeys didn't respond as expected. Taken from their mothers within hours of birth, they received milk from a bottle attached to the cage. Rather than becoming attached to the bottle or nipple (the source of the life-giving milk), they were fixated on the soft cloth diapers that lined the bottom of their cages. They seemed comforted not by the milk, but by cuddling with the soft cloth; this strange bond baffled the scientist and he began further experiments into the phenomenon.

He next presented the monkeys with two surrogate "mothers"; some monkeys had both and some had one or the other. Both "mothers" had a face with eyes; one was made entirely of wire and the other was covered with soft terry cloth material. Sometimes the babies received milk through a hole in the wire "mother," and sometimes through the cloth "mother." Regardless, the baby monkeys clung to the soft terry-cloth mother for comfort and security, whether that mother gave them milk or not. The baby monkeys who were raised with either a wire mother or a cloth mother gained weight at the same rate. However, the monkeys that had only a wire mother had trouble digesting the milk and suffered from diarrhea more often.

Whenever a frightening stimulus was brought into the cage, the monkeys ran to the cloth mother for protection and comfort, no matter which mother provided them with food; this response decreased as the monkeys grew older.

When the monkeys were placed in an unfamiliar room with their cloth mother, they clung to it until they felt secure enough to explore. Once they began to explore, they occasionally returned to the cloth mother for comfort. Monkeys placed in an unfamiliar room without their cloth mothers acted quite differently; they froze in fear and cried, crouched down or sucked their thumbs. Some monkeys even ran from object to object, apparently searching for the cloth mother, as they cried and screamed. Monkeys placed in this situation with their wire mothers exhibited the same behavior as the monkeys with no mother; without the soft mother to run to, they could not cope but would scream, run in circles and urinate.

If you spend enough time working with abused children, at some point you'll feel like you've stumbled into *Harlow's lab*.

Yes, it gets worse. Harlow next did isolation experiments on the baby monkeys. Partial isolation resulted in various abnormalities such as blank staring, repetitive circling in their cages and self-mutilation. Total isolation experiments produced monkeys that were severely psychologically disturbed. The damage was permanent; he was never able to successfully integrate them into society.

Since these experiments, much more research followed regarding nurturing and development of human children. Although the full truth will never be found in psychology because of its many false assumptions and reprehensible methods, there is truth in statistics. Studies clearly prove that humans are permanently impacted by their experiences during infancy and the first two years of life.

As if naked, wearing leaves and hiding from God weren't bad enough... if abused, neglected or isolated during this stage, without a miracle, the damage is lasting.

But of course, I believe in miracles.

Candlelight-Parenting

Nurturing Children with Attachment Disorders

"For we do not preach ourselves, but Jesus Christ as Lord, and ourselves as your servants for Jesus' sake. For God, who said, 'Let light shine out of darkness,' made his light shine in our hearts to give us the light of the knowledge of the glory of God in the face of Christ." (2 Cor. 4:5-6 NIV)

Mom, Dad, imagine you're a candlestick. Jesus placed His candle inside you and lit the flame. Now His love, (and *the knowledge of the glory of God in the face of Christ*), burns brightly inside your heart. Next, He placed a wounded child in your care; adorable, helpless and lost somewhere within the darkness of his soul. Welcome to the world of *Candlelight Parenting.*

COME and FIND ME WHERE I'M LOST.

Your mission is to help this lost and injured child find his way. You'll guide him to Jesus, so he might find inner healing. Before he arrives, you'll keep him within range of your candle's light at all times. While he's still separated from his Savior, you'll shine the knowledge of God's glory (Christ) and shelter him with the same affection you've received from Christ.

But here's the problem: Because of his wounds, he won't trust you. He'll refuse to follow. Your light may even make him cringe and run the other direction. He might even be tricked into working for the enemy, trying to *take you out.*

God gave parents the responsibility to guide and protect children, because they need both. The Bible teaches that all children are born with a sinful nature and that foolishness is bound up in the heart of a child. If you're raising a child who seems to go beyond even that, perhaps one who seems like he's come from *Harlow's lab* (as in the previous chapter), you probably have a child with invisible wounds and trust issues. In the world of adoption and foster care these are referred to as *attachment disorders.* There are different terms for different types and levels of this problem. Most likely you'll encounter plenty of information on this subject; I'd like to help you look at it from a biblical point of view.

Another word for trust is *faith.* Your child lacks faith. Babies who are nurtured and protected develop a natural trust, or faith, in their caregiver; they tend to assume other people are trustworthy as well, until they prove otherwise. A nurtured child sees the world through rose-colored glasses—joy, wonder and hope color everything; life is a melodic, vibrant, beautiful mystery! But a neglected or abused child can develop a bleak outlook and very debilitating lack of faith in others—the Bible describes this as *bitterness.*

Many adults are angry and bitter. Their hearts have grown cold; they view life through a lens of gloom. A sin-deadened, faithless, hopeless perspective often defiles people as they age. However, an abused or neglected child develops this heart-sickness much, much earlier. This is dangerously crippling because children are helpless and unaware; they need to trust in your judgment. This crippling lack of faith makes your child extremely vulnerable to the enemy of his soul.

"Children, obey your parents in all things: for this is well pleasing unto the Lord." (Col. 3:20 KJV)

"Obey your leaders and follow their orders. They watch over your souls without resting, since they must give to God an account of their service. If you obey them, they will do their work gladly; if not, they will do it with sadness, and that would be of no help to you." (Hebrews 13:17 GNB)

Parents who love a child who does not trust them can also become very discouraged over time. It's much easier to love when love is returned. But remember this:

"For when we were still helpless, Christ died for the wicked at the time that God chose. It is a difficult thing for someone to die for a righteous person. It may even be that someone might dare to die for a good person. But God has shown us how much he loves us—it was while we were still sinners that Christ died for us! By his blood we are now put right with God" . . . (Romans 5:6-9a GNB)

Your relationship with Jesus is your source of love; when you abide in Christ, and He abides in you, you'll have enough love to share—even with those who cannot return it.

"But now I tell you: love your enemies and pray for those who persecute you" . . . . "Why should God reward you if you love only the people who love you?" (Matthew 5:44, 46a GNB)

When a child's reality is hellish, or the world as he knows it suddenly disappears, he loses his way. He doesn't know what's real and what's not.

"When my thoughts were bitter and my feelings were hurt, I was as stupid as an animal; I did not understand you." (Psalms 73:21-22 GNB)

"Others have no happiness at all; they live and die with bitter hearts." (Job 21:25 GNB)

If your child has lost his way, he doesn't trust you, but often times he doesn't even trust his own eyes. He needs a miracle. God sends this miracle as someone who wants to hold him; a person who won't let go, even when he's bad. God sends you.

Enter joyful little you, wearing your cross and *Jesus-Loves-You* T-shirt.

What are you doing here? God bless you; thank you for coming! Your child might not overcome his distrust of people until he places his faith in Christ; once he's attached to the Vine, all will begin to heal. Meanwhile, your mission is to patiently lead him and shine, shine,

shine! Show him that Jesus is worthy of his trust by consistently letting that trustworthiness and love come through you. Mom, Dad, don't enter a traumatized or broken child's reality, and don't pretend that the lies he's believed are true, but stay close to him. Keep the light of Christ's love shining, so he can see the way out.

In order to stay close, you'll need to put away expectations. You'll need to let Jesus' love *cover a multitude of sins.* If you have expectations, he'll disappoint you—over and over and over again—then you'll grow bitter too. Be patient; he's a child; a lost child. Young children are not miniature adults. Pray for renewed joy if his negative behavior wears at you. Read your Bible daily so that God can renew your mind. If you do not, the child's tainted perception and behavior will change yours.

"Foolish children bring grief to their fathers and bitter regrets to their mothers." (Proverbs 17:25 GNB)

Surely you'll teach right and wrong, and teach him the gospel. But don't expect him to get it. Don't make him earn your affection. Don't make him think he can earn God's love. Remind him that God freely offers not only His love, but His Spirit to live in your child's heart—which will give him the ability to do what's right and good. When he sees *you* yielding to God's love, power and perfect plans, he'll be encouraged to do the same. But if he doesn't understand, that's alright. Pray for him, and teach it without expecting or demanding results. When raising foster or adoptive children, remember that this little person has a valid reason for his distrust and bitterness. It's your job to show him what real love is and where it comes from.

Because you didn't enter the relationship with a strong bond (as parents might with a baby who is born to them), you must be cautious. Tailor your parenting methods to his unique needs. Be encouraging and compassionate; do not insult or tease him, not even in the guise of a joke. Even if he's accustomed to it, do not play roughly. He may not know it, but He's scared. Frightened children show their fear through bizarre, ugly behavior. Your faithless child, with his wounds and weirdness, needs you to pray for him and enjoy him—and let him know you enjoy him!

Regarding discipline: Be gentle; he has unseen damage.

He might even have brain-damage that makes it impossible for him to behave, regardless of consequences. Punishment methods of parenting will not produce the same results seen in healthy children. Certainly he needs boundaries and guidance. But I strongly caution against using methods that require this unique child (in this unique relationship) to meet expected standards. Harsh or physical disciplines (such as the method in the book *To Train Up a Child*)[1] can be exceedingly dangerous for adopted children and illegal with foster children. The Bible teaches that we should love one another deeply, from the heart. Therefore, never withhold deep affection until the child performs well enough. When he feels alone and/or threatened, his bitterness and hopelessness will grow; his bad behavior will only increase.

"Let all bitter, sharp and angry feeling, and noise, and evil words, be put away from you, with all unkind acts; And be kind to one another, full of pity, having forgiveness for one another, even as God in Christ had forgiveness for you." (Ephesians 4:31-32 BBE)

If you can find where he's become lost, bring him back! Never leave him alone in the darkness of his soul. Stay close and shine the light of God's perfect love (which casts out fear) into his world and upon his face. Hold him often; kiss his cheeks daily; tell him he's beautiful to you and that you hear birds singing when you're together. Make him smile; make him giggle—not through foolishness or coarse jesting, of course, but make him blush by how sweet you are on him.

"For you created my inmost being; you knit me together in my mother's womb. I praise you because I am fearfully and wonderfully made; your works are wonderful, I know that full well." (Psalm 139: 13-14)

Don't be like the Pharisees who laid heavy loads on the people but wouldn't lift a finger to help them. If you can identify triggers to your child's harmful behavior, and if you can remove those temptations, then remove them! Don't set him up to fail. On that subject, many parents have found that the *Feingold diet* and/or a low-carb/high-fat *Ketogenic type diet* have drastically improved their troubled child's mental and emotional state, and their behavior. Although there are still many studies to be done, science and statistics indicate that many behavior problems are just sensitivities to chemical additives in foods, or toxic build-up in the brain due to inherited metabolic quirks that render people incapable of dealing with the high-carb, preservative-rich diet our society currently prefers.

Don't forget this child was likely damaged by chemicals in the womb and carries genetic material from people who were, at least for a time, rendered incapable of parenting—and many of these same adults recovered once their chemical or substance effects were corrected. So if you have a difficult to understand or control child, prayerfully research natural diets, additive/chemical sensitivities and other environmental improvements. (A full-blown *Ketogenic diet* also works wonders if you have a child prone to seizures or other neurological disturbances.) Also, home schooling increases a child's security-level and allows for much more together-time as you work on your relationship.

Remember, your child's full spiritual and emotional healing will come when he matures enough to understand and puts his faith in Jesus. Only Jesus can open blind eyes, revive our wonder and cure us of heart-sickness. That could be when your child is four, or maybe when he's forty. When he invites Jesus to light a candle in his own heart, you'll have accomplished your mission. Until then, be gentle, kind and compassionate, and let Jesus' love shine.

"Defend the cause of the weak and fatherless; maintain the rights of the poor and oppressed. Rescue the weak and needy; deliver them from the hand of the wicked." (Psalm 82:3-4 NIV)

---

1. I previously (mistakenly) called the authors an "Amish couple." They write of Amish parenting methods, but their neighbors tell me they're not Amish. I mean no disrespect to the authors or to Anabaptists; *To Train Up a Child* proclaims "less spanking," more joy. But the book has been implicated in the accidental deaths of *multiple* adopted children. Therefore, I must warn parents: their method is *not* a choice for your unique parenting role.

Medicine Men

"Man needs to be saved from his own wisdom as much as from his own righteousness, for they produce one and the same corruption." —
William Law

Americans are obsessed with drugs. Can you name ten people who are totally drug-free? Without even prescription medications?

Some drugs commonly used in American society treat physical ailments, but a vast number of prescriptions are intended only to modify behavior, awareness, thought patterns or emotional condition. For this reason, all parents—and especially those who do foster care and adopt—should fully understand the drugs that American's bodies are full of and that their doctors are offering them (sometimes not merely offering, but imposing upon them).

In order to understand prescription drugs prescribed for behavior modification, you must first take a look at *the dealers.*

Using drugs to change behavior, awareness, thought patterns or emotional condition (in our society) comes from the belief system called psychology. Once an obscure practice, psychology is now one of the most powerful systems of belief in America—if not the most powerful. Their teachings have saturated our culture, including the church. So you owe it to yourself to research this belief system before blindly letting it guide you.

In brief, it's core is atheistic philosophy; some call psychology a religion. Why a religion? Because its foundational elements are conclusions about God: we are animals; we are not made in God's image; we are not governed by any laws of God (because God does not exist), and we are definitely not under the curse of sin, because sin does not exist. Much of psychology attempts to convince us that we are not guilty of sin, when our consciences accuse us. Some sects of psychology assume that humans are born full of goodness; if left to themselves, they will develop into perfectly wonderful beings. However, psychology has over two-hundred contradicting schools of thought, which change constantly.

Even more confusing, just around the time secular researchers began putting less confidence in psychology, more professing Christians began pursuing it. Across America "Christian" counseling centers suddenly sprung up, offering what they believed was the perfect combination: Christianity plus psychology!

In their attempts to be relevant, thereby more popular, many preachers, teachers, counselors and writers began to promote a psychological perspective on life, rather than a biblical one. The beliefs of psychology overshadowed the cross of Christ, and psychological jargon contaminated the church. Because this has been ongoing for some time, if you grew up in church you may not even realize that *humanism* isn't Christianity—it's the opposite. [1]

"The time will come when people will not listen to sound doctrine, but will follow their own desires and will collect for themselves more and more teachers who will tell them what they are itching to hear." (2 Tim. 4:3 GNB)

Don't take my word for it; educate yourself. You can begin with the writings, videos and courses offered by The Institute for Nouthetic Studies, or through the Association of Certified biblical Counselors. (Both are Christian and reject the teachings of psychology.)

The use of drugs to change behavior, awareness, thought patterns or emotional condition entered our society (fairly recently) through psychology, but it's actually an ancient practice. Every pagan tribe and ungodly nation dabbled widely in this art. It's referred to in history and the Bible as pharmakeia, or in other words, witchcraft:

    pharmakeia (far-mak-i'-ah): medication (pharmacy), that
    is, (by extension) magic (literal or figurative):-sorcery,
    witchcraft. (Strongs Concordance, G5331, from G5332)

HOW PREVALENT ARE PSYCHIATRIC DRUGS?

Over 78 and a half million Americans are currently taking psychiatric drugs. A total of 8,389,034 kids, seventeen and under, are on psychiatric drugs. 1,080,168 of these are babies and children five years old or less. [2] I'm not aware of studies that count how many of these children are adopted or in foster care, but based on experience, I assume a very disproportionately high number of them are. Below are some of the drugs *medicine men* commonly prescribe to alter behavior, awareness, thought patterns and emotions. I've also included known side-effects. This is only a partial list and a brief overview. I'll discuss this in more detail in the chapter titled Emergency Response. For your own research, begin by downloading the free booklet "The Side Effects of Common Psychiatric Drugs," from CCHR International.

SOME PSYCHIATRIC DRUGS and THEIR SIDE EFFECTS

PSYCHOSTIMULANTS

(Note: The U.S. Drug Enforcement Administration (DEA) classifies methylphenidate, the generic name for Ritalin, Concerta, Metadate and Methylin, as a Schedule II narcotic in the same abuse category as morphine, opium and cocaine.[5])

Brand Names (Generic Names)

Adderall (amphetamine and dextroamphetamine), Benzedrine (amphetamine sulfate), Concerta (methylphenidate), Cylert (pemoline—removed from the market), Daytrana (methylphenidate—skin patch), Desoxyn (methamphetamine hydrochloride), Dexedrine (dextroamphetamine sulfate), Dextrostat (dextroamphetamine), Equasym (methylphenidate), Focalin (dexmethylphenidate), Metadate (methylphenidate), Methylin (methylphenidate hydrochloride), Ritalin (methylphenidate), Vyvanse (lisdexamphetamine)

Side Effects of Psychostimulants:

Abdominal pain, aggressive or hostile behavior, agitation, angina (sudden acute pain), anorexia, blisters or rash, blood pressure and pulse changes, changes in sexual appetite or ability, changes in vision or blurred vision, chest pain, depression, diarrhea, difficulty falling asleep or staying asleep, dizziness or faintness, drowsiness, dry mouth, fast, pounding, or irregular heartbeat, fever, hallucinations, headaches, heart attack, hives, hypersensitivity, impotence, increased irritability/feelings of anger, insomnia, involuntary tics and twitching, itching, liver problems, loss of appetite, mania, mental/mood changes, muscle or joint tightness, nausea, nervousness, painful menstruation, psychosis, purple blotches under the skin, restlessness, seizures, slow or difficult speech, sore throat, stomach pain, stroke, stuffed or runny nose, stunted growth, sudden death, suicidal thoughts or suicide, swelling inside the nose, swelling of the eyes, face, tongue, or throat, Tourette's Syndrome, toxic psychosis, unusual bleeding or bruising, unusual sadness or crying, unusual weakness or tiredness, violent behavior, vomiting, weakness or numbness of an arm or leg, weight loss, "zombie" demeanor. [4]

ANTIPSYCHOTICS

(Called Major Tranquilizers or Neuroleptics)

Brand Names (Generic Names)

Compazine (prochlorperazine), Haldol (haloperidol), Largactil (clorpromazine), Lidone (molindone), Loxitane (loxapine), Mellaril (thioridazine hydrochloride), Moban (molindone hydrochloride), Navane (thiorixene), Novo-Trifluzine (trifluoperazine), Nozinan (methotrimeprazine), Orap (pimozide), Permitil (fluphenazine), Phenergam (promethazie), Proketazine (carphenazine), Prolixin (fluphenazine hydrochloride), Repoise (butaperazine Maleate), Serentil (mesoridazine besylate), Sparine (promazine), Stelazine (trifluoperazine), Stemetil (prochlorperazine), Taractan (chlorprothixene), Thorazine (chlorpromazine), Tindal (acetophenazine), Trancopal (chlormezanone), Trilafon (perphenazine), Vesprin (triflupromazine)—Newer Atypical Antipsychotics: Abilify (aripiprazole), Clozaril (clozapine), Geodon (ziprasidone hydrochloride), Invega (palperidone), Leponex (clozapine), Risperdal (risperidone), Serlect (sertindole), Seroquel (quetiapine), Symbyax (fluoxetine and olanzapine—antidepressant/antipsychotic mix), Zeldox (ziprasidone), Zyprexa (olanzapine)

Side Effects of Antipsychotics:

Abnormal gait (manner of walking), agitation, akathisia, anxiety, birth defects, blood disorders, blood-sugar abnormalities, blurred vision, breastmilk production, cardiac arrest, changes in behavior, chest pain, confusion, constipation, death from liver failure, decreased sexual interest or ability, depression, diabetes, diarrhea, difficulty breathing, swallowing or fast breathing, difficulty falling asleep or staying asleep, difficulty urinating or loss of bladder control, dizziness, dreaming more than usual, drowsiness, dry mouth, dry or discolored skin, excess sweating, excessive weight gain, extreme inner anxiety, eye pain or discoloration, fainting, fast, irregular, or pounding heartbeat, fatal blood clots, fever, fine worm-like tongue movements, flu-like symptoms, headache, heart arrhythmia, heart failure, heart palpitation, heartburn, heat stroke, hemorrhage, high fever, hives, hostility, hyperglycemia (abnormally high blood sugar), hypoglycemia (abnormally low blood sugar), impotence, increased appetite, increased salivation, indigestion, insomnia, involuntary movements, itching, jaw, neck, and back muscle spasms, joint pain, lack of energy, light-headedness, loss of appetite, manic reaction, mood changes, muscle or joint stiffness, pain, or weakness, muscle twitching, nausea, nervousness, Neuroleptic Malignant Syndrome, nightmares, pacing, pain in arms, legs, back, or joints, pain in the upper right part of the stomach, painful erection that lasts for hours, painful skin rashes, pancreatitis (inflammation of pancreas), poor concentration, restlessness or pacing, seizures or convulsions, sexual dysfunction, shakiness, shaking hands that you cannot control, sleepiness, slow or difficult speech, slow, jerky movements, sore throat, spasms, suicidal thoughts or suicide, swelling of the arms, hands, feet, ankles, or lower legs, swollen and leaking breasts, tachycardia (heart irregularity), Tardive Dyskinesia, tremors, unusual behavior, unusual bleeding or bruising, unusual tiredness, violence, vomiting, weakness, weight gain, yellowing of the skin or eyes. [4]

NEWER ANTIDEPRESSANTS

(The newer antidepressants emerged in the late 1980s/1990s, marketed as being capable of selectively targeting a chemical in the brain that was theorized to influence depression. This has remained a theory only. There are no physical tests or scientific evidence to substantiate the theory.[4])

Brand Names (Generic Names)

SSRIs: Akarin (citalopram), Apo-Sertral (sertraline), Aropax (paroxetine), Asentra (sertraline), Celexa (citalopram), Cipralex (escitalopram), Cipram (citalopram), Cipramil (citalopram), Citopam (citalopram), Deroxat (paroxetine), Dumyrox (fluvoxamine), Eufor (fluoxetine), Faverin (fluvoxamine), Floxyfral (fluvoxamine), Fluctine (fluoxetine), Fluocim (fluoxetine), Fluox (fluoxetine), Fluvox (fluvoxamine), Gladem (sertraline), Ladose (fluoxetine), Lexapro (escitalopram oxalate), Lovan (fluoxetine), Lustral (sertraline), Luvox (fluvoxamine), Paroxat (paroxetine), Paxil (paroxetine), Pexeva (paroxetine), Prisdal (citalopram), Prozac (fluoxetine hydrochloride), Psiquial (fluoxetine), Sarafem (fluoxetine hydrochloride), Sercerin (sertraline), Serlift (sertraline), Seroplex (escitalopram), Seroplexa (escitalopram), Seropram (paroxetine), Seroxat (paroxetine), Sipralexa (escitalopram), Tolrest (sertraline), Veritina (fluoxetine), Zoloft (sertraline hydrochloride), Xydep (sertraline)—SerotoninNRIs: Ariclaim (duloxetine), Cymbalta (duloxetine), Dalcipran (milnacipran), Dobupal (venlafaxine), Efectin (venlafaxine), Effexor (venlafaxine), Ixel (milnacipran), Pristiq (desvenlafaxine), Yentreve (duloxetine)—SelectiveNRIs: Edronax (reboxetine), Outorin (nefazodone), Merital (nomifensine), Norebox (reboxetine), Serzone (nefazodone), Strattera (atomoxetine), Vestra (reboxetine)—NDRIs and OTHER: Odranal (bupropion), Wellbutrin (bupropion), Zyban (bupropion), Desyrel (trazodone), Dutonin (nefazodone), Ludiomil (maprotiline hydrochloride), Nedafar (nefazodone), Serzone (nefazodone), Symbyax (fluoxetine and olanzapine— antidepressant/antipsychotic mx)

Side Effects of Newer Antidepressants:

Abnormal bleeding or bruising, abnormal thoughts, agitation, akathisia (severe restless- ness), anxiety, black and tarry stools, blisters, blood in stools, bloody vomit, blurred or changes in vision, burning or tingling in the hands, arms, feet, or legs, burping, changes in ability to taste food, changes in sexual appetites or ability, chest pain, coma, confu- sion, constipation, cough, dark colored urine, delusions, diarrhea, difficult, frequent, or painful urination, difficulty breathing or swallowing, difficulty concentrating, dizziness or faintness, drowsiness, dry mouth, emotional numbing, enlarged pupils, eye pain or redness, fast, pounding, or irregular heartbeat, fever, flu-like symptoms, flushing, forget- fulness, gas or bloating, hallucinations, headache, heart attacks, heartburn, hives, hoarseness, hostility, hot flashes or flushing, hypomania (abnormal excitement), impo- tence, increased appetite, increased sweating, indigestion, insomnia, itching, joint pain, loss of appetite, lump or tightness in throat, mania, memory lapses, mood swings, mus- cle weakness or tightness, nausea, nervousness, Neuroleptic Malignant Syndrome, night- mares, numbness in your hands, feet, arms, or legs, pain in the back, muscles, joints, or anywhere in the body, pain in the upper right part of the stomach, painful erection that lasts for hours, painful or irregular menstruation, panic attacks, paranoia, problems with coordination, problems with teeth, psychotic episodes, rash, restlessness, ringing in the ears, runny nose, seizures, sensitivity to light, sexual dysfunction, slow or difficult speech, small purple spots on the skin, sneezing, sore throat, fever, chills, and other signs of infection, stomach pain, sudden muscle twitching or jerking that can't be con- trolled, sudden upset stomach, suicidal thoughts or behavior or suicide, swelling of the eyes, face, lips, tongue, throat, hands, arms, feet, ankles, or lower legs, swelling, itching, burning, or infection in the vagina, tightness in hands and feet, twitching, uncontrolla- ble shaking of a part of the body, violent behavior, vomiting, vomiting material that looks like coffee grounds, weakness or numbness of an arm or leg, weakness or tiredness, weight gain, weight loss, withdrawal symptoms include deeper depression, yellowing of the skin or eyes. [4]

ANTI-ANXIETY DRUGS & BARBITURATES

(Minor Tranquilizers, Benzodiazepines or Sedative Hypnotics)(British studies call Benzodiazepines more lethal than heroin, cocaine and methadone.(6) British professor C. Ashton reported cases of babybattering, wife-beating and "grandmother-bashing" could be attributed to people taking benzodiazepines.[7])

Brand Names (Generic Names)

Ambien (zolpidem), Ativan (lorazepam), Azene (clorazepate), BuSpar (buspirone), Centrax (prazepam), Dalmane (flurazepam), Doral (quazepam), Equanil (meprobamate), Halcion (triazolam), Klonopin (clonazepam), Lexomil (bromazepam), Lexotan (bromazepam), Lexotanil (bromazepam), Librax (chlordiazepoxide and flicinium), Libritabs (chlordiazepoxide), Librium (chlordiazepoxide), Lunesta (eszopiclone), Miltown (meprobamate), Niravam (alprazolam), Paxipam (halazepam), Placi- dyl (ethchlorvynol), Prosom (estazolam), Reapam (prazepam), Restoril (temazepam), Rivotril (clonazepam), Rohypnol (flunitrazepam), Rozerem (ramelteon), Serax (oxazepam), Serepax (oxazepam), Serestra (oxazepam), Sonata (zaleplon), Stesolid (diazepam), Stilnox (zolpidem), Temes- ta (lorazepam), Tranxene (clorazepate), Valium (diazepam), Valrelease (diazepam), Versed (midazolam), Verstran (prazepam), Vistaril (hydroxyzine), Xanax (alprazolam), Barbiturates: Amytal (amobarbital), Butalan (butabarbital), Butisol (butabarbital), Luminal (phenobarbitone), Mebaral (mephobarbial), Nembutal (pentobarbital), Seconal (secobarbital), Sodium Amytal (amobarbital), Solfoton (phenobarbital), Tuinal (secobarbital and amobarbital)

Side Effects of Anti-Anxiety Drugs & Barbiturates:

Acute hyper-excited states, aggressive behavior, agitation, agranulocytosis (susceptibility to infection), akathisia, amnesia, anxiety, blurred vision, changes in appetite, changes in sexual appetites or ability, chest pain, confusion, constipation, diarrhea, difficulty urinating, disorientation, dizziness or lightheadedness, drowsiness, dry mouth, epileptic seizures and death have resulted from suddenly stopping, fast or irregular heartbeat, fatigue, fear, feeling that the throat is closing, fever, frequent urination, hallucinations, hangover effect (grogginess), headache, heartburn, hives, hoarseness, hostility, increased salivation [drooling], insomnia, irritability, itching, jaundice, jaw, neck, and back muscle spasms, lethargy, liver problems, memory impairment, muscle tremors, nausea, nervousness, nightmares, numbness, problems with coordination, psychosis, rage, restlessness or excitement, sedation, seizures, severe depression, severe skin rash, sexual problems, shuffling walk, sleep disturbances, slow or difficult speech, slurred speech, stomach pain, suicide attempt, swelling of the eyes, face, lips, tongue, or throat, talkativeness, tiredness, transient amnesia, tremors, unusual movements of the head or neck muscles, upset stomach, vomiting, weakness, weight changes—Barbiturate side effects: Addiction, breathing difficulties, chronic tiredness, depression, disorientation, dizziness, fever, hallucination, kidney disease, lack of coordination, liver disease, menstrual irregularities, rash, slowed reflexes & response, sluggishness, tightness in chest, upset stomach, vision problems, swelling of eyelids, face, or lips. [4]

WARNING: It can be dangerous (or fatal) to immediately stop taking psychiatric drugs, due to potential withdrawal side effects. No one should stop taking any psychiatric drug without the advice and assistance of a competent, medical doctor.

IS THERE A BETTER WAY?

If these drugs are *gifts from God*, reinforcements sent to help us, why do they behave like *enemies*, raping and pillaging instead? Please think (and pray) about this.

Most cultures have had their medicine men. They're sometimes called healers, sometimes doctors. There have been healers who did good, but many whose help was actually serious abuse. They offered elixirs to treat their patient's inner mental and emotional disturbances. Many of these potions were later outlawed, but only after causing many deaths and wreaking havoc in societies. One such concoction was *laudanum*. It's name was derived from the Latin verb *laudare*, which means to praise. Initially, "laudanum" referred to any combination of opium and alcohol. In early and mid-Victorian Britain it was possible to walk into a chemist's shop and buy (without prescription) laudanum, cocaine and even arsenic. Opium preparations were also sold freely in towns on market halls and in the countryside by traveling hawkers.[8] Opium, and after 1820, morphine, was mixed with everything imaginable: mercury, hashish, cayenne pepper, ether, chloroform, belladonna, whiskey, wine and brandy."[10] Until the early 20th century, laudanum was sold without a prescription and was a constituent of many patent medicines; it was prescribed for adults and children as a cure for almost every ailment. Today, laudanum is recognized as dangerous and addictive; it's strictly regulated and controlled throughout most of the world.[9]

However, some of the same potions historically banned, or regulated, are still readily available — reformulated or relabeled; the secret recipes are the same. No, you cannot readily purchase laudanum, but you can pick up some alcohol at the grocery store, then swing by any emergency clinic (or dentist) claiming you're in a bit of pain. They'll write you a prescription for opium, otherwise known as Hydrocodone (a semi-synthetic opioid synthesized from codeine, one of the opioid alkaloids found in the opium poppy. It's a narcotic used orally for pain, but also commonly taken as a cough suppressant.[11]) The most commonly abused opioid painkillers include oxycodone, hydrocodone, meperidine, hydromorphone and propoxyphene. Oxycontin, one brand of oxycodone, is known as "Hillybilly Herione" because of it's current rampant abuse and destructive effects on society.[12]

Hypnotics, benzodiazepines, tranquilizers . . . cocaine, meth., heroine, etc. — they produce predictable, specific (demonic, evil) patterns of behavior. (See the side-effects lists above.) Alcohol too has a very predictable effect on people (like that of barbiturates). This legal drug is the gateway not just to sexual promiscuity, but complete abandon and ultimately bondage to sexual perversion. In advanced stages alcohol can cause psychosis and leads to suicide.[13]

"The thief comes only in order to steal, kill, and destroy. I [Jesus] have come in order that you might have life — life in all its fullness." (John 10:10 GNB)

Demonic activity is rampant in our world. The Bible illustrates that even children can be demon-possessed. Freedom from evil, and from evil spirits, is found only through Jesus. However, when preachers of psychology prescribe behavior altering drugs, they're often trying to cure symptoms of spiritual darkness and oppression by conjuring up more evil. This is like asking Satan to drive out Satan.

But if they're wrong, and if their drugs don't truly heal, is there a way? Is healing even a possibility? Can your family be free of darkness and chaos? Yes, I believe your family can escape bedlam and evil. By wholeheartedly surrendering to God and allowing Him to make changes in your family, however He sees fit, then persevering in that path, your home can become a place of light, joy, peace and security. Jesus is our Wonderful Counselor (Isa. 9:6); we should not be filled with potions which violate and ravage us, and lead us into sin, but rather be filled with the Holy Spirit. (Eph. 5:18) The side effects of being filled with His Spirit are love, joy, peace, patience, kindness, goodness, faithfulness, humility and self-control—because those are His attributes! (Yes, He's awesome and beautiful!) (Gal. 5:22-23)

"So then, submit yourselves to God. Resist the Devil, and he will run away from you. Come near to God, and he will come near to you. Wash your hands, you sinners! Purify your hearts, you hypocrites! Be sorrowful, cry, and weep; change your laughter into crying, your joy into gloom! Humble yourselves before the Lord, and he will lift you up."
(James 4:7-10 GNB)

But will this be harder than obtaining a *false-peace* by drugging an out-of-control child into compliance? Will it be harder than drugging a depressed mother into a state of glee (or at least apathy)? Yes, of course it will! It's much more work, in the beginning—but walking in faith and obedience to Christ produces abundant, joyful life and miracles! On the other hand, the drugged mother cannot hear clearly when the Holy Spirit warns her of danger or disobedience. And the drugged child cannot escape the bubble of dullness we've put him in. He CANNOT hear the voice of God calling to him, therefore he cannot respond!

". . . as soon as they hear the message, Satan comes and takes it away."
(Mark 4:15b GNB)

The drugged child cannot recognize and feel sorry for his sins, because his mind is hypnotized and his feelings are sedated. Therefore, he cannot repent of his sins, and thus he cannot receive forgiveness. If we keep him drugged up long enough, he'll come to the end of his days, separated from God, and he'll pass into eternal punishment . . . without ever realizing he was here.

Yes, I know the popular crowd is pushing mind-altering drugs on you and your children. But the social crowd, with their fake smiles and condescending speech, has always been mean and cruel; they're the devil's hands. Shame on them, but shame on us for wanting their approval.

"Unfaithful people! Don't you know that to be the world's friend means to be God's enemy? If you want to be the world's friend, you make yourself God's enemy." (James 4:4 GNB)

Jesus loves the people of our confused, ravaged and pillaged society; pray for them. But we must not participate in practices that will displease our God and hurt our families. We must, instead, follow the Holy Spirit of God. His ways are perfect.

"You are to open their eyes and turn them from the darkness to the light and from the power of Satan to God, so that through their faith in me [Jesus] they will have their sins forgiven and receive their place among God's chosen people." (Acts 26:18 GNB)

To read more on this subject, please see the chapter titled "Emergency Response." If your family needs counseling, contact the Association of Certified biblical Counselors for recommendations:

ACBC Headquarters
2825 Lexington Road
Louisville, KY 40280
502-410-5526

1: PsychoHeresy: The Psychological Seduction of Christianity, 1987 by Martin & Deidre Bobgan

2. IMS, Vector One: National (VONA) and Total Patient Tracker (TPT) Database, Year 2013, Extracted April 2014.

3: FDA: "FDA Directs ADHD Drug Manufacturers to Notify Patients about Cardiovascular Adverse Events and Psychiatric Adverse Events." FDA: "FDA Proposes New Warnings about Suicidal Thinking, Behavior in Young Adults Who Take Antidepressant Medications." National Resource Center on ADHD: "Managing Medication for Adults with ADHD." National Resource Center on ADHD: "Medications Used in the Treatment of ADHD." Pliszka, S. and the AACAP Study Group, Journal of the American Academy of Child and Adolescent Psychiatry, July 2007. WebMD Health News: "New Heart Alert for Some ADHD Drugs." Medscape: "Once-Daily Guanfacine Approved to Treat ADHD." Intuniv web site. 2014 WebMD.

4. The Side Effects of Common Psychiatric Drugs, Citizens Commission on Human Rights International, 2016; Physicians' Desk Reference, http://www.pdrhealth.com; "Adderall," DrugStore.com, Internet URL: http://www.drugstore.com; "Study Suggests Focalin (TM) LA Capsules (d-MPH-ER) Are Safe and Effective for ADHD in Adults," PR Newswire, 5 May 2004; A.D.D. Warehouse website; ADHDHelp, Internet URL: http://www.adhdhelp.org/metadate.htm. Journal of the Royal Society of Med., Vol 92, Mar. 99 "letters to the editor" p. 156. Medline Plus, www.nim.nih.gov/medlineplus: Millichap, J.Gordon "Methylphenidate Role in Tourettes Syndrome Prevalence.

5. "Drug Scheduling," U.S. Drug Enforcement Administration Online, Internet URL: http://www.dea.gov.

6. Op. cit., Tracey McVeigh.

7. Benzo.org.uk, citing Professor C. Heather Ashton, Benzodiazepines: How They Work and How To Withdraw, Feb. 2001.

8. Victorian Drug Use, Dr Andrzej Diniejko, D. Litt.; Contributing Editor, Poland

9. Article entitled "Laudanum," from Wikipedia

10. "In the Arms of Morpheus: The Tragic History of Laudanum, Morphine, and Patent Medicines", by Barbara Hodgson. Buffalo, New York: Firefly Books, 2001

11. Karch, Steven B. (2008). Pharmacokinetics and pharmacodynamics of abused drugs. Boca Raton: CRC Press.

12. Foundation for a Drug-Free World, 2006-2016

13. Pediatric HouseCall, 1995 by Applied Medical Informatics

1

Emergency Response

"Then Peter spoke up, 'Lord, if it is really you, order me to come out on the water to you.'
'Come!' answered Jesus. So Peter got out of the boat and started walking on the water to Jesus. But when he noticed the strong wind, he was afraid and started to sink down in the water. "Save me, Lord!" he cried. At once Jesus reached out and grabbed hold of him and said, "What little faith you have! Why did you doubt?'"
(Matthew 14:28-31 GNB)

REMAIN CALM; ANALYZE THE SITUATION; KNOW WHO TO CONTACT and WHAT TO REQUEST:

Peter was brave and filled with faith, but then he doubted. We do that. We're ready to swim great oceans for Jesus! Then life happens; we're tossed this way and that; we take our eyes off of Jesus . . . and we sink. Thank God we're told the rest of the story: as Peter sank, he cried out to Jesus; the savior took his hand and lifted him up.

It's wise to have an action plan before you need it, so if your skies are blue and the birds are singing, you may want to read this chapter anyway. If you choose not to, I'll understand. Keep it tucked away in case you need it in the future.

However, if you're sinking now, sirens are going off, people are sobbing and screaming and things seem hopeless, then you can already relate to Peter; you're probably crying out, "Save me, Lord!" Believe that He'll answer, but let me give you some practical advice too. I've been in that same water; consider this part of God's response to your cry: If God is for us, who can stand against us? No one and nothing. However, what if God is *not* for us? Really, think on that. What if God sets His beautiful face against you, because of your sin? Then who can stand against you? Well, just about anyone. There are many examples in the Old Testament of God abandoning His people to be oppressed by their enemies because they stopped worshiping Him and began worshiping idols.

RECOGNIZE the THREAT:

In 2009 (the now late) pastor and author David Wilkerson said, "What we're now experiencing is not a recession, not even a depression. We are under God's wrath." Beginning in the 1970's and continuing until his death in 2011, this pastor's voice joined the voices of many other godly men who claimed the Lord was warning them through the Bible and dreams and visions about the upcoming collapse of America. In careful details, David Wilkerson described the downward slide (to come) of America into the same immorality and chaos that we now see today. When he began his warnings in the 70s, most of the things he described seemed very hard to believe. Would America really change that much? Impossible! People laughed, at first. It isn't funny anymore; America is unstable, morally filthy, corrupt and suffering exactly as he said it would be.

Does this apply to you as an adoptive or foster parent? Yes, very much so. Let me explain:

In 1985 Pastor Wilkerson said, "Sudden destruction is coming and few will escape." Later in his warning he said, "It is because America has sinned against the greatest light. Other nations are just as sinful, but none are as flooded with gospel light as ours. God is going to judge America for its violence, its crimes, its backsliding, its murdering of millions of babies, its flaunting of homosexuality and sadomasochism, its corruption, its drunkenness and drug abuse, its form of godliness without power, its luke-warmness toward Christ, its rampant divorce and adultery, its lewd pornography, its child molestations, its cheating, its robbing, its dirty movies and its occult practices."

These sins are deadly for society and for families. Most likely these are exactly why your foster or adoptive children needed new families. Recognize that these sins will also destroy *your* family — your enemy is attempting to lure your family into these same minefields.

Maybe your family was thriving before you adopted or brought in a certain child. Maybe you're only in *over your head* because you were trying to heal wounds caused by others, without any guilt on your part. Maybe you've followed close on the heels of your Commanding Officer (Jesus). However, we're human, we can be deceived and we can deceive ourselves, therefore, when I'm ambushed, or feel like I'm sinking, the first thing I do is question whether I've strayed from the path and need to repent. There's never any risk in taking this first step during a crisis. What's the worst thing that can happen? God can tell you that you don't need to repent; you're right on track. However, if you don't take this first step, and there is an idol in your heart, or hidden in your tent, things can only get uglier.

RECOGNIZE your CHAMPION:

If your family's sinking, whether or not you hear sirens, you need a champion. Your Christian brothers and sisters can support you, but ultimately they cannot save you. God may use authorities or ministries to hold up your arms during battle, but they cannot save your family. Even your pastor cannot save you. You have only one true hero; cry out to Jesus: "Save me, Lord!" Then believe that He'll answer—but understand who He is; He won't defeat your enemies if you have *sin in your camp*. (Please read the Old Testament; God warned His people many times about their worship of other gods; He told them that if they didn't repent, He would have to fight against them . . . they didn't listen.) I don't know the god whom many people preach and believe in—that cheerful little fellow who winks at your sin and tells you that as long as you're trying your hardest, it's all good; he then praises you to help you feel better about yourself. That strange, inconsistent and unholy little character is definitely not the God of the Bible—that imposter cannot save. If you want to be rescued, you'll need to come to the real Jesus—He who will judge the living and the dead and who's coming to rule as King (2 Tim. 4:1). When Joshua met Him in the desert, it went like this:

"Now when Joshua was near Jericho, he looked up and saw a man standing in front of him with a drawn sword in his hand. Joshua went up to him and asked, 'Are you for us, or for our enemies?'

'Neither,' he replied, 'but as commander of the army of the Lord I have now come.' Then Joshua fell facedown to the ground in reverence, and asked him, 'What message does my Lord have for his servant?'" (Joshua 5:13-14)

No, he won't *get your back*; when you realize who He is, you'll fall on your face before Him, waiting for directions. If you'll do this, He'll raise you up. But when you approach this Jesus, who happens to be creator of the universe and Captain of the Lord's Armies, approach Him with fear and trembling, a repentant heart and a willingness to tear down your altars to foreign gods. Yes, His offer of salvation is free—you cannot be good enough, so He had to die to redeem you—but accepting His offer requires that you stop fighting Him, take His outstretched hand and allow Him to lift you out of what you're drowning in.

REFINER'S FIRE–GOD'S EMERGENCY DETOX:

"And I will make the third part go through the fire, cleaning them as silver is made clean, and testing them as gold is tested: and they will make their prayer to me and I will give them an answer: I will say, It is my people; and they will say, The Lord is my God." (Zech. 13:9 BBE)

"Happy are those who remain faithful under trials, because when they succeed in passing such a test, they will receive as their reward the life which God has promised to those who love him." (James 1:12 GNB)

"The LORD your God is using them to test you, to see if you love the LORD with all your heart. Follow the LORD and honor him; obey him and keep his commands; worship him and be faithful to him." (Deu. 13:3-4 GNB)

If God is for us, who can stand against us? No one and nothing. However, He prepares us for victory; one of His methods is to take us through the fire. These trials produce perseverance and hope, but they're also intended to detoxify (or purify) us. Only those whose hearts have been purified by faith will see Him. He wants us to see

Him. But we're in a battle with real enemies who do not want us to see God. While you're under fire, be brave; follow your Commander's orders, and He'll lead you safely out the other side.

RECOGNIZE the ENEMY'S STRATEGY:

In the book of Numbers we read about a traitorous, donkey-riding prophet named Balaam. Israel's enemies tried to get the prophet to curse Israel, but God wouldn't allow him to. However, in the end, the *good prophet* found a way. Balaam taught Israel's enemies how to lead the people of Israel into the sin of idolatry and sexual immorality; once they participated in these things, their own God cursed them.

> ". . . Balaam, who taught Balak how to lead the people of Israel into sin by persuading them to eat food that had been offered to idols and to practice sexual immorality." (Rev. 2:14b GNB)

> ". . . it was the women who followed Balaam's instructions and at Peor led the people to be unfaithful to the LORD. That was what brought the epidemic on the LORD's people." (Num. 31:16b GNB)

The enemy of your soul is intent upon destroying your family; he knows this trick. In fact, he (the devil) invented it, and he's trying to use it against you even now.

I recently watched the movie *War Room;* it was great. I especially enjoyed the scene where the woman realized Satan was destroying her family, and she "kicked him out" of her house. She began reading her Bible, praying, standing on God's promises and refusing to allow sinful attitudes into her marriage. But there was something missing: people have junk, but this make-believe family had none. Ungodly junk seeps into our homes even when we're attentive—or rushes in like a flood when our guard is down. The script-writer forgot to show the necessary *purging* of their home.

At least in America, homes are filled with unholy books, movies, video games, music and gadgets that connect us to a never-ending stream of even more. The world is wicked—even a huge percentage of children's toys these days are demonic and evil, with themes of witchcraft/occult, violence and warfare, pride and vanity, greed, sensuality and immorality, etc. Even if our home is only filled with "Christian-labeled" books, games, movies and music, the message in some of those is suspect; many contain outright heresy and profane propaganda. Satan masquerades as an angel of light; he writes many spiritual books and preaches countless sermons that don't quite line up with all of the Bible. Every person I know (who isn't actively, aggressively, consistently purging their home) has possessions that God hates; things God will not tolerate. Satan constantly entices us with items that attract the wrong spirits and things that disgust and repel the Holy Spirit of God. We are not make-believe families, so on top of learning to read our Bibles, to pray, to stand on God's promises, and to avoid ungodly attitudes, we also need to *clean house*. Then we'll have to fight hard to keep it clean.

FRIENDLY FIRE:

I know it's hard to be *in the world, yet not of the world* — but we're commanded to do just that. In my misguided "freedom in Christ" I've brought home stumbling-blocks, things that led my loved ones into sin and into spiritual-captivity. Yet more often, we've been the victims of *friendly-fire*, as our friends and relatives unknowingly carried these dangers into our homes — wrapped in pretty paper with bows on top. In our apathy we can easily allow our children to do things that bring God's wrath upon them and upon us. (Read 1 Samuel Chapters 3 and 4.) This is especially true when we're parenting children whose former homes taught them to accept the very things that destroyed their families.

We're not stronger, faster, or somehow better than the biological families we've replaced. We're simply here, by God's grace/still in the race. But if we're not fighting, we're losing; if we're not fighting to keep our environment filled with only things that please and welcome the Holy Spirit of God, the enemy's seductive weapons of mass destruction will overtake us too. Yes, this is a race that God intends for us to win! He is able to make us stand! Therefore, if we fall, it won't be because victory was unattainable. It'll be because victory was impossible *for us,* yet we refused to let God's will and mighty power overtake us and carry us across the finish line — for His glory.

If you're not willing to heed this warning, may I suggest you're doubting He's real, doubting He's Holy and doubting that He has a very strong opinion on how you live your life? But if you've been purchased by His blood, He owns you; you're His slave to righteousness. If He gives you the gift of clear vision (ask for it!) you will no longer doubt; you'll be overwhelmed by the dazzling light of the Lord's presence.

"Then Moses requested, 'Please, let me see the dazzling light of your presence.'" (Exo. 33:18 GNB)

"Other nations will be covered by darkness, But on you the light of the LORD will shine; The brightness of his presence will be with you." (Isa. 60:2 GNB)

It is possible to remain stubbornly in the dark; it's also possible for a family to sink all the way. Please don't let that happen. Call out to Him; beg Him to save you and your family from whatever's threatening to swamp you—and do whatever it takes to keep Him close.

"'If you are going to turn to the LORD with all your hearts, you must get rid of all the foreign gods and the images of the goddess Astarte. Dedicate yourselves completely to the LORD and worship only him, and he will rescue you . . ." (1 Sam. 7:3b GNB)

BALAAM RIDES AGAIN:

"They have left the straight path and have lost their way; they have followed the path taken by Balaam son of Beor, who loved the money he would get for doing wrong." (2 Pet. 2:15 GNB)

If God is for us, no one and nothing can stand against us. But beware of secret-agents; they're coming. If our enemy can get us to take the wrong path and to forsake (or turn away from) our Captain—our Tower of Refuge and strong defender—we're in a grave predicament.

In Pastor David Wilkerson's earlier warnings he claimed, "There will be a new drug that will be popular with teenagers that will break down resistance and will encourage sexual activity." A confusing claim; it makes me think, *Really, David? You're a preacher of the 70s, and you say there are dangerous drugs coming?* The youth of the 1960's and 70s were more prone to experiment with drugs and sex than any generation before them. Thank God they grew up and sobered up.

Or, did they? The youth of the 60s and 70s grew up; they became the adults and workforce of America—the lawyers, teachers, doctors, scientists, psychiatrists and owners of pharmaceutical companies etc. Within a couple of decades, America was awash with pills, sexual immorality—and mental illness.

Prior to WWII, prescription mood and mind-altering drugs were rare in America, but after 1950 tranquilizer usage became common among men first and then women (in the 60s and 70s) who were disappointed with their dull, meaningless and "stifling" lives. By the year 2000 (after the 60s and 70s youth had been "in office" for thirty years) nearly 80 million Americans were on doctor-prescribed mind-altering psychotropic medications. Their tranquilizers, benzodiazepines and antidepressants (SSRIs) are the heirs of opium, marijuana and morphine, which were widely available in the 19th century. Through clever marketing to *culturally respectable users,* pharmaceutical manufacturers successfully separated psychotropic drugs from the reputations of their discredited (and now illegal) forefathers. Psychotropic drugs became viewed as respectable treatments for specific ailments, instead of quick ways to attain more pleasurable states of mind.[1]

This change in America caused great suffering, including an epidemic of mental illness. Over the last few decades there's been a 600 percent increase in Americans on government disability due to mental illness. In fact, mental illness is now the leading cause of disability in children, well ahead of physical disabilities like Cerebral Palsy or Down's Syndrome—and respected professionals believe this was caused by the use of psychotropic medications.[9]

Chances are that this has nothing to do with your family; hopefully you're not even in a grave predicament—but many foster and adoptive children are the casualties of these changes in America.

They and their biological parents are the faces of these statistics. What's even worse, these drugs very clearly and powerfully pervert sexuality—and Gcd, who is holy and unchanging, punishes nations for allowing perverted sexual practices.

Psychotropic medicines can produce sexual disability, but they're also proven to cause feelings of intense sexual lust, insatiable erotic perversion and deviation, irregular arousal, gender-identity disorders and even spontaneous erections and orgasms. Some of the worst *sex offenders* are antidepressants, the drugs with a reputation as mild and harmless.[2] Whether this is unintended friendly-fire, or the work of secret-agents, antidepressants are currently the most commonly prescribed class of medications;[3] one in eight adult Americans have been on an antidepressant over the last ten years.[4] Two-hundred-thirty million prescriptions per year are written for this one type of psychotropic medicine alone; eleven million of these are for children.[5] All this, despite the fact that scientific studies have proven them no more effective than a placebo and far more damaging[9]—in fact, a well-respected researcher, Nancy Andreasen, and her colleagues published evidence proving that the use of some psychotropic drugs causes shrinkage of the brain. Adults and children experience the same side-effects, but children may suffer even greater harm to their psychosexual development.[7] While sexual corruption by these drugs is acknowledged as a significant treatment risk, American children (who have no say in the matter) are forced to ingest the chemical poisons anyway.[6] Not every person who takes these medicines will have their sexuality perverted (and be given over to a *debased mind*), but studies admit that between 30 and 73% clearly will—and (even if the drug is discontinued) the unsavory side-effects can remain for years, or even indefinitely.[8]

In an unexpected turn of events, Pastor Wilkerson's prediction became reality; not as we'd expected (only among illegal drug-users) but within the law-abiding families who were simply following the *good doctor's* advice.

> "The angst that drives the voracious and profitable consumption of psychotropic drugs is, however, unlikely to subside. Educated consumers and their physicians would be well advised to take a careful look at the history of

tranquilizers before seeking or providing a prescription for the newest miracle drug that reputedly will relieve the perennial pains of human existence."–Allan V. Horwitz, Ph.D. (Rutgers University).

(Please study Acts 15:29, 21, 23, Rom. 1:27, 1 Cor. 6:13, 18, 2 Cor. 12:21, Eph. 5:3, Col. 3:5, 1 Thes. 4:3, 7, 1 Tim. 1:9-10, Jude 1:7, 1 Pet. 4:3 and Rev. 2:20-21—if any of these things apply to your family or the children in your care, please deep clean and ask God to purify and forgive your loved ones.)

"But there are a few things I have against you: there are some among you who follow the teaching of Balaam, who taught Balak how to lead the people of Israel into sin by persuading them to eat food that had been offered to idols and to practice sexual immorality." (Rev. 2:14 GNB)

ABOUT THOSE DEMONS IN THE WALLPAPER:

They're real, you know. We're all adults here; we all have some interest in a biblical world view. So let's talk about demons.

"This man had an evil spirit in him and lived among the tombs . . . . . He was too strong for anyone to control him. Day and night he wandered among the tombs and through the hills, screaming and cutting himself with stones. He was some distance away when he saw Jesus; so he ran, fell on his knees before him, and screamed in a loud voice, "Jesus, Son of the Most High God! What do you want with me? For God's sake, I beg you, don't punish me!" (Mark 5:2b, 4b-7 GNB)

Many parents wonder if the out-of-control child in their care is demon-possessed. You wonder, your relatives wonder, and sometimes your neighbors wonder. I know you've wondered, because I hear you say it out loud when you're around trusted friends or when you think nobody is listening. I'm not (in any way) declaring that your child is possessed by the devil, a demon, or a mob of demons, but since many people wonder, I think it's healthy to address it.

(DISCLAIMER: I am not saying that your child is demon-possessed. I am not implying that your child is demon-possessed. By addressing this subject, I'm merely acknowledging what many people wonder because of the biblical accounts.)

But, pressing on, demons are real, and demon-possession is real—if you believe the Bible, you believe that. And if you read the Bible, you know that demons are no respecter of persons; they indwell children when opportunity presents itself. In fact, they've even been known to inhabit animals—such as pigs. (Mark Chapter 5)

Before I go further, I want to remind you: regarding spiritual or unseen matters, if it isn't biblical, *it isn't reliable.* Let me rephrase: You're in a battle with devious spiritual creatures who want to trick and destroy you. Hold fast to what God's Word (the Bible) teaches. Allow *the Bible* to interpret *the Bible,* and ask God to give you a discerning heart. Treat all non-biblical information as a potential deadly trap set by your enemy. When it comes to demons and demonology (what we believe about them), the world is incredibly saturated with false information; of course it is—your enemy uses subterfuge to throw his victims off. Study your Bible, and study under one of the safe Bible teachers that I recommended earlier.

REMEMBER WHO YOUR REAL ENEMY IS:

During the Dark Ages, there was much confusion and false-information on the subject of demons. People who were accused of "having a demon" were treated as if they *were the demon.* Men, women and even children were burned at the stake due to fear. (It wasn't called the dark ages for nothing!) But in the Bible it wasn't so. We have the Bible now, in our own languages—we can know the truth. In the biblical accounts the parents of demon-possessed children were heartbroken, distraught and highly-protective of their poor, suffering children. They loved their children, despite the demon; they stayed close, fighting to protect them from the evil creature. These anguished parents ran to Jesus, fell at His feet and begged Him to set their beloved children free from the clutches of evil. Jesus responded mercifully; He cast the evil spirits from these cherished, tormented little souls.

"For we wrestle not against flesh and blood, but against principalities, against powers, against the rulers of the darkness of this world, against spiritual wickedness in high places." (Eph. 6:12 KJV)

What are the signs of demon-possession, according to the Bible? You might be surprised. Yes, there's often LOUD SCREAMING, with super-human strength and anti-social, even violent, behavior (1 Sam. 16:14, 23, 18:18, 19:9, Matt. 8:28, 12:43-45, Mark 1:23-26, Mark 5:3-7, Luke 8:29, Acts 19:16). But other times the demon caused muteness (Matt. 9:32, Mark 9:17, Luke 11:14), muteness and blindness (Matt. 12:22), convulsions and suicide attempts (Matt. 17:15, Mark 9:17-18), a hunched-back (Luke 13:11-12) and uncanny, accurate knowledge of unseen spiritual things (Mark 1:34, 5:7, Luke 4:34, Acts 16:17). But just when you think you've figured it out, you read Scriptures like 2 Corinthians 12:7 where the apostle Paul—very much a born-again believer—receives a "messenger from Satan" to constantly torment him; in some translations this messenger is said to be a "painful physical ailment." I doubt we're intended to fully understand the unseen world. Nevertheless, we do know when we're outnumbered. Yes, we're up against an enemy too strong and stealthy for us. But we have a strong defender.

"But the LORD is my defense; and my God is the rock of my refuge."
(Psalm 94:22 KJV)

". . . when the Lord Jesus comes, he will kill him [the Wicked One] with the breath from his mouth and destroy him with his dazzling presence."
(1 Thes. 2:8b GNB)

No, I'm not saying the child in your care has a demon. But if *you think* this child acts like the devil's taken up residence in him, you certainly have biblical grounds for your suspicion. I won't deny you that. But you must react as the parents in the biblical accounts did:

"Son of David!" she cried out. "Have mercy on me, sir! My daughter has a demon and is in a terrible condition." (Matt. 15:22 GNB)

"A woman, whose daughter had an evil spirit in her, heard about Jesus and came to him at once and fell at his feet. The woman was a Gentile, born in the region of Phoenicia in Syria. She begged Jesus to drive the demon out of her daughter." (Mark 7:25-26 GNB)

"A man shouted from the crowd, "Teacher! I beg you, look at my son— -my only son! A spirit attacks him with a sudden shout and throws him into a fit, so that he foams at the mouth; it keeps on hurting him and will hardly let him go!" (Luke 9:38 GNB)

A child is not a demon; never, ever, demonize a person. A human is never a demon, not even if they're possessed! Granted, people can bear some blame; they open the door to demon-possession through vile sins and sorcery, including pharmakeia (the use of mind-altering substances). But a demon-possessed person is a helpless victim held captive and tortured by invisible, evil beings. If you suspect this has happened to your loved one, take that person, run to Jesus with them, fall at His feet and beg Him to heal them!!!!!

"He said to them, "Go throughout the whole world and preach the gospel to all people. Whoever believes and is baptized will be saved; whoever does not believe will be condemned. Believers will be given the power to perform miracles: they will drive out demons in my name. . . " (Mark 16:15-17 GNB)

DAMAGE CONTROL; EVASIVE MANEUVERS; FUTURE STRATEGY; EVACUATION PLANS:

Whether your catastrophe is an enemy invasion, an Act of God or mutiny of the troops—or even the result of your own oversight (or violation of orders), what's done is done. Now you need damage control, evasive maneuvers, and a future strategy; hopefully you won't need to evacuate

You've sought the Lord humbly, asking forgiveness for any possible mistakes, and you've cried out, "Save me, Lord!" You're willing to follow His lead; you believe He'll move mountains on your behalf, not because you deserve it but because He's cool like that. Now what?

DAMAGE CONTROL in an ADOPTION-CRISIS:

The current rate of adoption disruption or dissolution is roughly 10% to 20% in America; rates vary from 3% to 53%, depending on the group being studied and the calculating techniques.[10] Dissolution describes an adoption that fails after finalization, resulting in the child returning to foster care and/or another set of adoptive parents. Not every adoption crisis has an easy resolution; if possible, I'd like to help you make it through your *zero hour* victoriously. Below are a few practical maneuvers that have helped parents of mutinous recruits to clean up existing damage and avoid further destruction:

LOWER-RISK THREATS:

EVASIVE MANEUVERS in the NURSERY-ROOM:

Babies with trauma and brain damage may need extra measures to keep them safe and sanitary. Two common problems parents mention are climbing out of cribs (by babies who cannot yet land safely, or who aren't safe once they escape unnoticed) and babies or toddlers who have an unsafe fascination with their own bodies and waste.

THREAT: climbing from crib.

EVASIVE MANEUVER: Dress him in an outfit that prohibits climbing. I've seen parents create mesh-lids for cribs and other curious contraptions to stop babies from climbing when they weren't yet safe climbers. I don't recommend these; various lids and fencing can create more serious safety-concerns—like strangling or suffocating when entangled in a home-made contraption. Safety-clothing may be a simpler, safer option. For climbers who need to lift one leg high (while balancing on the other) in order to vault themselves over the side of their crib, some parents choose clothing that prohibits the legs from separating any farther up than necessary, such as above the knee. Safer sleepwear allows for adequate night-time movement and comfortable sleeping, but may keep baby from falling out of the crib onto his head.

THREAT: removing diaper.

EVASIVE MANEUVER: Dress him in clothing that prohibits diaper-removal. I once read about parents who were charged with abuse or neglect because they used duct-tape to keep their foster baby's diaper on. They argued that the baby would remove his diaper and smear himself (and the walls and crib) with feces; they were trying to keep him and his environment sanitary. Don't use duct-tape, but if you encounter this problem, consider shortening the amount of time the baby is left alone in his crib, and explore safe and healthy ways to keep his diaper where it belongs. Parents who use back-zipping, one-piece sleepwear report great success, especially when the sleepwear also incorporates a complicated button-closure with the zipper. With prayer, imagination and a sewing machine (or a seamstress friend), safer clothing possibilities are endless.

HIGHER-RISK THREATS:

THREAT: habitual lying.

EVASIVE MANEUVER: Don't call him as a witness, don't ask him to deliver a message, and don't designate him as the lookout. Decrease lying by removing the opportunities; if you have a habitual liar, avoid asking them questions until you believe they can withstand the temptation to lie. Some children, due to brain damage, have trouble distinguishing reality from imagination. Be patient and steadfast in prayer for your child; teach them the dangers of lying, but be calm and loving when they don't seem to understand or care.

**** *NOTE: If your child has taken psychotropic medications, they may be experiencing side-effects, drug-induced mental instability, or withdrawal symptoms. It can be fatal to discontinue a psychotropic medicine; please do so only with the assistance of a competent professional.*

THREAT: stealing.

EVASIVE MANEUVER: Don't ask him to carry the money bag, don't send him into the supply-room, and don't designate him to distribute the goods. Children who steal will steal, you may not be able to stop it. However, you can minimize the opportunities, and you might redirect him toward "safer" types of stealing. For example: a child who steals money from a neighbor is in great danger, but a child who only steals random items from his adopted parents is in less danger. Children who are in the first category should be more closely supervised (no more visiting at the neighbor's) and could be switched to a non-monetary shopping system, etc. A child who steals money doesn't usually want money; he wants the things he'll purchase with it. Instead of allowing him to shop and purchase things with money, develop an activity where he earns items (that you will purchase) by racking up "hours" (or minutes) on a chart as he performs chores, jobs or other activities. He cannot easily steal "hours," so you'll have minimized his temptation to steal.

THREAT: sexual-aggression

EVASIVE MANEUVER: Don't allow him to oversee the younger recruits or troops, and avoid all one-on-one encounters. When parents consider ending an adoption there are many causes, but quite often sexually aggressive behavior (by the adopted child) toward younger children is involved. This assertive sexual behavior, or vile-accusations, may be directed toward adults as well. If your family is ambushed in this manner, you'll probably need respite-care while you regroup. Be aware that if the perpetrator of this sexual-indecency is less than five years older than the victim, this is a non-criminal incident; no reports are necessary. However, if he is five years older than the victim (or more), it is an illegal act; this is the accepted medical definition.[11] Although it isn't godly, acting-out sexually is normal for children when they are unsupervised and playing with non-relatives—and quite common for children with trauma and tainted beginnings. I'm not saying it's good, nor am I saying that all children will do this—but it's well within the scope of childhood behavior when unsupervised, playing with non-relatives. Remember that your adopted or foster-child views your other children as non-relatives, regardless of what any paperwork now declares. Supervise your child vigilantly; if their sexual exploration of another child did not break the "more than five years age difference" rule, then they are not necessarily a sexual-predator, and they are not a criminal, therefore this offense does not have to be shouted from the rooftops.

**** NOTE: If your child has taken psychotropic medications, they may be experiencing perverse sexual side-effects, drug-induced mental instability, or withdrawal symptoms. It can be fatal to discontinue a psychotropic medicine; please do so only with the assistance of a competent professional.

THREAT: violent outbursts

EVASIVE MANEUVER: learn not to push the buttons that detonate him, learn to de-escalate a conflict, and avoid putting victims in his path. Only through prayer and observation will you know your child's triggers. But do pray, and do observe. Triggers can be certain trauma-inducing, frightening situations, or something simpler like low-blood sugar or a reaction to breathing or ingesting chemicals, dyes or preservatives. Study him to learn what frustrates and angers him; be sensitive to these weaknesses and help him to overcome them. Violence can also be a learned behavior; by modeling peaceful, loving relationships for him, you can help his violent behavior to recede.

**** NOTE: If your child has taken psychotropic medications, they may be experiencing violent side-effects, drug-induced mental instability, or withdrawal symptoms. It can be fatal to discontinue a psychotropic medicine; please do so only with the assistance of a competent professional.

Special Note about sexual aggression and violence:

When parents dissolve an adoption, in many cases it's because they believe the adopted child is a definite danger to other children in the home, and they've run out of options. As I've spoken with these parents, and as others have found in their research, there's a reoccurring theme: the adopted child was victimizing, or seriously threatening to victimize another child in the family or extended family—usually in a sexual manner. It isn't that these parents loved the aggressive child less; they were incapable of safely and humanely raising severely incompatible children under the same roof. Most families cannot run two house-holds at once; it may be negligent to continue raising a child who is damaging to the others. While there have been instances of this behavior in biological families, the incidence is overwhelmingly greater among children who view each other as *unrelated*. Even in the Bible, the instances of inter-family violence and molestation are in *blended families*, where the husband took more than one wife, or (think Abimilech) had a child from his sex-slave etc. In traditional, loving, godly families, you will not need to fear that sibling rivalry and other behaviors will escalate to such bizarre levels. But when you adopt, you may enter a different realm of child-rearing.

THREAT: prowling.

EVASIVE MANEUVER: Sound the alarm; alert the whole camp! Beyond sexual aggression and violence, next of the list of troubling behaviors is probably night-prowling. Incidentally, the kids who prowl are often the same ones who act out sexually, or violently. Kids will be kids, but there's something extremely unnerving about sharing your home (your refuge from the world) with a child who prowls about with wicked intent while you're sleeping. This can be spooky and dangerous, especially if there are younger or vulnerable children in the home. If you have a habitual prowler, parents report that the best way to keep everyone safe (including your little prowler) is to install door and window alarms. They're available at most hardware stores at a reasonable price. Using alarms that sound when the child prowls is both a deterrent and a kind way to minimize the temptation.

THREAT: the ship's sinking, the sky's falling; we're about to die.

EVASIVE MANEUVER: If you cannot call in adequate reinforcements, you may need to evacuate, either temporarily, or for good. When things seem hopeless, beyond control, irreparably unsafe and/or criminal, you might panic and look for the first life-boat. However, the first life-boat might not be going in the right direction, or it might not be sea-worthy. So slow down, be calm, and prayerfully examine these boats and rafts before you choose one. In terms of adoption, never jump directly onto the "adoption disruption or dissolution" raft *first*. Rather, look for the boat named "Respite."

Sometimes your adoption agency will help you find respite, sometimes not. Don't despair if they're not helpful. Look for networks of other adoptive parents who are "in the trenches"—they can usually direct you to trustworthy respite resources. Here are some things to remember when seeking a respite-provider: Just because they provide respite, doesn't mean they understand. They might not understand why you're so overwhelmed, distraught or panicked; don't try to explain it. In fact, less is better. When emotions and accusations run high, it's wise to ask God to put a guard over your lips and not let any unloving, nor-edifying words escape. Share only things that are vital for the safety of your child and others; leave everything else unsaid.

Whether you approach an individual who does respite-care, or a youth ranch or home, remember to carefully check their references. Also, understand that many of them will refuse to help if your child sounds too difficult (or if you mention autistic-tendencies). They only want to hear that you're overwhelmed, burnt-out and you need a break, period.

Sometimes the help of a respite home will give your family that much needed time to regroup, and you'll experience a second-wind. If not, you may come to the very unfortunate conclusion that this child isn't a healthy or safe fit for your family, nor is your family the correct place for them to grow up. Never take this step without asking godly men and women to pray along with you for God's guidance.

If you do decide to pursue dissolution, remember to keep the child's safety and best interests at the forefront of the search. Many families reach this point overwhelmed and surrender the child to DHS/Child Protective Services. In so doing they're often charged with abandonment, and they usually have no say in choosing the child's new home. Far better, for the parents and the child, is the arrangement wherein adoptive parents find a temporary respite provider, and then approach an attorney (who specializes in adoption) and allow him or her to locate a suitable second-family. Although the attorney suggests a potential second-family, the parents have the final say.

Whether your evasive maneuvers succeed, and you avoid a calamity (or successfully control the damage), or your crisis ends with retreat and permanent evacuation, remember to protect this child to the best of your ability. You may not be able to claim a victory, you might be forced to retreat after suffering casualties, but attempt to *do no harm* to those entrusted to your care.

Whom shall I fear? None but you, Lord. But (with the help of your Holy Spirit) I will definitely fear you and treat you with the honor, respect and obedience you deserve.

1. Happy Pills in America: From Miltown to Prozac By David Herzberg. 279 pp., illustrated. Baltimore, Johns Hopkins University Press, 2009; The Age of Anxiety: A History of America's Turbulent Affair with Tranquilizers By Andrea Tone. 298 pp., illustrated. New York, Basic Books, 2009; Before Prozac: The Troubled History of Mood Disorders in Psychiatry By Edward Shorter. 304 pp. New York, Oxford University Press, 2009.
2. :antidepressant medications, including the Selective Serotonin Reuptake Inhibitors fluoxetine (Prozac), paroxetine (Paxil), sertraline (Zoloft), citalopram (Celexa), escitalopram (Lexapro), and fluvoxamine (Luvox), and the Serotonin Norepinephrine Reuptake Inhibitor (SNRI)1 venlafaxine (Effexor) according to: Sexual Side Effects of Antidepressant Medications: An Informed Consent Accountability Gap, by Audrey S. Bahrick Æ Mark M. Harris—Springer Science+Business Media, LLC 2008; Medical Disability Advisor <http://www.mdguidelines.com/medical-topics>
3. Burt, C.W., McCaig, L. F., & Rechtsteiner, E. A. (June, 2007). Ambulatory medical care utilization estimates for 2005. Advance Data from Vital and Health Statistics, Number 388. Retrieved from http://www.cdc.gov/nchs/data/ad/ad388.pdf. Accessed Jan 7, 2008.
4. Raz, A. (2005). Perspectives on the efficacy of antidepressants for child and adolescent depression. Public Library of Science: Medicine, 3(1), e9.
5. Goode, E. (2004, February). Stronger warning is urged on antidepressants for teenagers. New York Times, p. A12.; Centers for Disease Control and Prevention (CDC).
6. Rivas-Vasquez, R. A., Rey, G. J., Blais, M. A., & Rivas-VAsquez, A. A. (2000). Sexual dysfunction associated with antidepressant treatment. Professional Psychology: Research and Practice, 31(6), 641-651.).
7. (Sexual Side Effects of Antidepressant Medications: An Informed Consent Accountability Gap, by Audrey S. Bahrick Æ Mark M. Harris—Springer Science+Business Media, LLC 2008.
8. Mon Montejo-Gonzalez, A. L., Llorca, G., Izquierdo, J. A., Ledesma, A., Bousono, M., Calcedo, A., et al. (1997). SSRI-induced sexual dysfunction: Fluoxetine, paroxetine, sertraline, and fluvoxamine in a prospective, multicenter, and descriptive clinical study of 344 patients. Journal of Sex and Marital Therapy, 23(3), 176-194.; Montejo, A. L., Gines, L., Izquierdo, J. A., & Rico-Villademoros, F. (2001). Incidence of sexual dysfunction associated with antidepressant agents: A prospective multicenter study of 1022 outpatients. Journal of Clinical Psychiatry, 62(Suppl 3), 10-21.
9. The Epidemic of Mental Illness: Why? by Marcia Angell, 2011; The Emperor's New Drugs: Exploding the Antidepressant Myth by Irving Kirsch; Anatomy of an Epidemic: Magic Bullets, Psychiatric Drugs, and the Astonishing Rise of Mental Illness in America by Robert Whitaker; Unhinged: The Trouble With Psychiatry-A Doctor's Revelations About a Profession in Crisis by Daniel Carlat.
10. Barth, R.P. and Berry, M. (1988). Adoption and disruption: rates, risks, and responses. Hawthorne, NY: Adline de Gruyter; Boyne, J., Denby, L., Kettenring, J.R., and Wheeler, W. (1984). The shadow of success: A statistical analysis of outcomes of adoptions of hard-to-place children. Westfield, NJ: Spaulding for Children; Groza, V. and Rosenberg, K. (1998). Clinical and practice issues in adoption: bridging the gap between adoptees placed as infants and as older children. Westport, Connecticut: Praeger; Groze, V. (1986). Special needs adoption. Child and Youth Services Review, 8(4), 363-373; Stolley, K.S. (1993). Statistics on adoption in the United States. The Future of Children: Adoption, 3(1), 26-42.
11. Child Molestation Research & Prevention Institute, Inc., 2016.

Who's Got My Back?

A Message to the Church

The Lord's Army?

*"'The Lord knows those who are his' and 'Those who say that they be-
long to the Lord must turn away from wrongdoing.'
. . . . . . Those who make themselves clean from all those evil things, will
be used for special purposes, because they are dedicated and useful to
their Master, ready to be used for every good deed. Avoid the passions of
youth, and strive for righteousness, faith, love, and peace, together with
those who with a pure heart call out to the Lord for help." (2 Timothy
2:19b, 21-22 GNB)*

PRAYER-WARRIORS URGENTLY NEEDED. APPLY HERE!

Dear Church,

Are we praying for those who work with vulnerable children?
We say we are—but is God answering our prayers? If we're living
hypocritical lives, disobedient to the one we call *our Master*, then He's
not listening to us; we're not helping anyone.

*"For the eyes of the Lord are on the upright, and his ears are open to
their prayers: but the face of the Lord is against those who do evil." (1
Peter 3:12 BBE)*

*" . . . the Lord your God is full of grace and mercy, and his face will not
be turned away from you if you come back to him." (2 Chro. 30:9b BBE)*

*"The effectual fervent prayer of a righteous man availeth much." (James
5:16b KJV)*

If a parent comes to us asking for help getting a painful speck out of their eye, can we help? Have we prepared ourselves to help, by removing our own log?

"How can you say to your brother, 'Please, brother, let me take that speck out of your eye,' yet cannot even see the log in your own eye? You hypocrite! First take the log out of your own eye, and then you will be able to see clearly to take the speck out of your brother's eye." (Luke 6:42 GNB)

My brothers and sisters in Christ, those who are active in orphan-care (and other ministry) need our effective prayers. They really do. If we humbly walk in obedience to God's Word—by His Spirit, His power and His grace—we must pray for them and for the orphaned and suffering children of the world. Our prayers will be heard and answered. However, if we've been proud and hypocritical, allowing hidden sin in our lives or outward disobedience, we should ask the Lord Who Sees to purify our hearts and help us to change (by His mighty power). Then we can pray for them and help when they have specks in their eyes.

NEEDED: A CHURCH WHO *doesn't* SAVE

The other day I read an article in The Navajo Times about domestic violence; the Native-American author called it a "cancer" that's destroying his people. This past year when we met Eugene Cody, a Navajo evangelist, he described reservations that are covered with Christian churches. How can a nation be covered with Christian churches and be eaten-up with the cancer of domestic violence (not to mention drug and alcohol abuse)?

When the Lord called Eugene, he expected it would be to a jail ministry, or something similar. God saved him from a former life of jail and alcoholism. But instead, the Lord put a burden into his heart to wake up sleeping churches—to light a fire among Christians, so that they will chase the darkness from their nation. He travels roughly four-thousand miles each month across reservations, teaching his people what the Bible says about false prophets and about the characteristics of a true, godly leader. (Eugene is always in need of new tires and a wheel alignment; if you'd like to bless him, look him up in Arizona. The Southwest Indian Missionary Association can tell you how to find him.) One verse that really stands out for Eugene is Isaiah 56:10.

"His watchmen are blind, they are all without knowledge; they are all dogs without tongues, unable to make a sound; stretched out dreaming, loving sleep. Yes, the dogs are for ever looking for food; while these, the keepers of the sheep, are without wisdom: they have all gone after their pleasure, every one looking for profit; they are all the same." (Isa. 56:10-11 BBE)

The writer of the article about domestic violence speculated that the Native people learned their violent behavior from the many movies (condoning men hitting women, or abducting them) that they were made to watch when they were children growing up in boarding schools. I offer that the cause wasn't just the movies, but (more importantly) the fact that they grew up in boarding schools, never knowing the loving care of a mother (or father) as God intended. The Native-American people have been (for the most part) "motherless children" since (at least) the 1800s, and the church played a big part in this tragedy.

"How terrible for you, teachers of the Law and Pharisees! You hypocrites! You sail the seas and cross whole countries to win one convert; and when you succeed, you make him twice as deserving of going to hell as you yourselves are!" (Matthew 23:15 GNB)

Many countries today are covered with sleeping churches and with overflowing orphanages—but the children's parents are still alive. Thus was the case in America when some parts of the church decided that the best way to remove heathen-tendencies from Native-Americans was to steal their babies and children away from them and raise them as "Christians." There were many good examples in history of missionaries who did not partake in these cruel practices, but as early as the 1500s Spanish missionaries removed Indians from their relatives to indoctrinate them; they held Indians captive on their mission-work farms in an attempt to keep them *Christianized.* The Virginia Company, in the 1600's, attempted to educate Indian children by placing them in English homes and then introducing them to Christian churches and colleges. However, the Indians didn't want to part with their children; they fought back, and the missionaries eventually gave up. When the Puritans first came to America in 1628, they too intended to convert the Indians to Christianity. However, they soon concluded that the Indians were *a cursed race and therefore prime subjects for slavery instead.*[1] Later, the United States government adopted the same practice. The federal government began forcibly sending Native Americans to off-reservation boarding schools in the 1870s. Army officer Richard Pratt, who founded the first school for these *precious little souls,* based it on an education program he developed in a prison! He described his philosophy in 1892: "A great general has said that the only good Indian is a dead one," Pratt said. "In a sense, I agree with the sentiment, but only in this: that all the Indian there is in the race should be dead. Kill the Indian in him, and save the man."

The late performer and Indian activist Floyd Red Crow Westerman was haunted by his memories of growing up in a boarding school. As a small child, he left his reservation in South Dakota for the Wahpeton Indian Boarding School in North Dakota. Sixty years later, he still remembers watching his mother through the window as he left. At first, he thought he was on the bus because his mother didn't want him anymore. But then he noticed she was crying. "It was hurting her, too," Westerman says. "I'll never forget. All the mothers were crying."

The government operated as many as 100 boarding schools for American Indians, both on and off reservations. Children were taken forcibly, by armed police when necessary. "Only by complete isolation of the Indian child from his savage antecedents can he be satisfactorily educated," they stressed. Nearly one hundred years after the government began forcing American Indian children to grow up isolated from their families in boarding schools, this method of Indian education was finally declared *a national tragedy.* For decades there had been reports that children in the boarding schools were abused and that they were not educated in basic concepts, such as Math or

English. Instead, children were beaten, malnourished, forced to do heavy labor and physically-drilled (regardless of age) with a scheme of military training that was largely obsolete even in Army training camps. In the 1960s, a congressional report found that many teachers still saw their role as civilizing Indians, not educating little children. The report said the schools had a "major emphasis on discipline and punishment." Since the 1960s funding has gradually declined and many of the schools have shut down.[2] But the wounds of mass institutionalization have not yet begun to heal.

I hope it horrifies you to think that young boys and girls have been stolen away from their mothers in the name of evangelism. I hope you can see that many of the problems in current societies were caused by those who tried to help. But no one has the right to break up a family in the name of religion. I'm sure you agree.

But, now, here's the point where I step on some toes. (As if I haven't already!)

STRENGTHEN PARENTS; HELP CHILDREN

"You are like light for the whole world. A city built on a hill cannot be hid." (Matthew 5:24 GNB)

Church, do we love families, even when they don't fit neatly into our programs? Do we pray for them and ask God how we can serve and strengthen them? Or are we simply counting heads and corralling them into pens we created before they arrived?

I visited a Sunday School class once where a dark-haired little charmer, with a twinkle in his eyes and mischievous grin, was teaching the other children how to dance like a gigolo to "This Little Light of Mine." This little boy had all the moves; it was impressive and horrifying. The volunteer-teacher had too many children to oversee, so she didn't seem to notice. Meanwhile, on the other side of the sound-proof wall, the parents were diligently studying their Bibles and praising God. Unfortunately, children weren't allowed in the room with the Christians.

In many churches today, children never get to see people who've been set free from the power of Satan adoring and worshiping their

Savior. They never see born-again believers devouring God's Word together. Instead they're isolated with the other non-regenerated little people in classes with overseers. I'm not saying there's never a time and need to provide fun activities for children at church. But all too often, the purpose degenerates from teaching children to know Christ, to simply keeping kids entertained (and full of candy)—so we can keep the *little distractions* out of our peaceful sanctuary! Many parents of special-needs children, or adopted and foster children, say that the hardest place to take their child is their local church, unless they're fortunate enough to find a church that elevates people above programs.

Dear Church, we have a tendency to get hung up on man-made traditions and programs (even if they're hurtful) and, in so doing, sometimes we ignore the heart of God. I won't spend time here documenting the high rate of abuse and child molestation within churches (though it's alarming), nor even discuss the fact that a great deal of heresy enters the church through well-meaning, uneducated Sunday School teachers, not pastors (vulnerable children don't know the difference). I only want to talk about the church's responsibility to encourage and strengthen families, *by encouraging parents to parent*—by applauding and enabling parents who keep their children close, who nurture, protect and teach them the ways of God. It's the biblical duty of the parent to teach spiritual truth to their own child. We might take up the slack when they're lacking, but ultimately it's our duty to build parents up by pointing them to Jesus and reminding them that *they can do this*, with His help! God chose them as the parents of this child; He will enable them.

We are servants of a mighty God who saves! But if we're not careful, we become egotistical people whose "savior complex" makes us interfere in hurtful ways. We are like light for the whole world—but the light is the knowledge of the glory of God, who is Christ. If we are not pointing people to Jesus, we're not shining.

There's a fine-line between offering to help and taking over. Sometimes the church accidentally slips over that line. After all, we can do this so much better than they can!! For example: 80% of children in institutions around the world—orphanages—have at least one living parent. In some countries the number is higher; in the

Czech Republic 99% of institutionalized children have a living parent; 98% in Bulgaria; 95% in Russia, etc.[3] Most of these children are wanted by their parents; they could return to their families given the right support (usually poverty is involved). We know that nothing is better than growing up in a family, even a poor family. Eighty years of research has proven that orphanages are not safe, nor healthy for children; institutionalization always has a very negative impact.[4] And yet the statistics remain steady. In some countries poor parents are offered money to give up their children. Many corrupt institutions and unethical adoption agencies profit from the children through donations to their orphanage or through child trafficking.[3]

Yes, our world is undeniably broken; there will always be some children who need a form of alternate care during part or all of their childhood, even if they have a living parent. We cannot simply run about removing children from orphanages and expecting their broken families will rise to the occasion and nurture them. There will always be a need for foster parents, for adoptive parents and for those who will reach out to street kids, the "social orphans" (those who may have parents, but live as if they have none.) But the numbers above are something else entirely. This is clearly help gone wrong—maybe of forgetting that Jesus saves and thinking that *we save*. Or perhaps it's something less noble.

Whether you're involved in building orphanages, doing-away-with orphanages (deinstitutionalization), or teaching Sunday School, please remember to support and strengthen the children's parents whenever possible. Encourage them, pray for them and point them to Jesus. The absolute best outcome would be for parents to rise up and put us out of a job! If these parents will put their trust in Christ, they'll be better at it anyway because it's their job—God created them for good works, and the first of these works is to care for their own family.

To explore a model that's producing excellent fruit, take a look at the *Bridge of Hope* program of Gospel For Asia. Instead of taking children away from poverty-stricken, non-Christian parents, they take the message of salvation and hope in Jesus to depressed areas, and, with it, they offer free Christ-centered education, meals and medical care. They include parents in the educational process; parent training sessions are an integral part of the program. In addition, one-hundred percent of the child sponsorship donations go directly to the *Bridge of Hope* programs on the mission field. People involved in administrative work do so as missionaries, raising their own support—we have a number of good friends who've participated in this way. The harvest has been great; 74,000 children have been helped so far and thousands of families have found faith in Christ; as a result, new churches have been born.

However the Lord calls you to help, remember that God wants parents to raise their own children. We must not encourage them to disobey Him in this; we must tread lightly, careful not to come between parents and their children. We must not make the parents feel hopeless, inferior or inadequate by always outshining, out-giving and outperforming them. Instead, we can help them to become more adequate. We can bring hope and tools to these parents so that *they* can shine, give and perform!

WRAP-AROUND GONE WRONG

Not only biological parents suffer when we offer our help in the wrong way. Some of our *support* hurts adoptive families too.

Do you remember the story of the man who lured people's children away with enticing music? No, I'm not talking about your youth pastor—I'm talking about the *Pied Piper*. Throughout history the men offering treats, stimulating beverages, shiny trinkets or mesmerizing entertainment have usually been deceivers with an unholy agenda. While the church has a history of mistakes, of acting more like the Pied Piper than like Jesus, the church has entered a new season; some of the forward momentum is confusing, but much of what I see is very promising. Worldwide, more Christians now realize their responsibility to care for and protect orphans. This is evident through the growth of things such as *Orphan Sunday*—practiced in only two countries six years earlier, it was celebrated in more than seventy-five countries in 2015. Many Churches and Christian networks across our nation are now involved in their local foster care systems as well. Whereas the difficulties of adoption and orphan care used to be taboo subjects, there's now a greater understanding and acceptance of the struggles that accompany the blessings. Although not everyone will foster or adopt, churches have begun to realize and to proclaim that all Christians have a part to play by supporting the families who do. From running errands and cooking meals, to prayer and words of encouragement, supporting an adoptive or foster family can literally make the difference between tragedy and victory. This concept is sometimes called the *Wrap-Around* movement; it's one of the most positive developments I've seen. Nevertheless, it also seems to have a blind spot. Church, will you allow me to speak to this?

As a foster and adoptive mother, and as someone who's made mistakes and learned the hard way, I have a warning and a request for church leaders: Please teach your members how to properly *Wrap-Around* adoptive families without causing setbacks, discouragement or harm. And please don't ask volunteers to spiritually educate our beloved children unless they are biblically-qualified to educate and pastor adults as well. (A background check to see if they've been caught molesting children yet is not enough.) Teachers should prove an in-depth biblical education, a calling from God, and their lives must show the fruit of the Holy Spirit; please assure they meet the biblical requirements for spiritual leaders (deacons, elders, pastors etc.) If you cannot find qualified, godly leaders, please don't compromise.

The world will always have orphans and children whose families are incapable and disinterested in their care. But many more children have caring parents. Church, please discern between these two groups. When we insert ourselves where our presence isn't needed, or in the wrong way, we hurt the vital parent-child relationship! In many cases, adoptive parents are working on strengthening a blossoming (or not blossoming), very weak, tentative bond with their adopted child. The last thing this flimsy bond needs is for church volunteers to act like we love their child more than they do, while we totally overlook Mom and Dad. (Yes, I have seen this many times.) They're already hurting because their child doesn't trust them and doesn't return their love. They might also be trying to keep a child with destructive behaviors safe through restrictive measures. Even if we mean well, our ignorance hurts.

Additionally, some parents improve physical/emotional or mental health through a careful diet (it actually works!) Some children need a "line of sight" form of parenting—and no one (except Mom and Dad) needs to know why. Also, some of the lessons and games at church are disturbing, maybe because of the child's past, or maybe just because the volunteers don't understand childhood development or even Christianity. It's often necessary for a parent to stay close and interpret disturbing things for their sensitive child. I once sat in on a Sunday School class for three and four-year-olds where the lesson was all about killing babies. Oh, but it was biblical!! One of the four-year-olds enhanced the lesson by telling the other children how to cast spells; she'd learned it from a witch movie or television show. Just down the hall, another volunteer teacher was leading two-year-olds in a song about a Good Fairy coming along . . . And the pastor of this church always teaches sound, biblical sermons. (Parents, do you know what's being taught in your child's Sunday School class?)

Adoptive parents long for fellowship and edification, but when they go to church, (even without the negative elements just mentioned) they might encounter people who act like they're invisible as they rush to Wrap-Around and "love on" their child. After church is over, the parents have to go home and endure another spike in their child's negative behavior and rejection. Church—please look up! Do you see Mom and Dad standing there, ignored—perhaps friendless, perhaps even feeling hopeless—while you've been "loving on" their child? This behavior is counterproductive. I'm no better; I've made mistakes. However, God delights in showing us the error of our ways and then sending us in the right direction. So please take this advice: if you're a woman, wrap-around this needy mother. Get to know her, and pray for her!!! What can you do to strengthen Mom; to make her chores more possible; to encourage her? If you are a man, wrap-around this adoptive dad. He needs godly friends who will communicate with him, pray with him and encourage him. The family might need help with house-repairs, car-repairs, or even groceries.

Dear church, these parents adopted because they care. Trust them to care for their children (do not interfere unless they ask you to). Our responsibility is to Wrap-Around and *love on* the parents. Let's really get their backs, instead of rushing out front—outshining, out-giving, and outperforming them, making them feel like they should give us their kids and go home.

"Help carry one another's burdens, and in this way you will obey the law of Christ." (Galatians 6:2 GNB)

1. Changing Frontiers—A History of the United States, Christian Light Education, 2014, page 37, page 65
2. American Indian Boarding Schools Haunt Many, Charla Bear, May 19, 2008
3. Csáky, C., Keeping children out of harmful institutions: why we should be investing in family-based care, Save the Children, 2009
4. Berens, A., Nelson, C., The science of early adversity: is there a role for large institutions in the care of vulnerable children?, The Lancet, 2015.

War Stories

Introduction to Part Five:

Congratulations, you've reached the final part of the book! I hope you're feeling more prepared; I apologize if you're now terrified at the prospect of adopting or doing foster care. However, it gives me great hope to see you here, still reading.

Maybe you're scared, excited, or both. Maybe you've decided to enlist, or you're pretty sure you've been drafted. In any event, you're here with me now and you may get orders soon. Before you go, you've earned the right to come in to the circle, sit down and listen as we swap war stories. Some of these stories appeared in my first adoption book in 2010. The authors have now written updates for you—I'm happy to announce they're mostly praise reports! I greatly admire those who've shared here—many others are not ready. They entered adoption as close-knit, happy families—some already had well-adjusted biological children. These parents were excited, per-haps idealistically so, and were going to save a child! Now, many are divorced, their biological children have been abused and molested and, in some cases, even taken away from them because their homes became unsafe. They went into adoption or fostering unprepared; they experienced frustration, confusion and heartache. They were already experienced, good parents, so they couldn't understand why their parenting methods failed this time.

Other parents are grieving because they fell in love with a child and then lost them. One thing I'm repeatedly asked by hopeful parents is this, "Is there a risk that I'll care for a child and then have to give him/her back?" My answer is yes, if you're doing foster care, and maybe if you're adopting another way. There's always a risk that you'll love a child that you can't keep. Even our biological children can leave us long before we want them to. Any time you choose to love another, you become vulnerable to heartbreak. But if you do foster care long enough, you'll usually end up adopting. If you're a "regular foster" parent, you usually care for a few that go home before one sticks. The instance of this is lower in "fost-adopt" placements— please see an adoption glossary for clarification. Not every parent is okay with this, but I viewed my temporary foster parenting as a type of much-needed babysitting. I enjoyed the children while I had them, pray for them still, and I hope I brought some light into what might have been their darkest days. But I understand, from all angles, why some parents aren't ready to share their stories. If not for the constant urging of the Holy Spirit, I wouldn't share either. I honestly would not. I fostered and adopted troubled kids, and I wasn't always prepared. I had many moments where I felt I was doing a pitiful job with the children entrusted to me. Nevertheless, eventually (prayerfully) I always returned to this thought: If I were a child—without family or love—and I had the choice of being without a family forever or having Cheryl (pitiful as she is) as my mommy, what would I choose? So we survived and continued on, but I still struggled with guilt because they didn't seem to be getting "better," or I didn't feel as strong of a bond as I thought I should. In my mind, I was passionate about being a loving mother, but my emotions felt anemic. I prayed, asking for forgiveness for my feelings of apathy and for help to feel a deep parental love for these kids; still it was lacking. Then one day, I realized something vital: The only love that was missing was the "natural" love—the feeling of a bond between mother and child. Under natural circumstances, this strong emotional bond motivates and guides the parents as they raise their child. However, adoption isn't natural; my lack of strong emotion was actually the natural response to this situation! Not only was it my natural response, I've since learned that many adoptive parents (especially of severely troubled children) experience the same condition. This revelation was liberating and encouraging. No, we might not form a strong emotional bond with each other, but that's okay. God wants to enable us to have something higher than natural love—He wants us to share His love, which is *supernatural*.

Since that realization my goals became clearer; it's a mission—or ministry. Yes, it's parenting, but it isn't typical, and it's not my job to fix people. I am incapable of fixing anyone. But if I follow the Holy Spirit toward orphans, foster children and street kids, sharing God's love and sowing the seeds of His Word as I go, He'll make His seeds grow—He promises His Word won't return void. It will accomplish His purposes. As I mentioned earlier, there will be a harvest of souls! People will be saved, set free from their sins, delivered from the power of darkness and brought into His glorious light; they'll enter the kingdom of heaven and live forever in paradise, instead of burning in hell! Just because I bothered! Could anything else matter more than this?! My mission is to nurture children and pray God will touch them and call them into a relationship with Himself. Yes, this mission has been hard and will continue to be so—because I'm weak. But God is strong and faithful; He answers prayer, and I truly and wholeheartedly believe in miracles.

I pray that you'll be blessed by the following stories. I apologize for the disturbing elements in some; I can't fix that either.

"Therefore, as God's chosen people, holy and dearly loved, clothe yourselves with compassion, kindness, humility, gentleness and patience. Bear with each other and forgive whatever grievances you may have against one another. Forgive as the Lord forgave you." (Colossians 3:12-13)

He Was Full of Fun

by Linda Rollins

He was full of fun and laughter—playing and running— happy on his skinny little legs to be with people in a safe and light and loving place. He never cried. He had learned not to cry.

He had been alone many a dark night, many a dreary, lonesome day in his four short years—in a cold, filthy ghetto apartment, with little if any furniture, no housekeeping, no homemaking, no door even to the hallway. Alone in a dirty crib with a bottle of soured milk, sometimes a cookie or cold wiener. His mother worked nights. Two older sisters and brother made up the family. The siblings were expected to stay and care for him, but they had not.

Rusty's legs were like twigs and his tummy distended with malnourishment when he came to our home for a two-week stay while his mother traveled somewhere for "job training". He loved the warm house and the family and all the attention. He ran, and played, and laughed. We all grew to love him.

His mother never returned for him. She sent a letter asking my parents to adopt him. She was about to lose custody because of neglect; she wanted him with a Christian family, where she knew he'd be cared for and loved. Under Mama's good care Rusty soon gained weight and his health blossomed.

By the time he was in high school, he was star of the local high school's wrestling team. He loved the wrestling, one-on-one, grappling, fighting, playing, touching. He loved it too much.

We didn't understand the problems until after he was grown and came to live with my young husband and I, and our three little girls. Though he went to church, prayed with us at meals, and joined in our Bible study; though he professed Christ, wore Jesus t-shirts, played a guitar and sang church songs, his demeanor was odd. Something was amiss. We were naive. I was in my own happy, little bubble and had not so much as heard words like pornography, rape, and child molesting.

I was naive and had no idea about the crimes committed against my own child until it was too late.

There was peculiar behavior, like Rusty missing for a few hours at times now and then, and money missing. That, I think now, should have spelled a pornography addiction to me. One night, after he had gone to Bible Study, I caught Rusty lurking in the dark kitchen instead. He snuck in the back door just to scare me, he said. "Boo!" Just a little joke, right? Or maybe a trip to my daughter's bedroom? Still, I missed all the warning signs.

A few years later our little girl, with her innocence destroyed, told a church friend how her uncle had hurt her—how he had molested her many times and warned her that her sisters were next if she reported his crimes. Once she had told us, we could protect our girls and warn others, but damage and grief had already been done.

Our girl has suffered a scarred and battered life, with self-destructive patterns and a string of abusive men in her wake. She coped with her pain and shame by developing habits of lying, stealing and hiding. We all have suffered because of her suffering.

My parents saved one boy, who was very much in need of and deserving of a decent home and family. I still call him my brother. I still love him and feel that it was the right thing to do to take him in, but at such a price! We can't ever let him in our home. He wasn't and still isn't welcome in the extended family, except by my parents. I have watched him lose his wife and his own children because of his sinful behavior. He is still avoided and rejected by those around him.

My parents saved him, but he destroyed their grandchild and the hurt continues in her life, her siblings lives, and her children's lives, and in my own and her Daddy's lives. This danger is very real in many adoptive and fostering families. It should be guarded against. This child was adopted young. But who knows what grievous things happened to him in the few years before he came to our family, that warped his mind and perverted his sexuality? He was irreparably damaged by the lack of a father to claim him, neglect and rejection by his mom and siblings, and probably abuse by several of them or others. Healing his malnutrition was not enough; he needed healing of his heart and spirit. Then he could have been salvaged and not endangered other innocents.

How could a good and wonderful, godly thing—adoption— become such treachery? How could so fine a thing as opening your heart and home to an unloved child, destroy lives and leave a path of pain and heartache behind? How can we save the many who need homes without bringing on our selves and families untold grief? How?

SuperMom Meets Fetal Alcohol

By Emily LeChene

When I was asked to share my story as a foster and then adoptive parent I thought, no way! Words cannot describe what a difficult season this is for me. Share my story? I didn't even want to think about my chaotic life, let alone tell the world. To encourage me to share, Cheryl gave me a rough-draft copy of her first adoption book. Even opening the book terrified me, so I put it aside and didn't read it.

The author knows my experiences more than most. As a close friend, I've shared my frustrations and anxiety with her over the past five years—since I began my journey into foster care and later adoption. She was there when we were a happy family with five biological children. She was also there after we adopted, as the stress began to break our peaceful, close-knit family to pieces.

When I finally broke down and read her book, it opened my eyes. I was encouraged and strengthened through the knowledge that I'm not alone. I realized that my story also has the power to help others as they prepare to foster or adopt—or who may feel alone in the battle—as I so often have; for these reasons, I've decided to share.

Cheryl and her family are long-term friends of our family. In earlier years, Cheryl called me her "home-schooling mentor." I was home schooling for years before most people had even heard of the concept. Before her own babies reached school age, Cheryl determined that she also would home educate her children. Our worlds revolved around loving God and family, home schooling our children and the tight budget that so often comes with the decision to be a stay-at-home mom; it was great to have a friend with whom I shared so much in common.

The role of mentor later reversed as Cheryl was there to guide me through the process of fostering and then adoption. She is a woman who hangs on and trusts God through the impossible. She's given me courage to go on when I knew I was too weak to continue. If there's one lesson I've learned about mentors, it's that you really should listen when they give advice. I missed a good deal of the warnings and advice in the beginning of this reversed mentor role due to my high self-opinion of my parenting skills. Regardless of your skills as a parent, take the advice and stories in this book to heart. Heed the words of caution and educate yourself! I have found that raising biological children—for whom I cared from the womb with nourishing food, healthful beverages and vitamins—is far different from parenting little ones whose mothers had poor nutrition, drank alcohol and, in lieu of vitamins, took drugs.

As Cheryl and Mike began foster parenting, my husband and I watched with amazement. We admired this young couple with their happy brood of biological, foster and adopted children. Our own children were now growing up and we'd always considered that some day, we too would like to adopt. As we witnessed the ministry in action taking place in the Ellicott home, we were encouraged. "One day," we said, "we too will add to our already big, happy family!"

We finally believed the time had come—that the Lord was calling us to foster care and the possibility of adoption—in the year 2000. It was a beautiful Sunday afternoon and we were relaxing after church. The kids were here and there throughout the home; my husband and I were in the family room listening to Christian music. When the song "He," by Jars of Clay, came on, the lyrics went straight to our hearts. The song is about child abuse from a child's perspective. The singer sang in heart-wrenching tones as he unburied the hurting heart of an abused child. On our coffee table, The Sunday newspaper lay open to Societies Child. The entire page was covered with pictures of children waiting to find families. Our biological children's happy voices floated through the house as we stared down at these lonely faces. "Why do you hurt me," the singer cried out through the speakers of our stereo. I looked at my husband; he was trying not to cry, but tears filled his eyes.

"It's time," I said. "God's calling us to rescue children and bring them home." My husband nodded and then we both cried.

Right away, I called my dear friend who was both a foster mom and an adoptive mom by now. "Cheryl, how do we get set up to do foster care?" I asked. She explained that my first step was to call a local agency that would take us through the licensing process. We contacted the one she worked with and met with a home-study caseworker. Oddly enough, with one thing after another coming up within our family, it took us two full years before we actually became licensed foster parents; normally, it takes just a matter of months. Now I know that God was protecting us. We really had no idea how stressful our home would become after the foster children finally began to arrive.

As we purchased children's furniture, outdoor play equipment and cute wall borders for the "nursery," which was half of our master bedroom, we were filled with excitement. We were going to provide a happy home for little children who otherwise might have ended up in the Sunday newspaper! Visions of sugarplums danced in our heads as we set up the bassinet beside our own bed.

When our friends, Cheryl and Mike, came over for dinner with their beautiful family I felt I'd explode with excitement as I watched those beautiful children play. I've always adored children, and as the time to add to our family soon approached, the joy I felt that day as we visited with the Ellicott family is still etched in my mind forever. I stepped out of the room for some reason or other and Cheryl confided to my husband that she didn't know if I was strong enough to be able to do this. "She'll fall in love with every child and adopt every one that comes up for adoption no matter what..." she told him. "I really don't think she knows what she's getting into!"

They did try to teach me. Both Cheryl and Mike warned us about the serious issues of FAS, FAE, FAES and others. Was I intimidated by these serious issues? Not at all. I believed that there was no issue or condition our God, our family and good food, etc., could not cure. When I filled out the questionnaire, or "Christmas wish list" as Cheryl puts it, I checked yes, yes, yes, yes, yes to so many challenging issues, despite the warnings. I was the older woman; I had it all together! We'd been successful with our biological children and now we were enthusiastic about bringing in some of the babies who were deemed the most difficult.

In hindsight, I was way too plucky; this over-confidence was soon plucked from my heart as I realized I'd landed my entire family in a situation that changed our lives forever. SuperMom came crashing down to earth and found out the cape she wore was only an apron after all.

Within a year of our foster/adoption placements, three of our biological kids had moved out. The stress in our home put their dreams for college on hold as they went to work to pay for their apartments. One biological daughter suffered what seemed to be a nervous breakdown, and for the next few years, she faced extreme difficulties. Then our youngest biological daughter couldn't take the turmoil anymore. Home life as she'd known it had evaporated and she didn't take the changes well. Formerly an "A" student, she got involved in an unhealthy relationship, dropped out of high school and ran away from home. Time has passed now and she'd really like to return home and to school, but she has trouble even visiting us for more than a few hours; the stress level in our home is still too intense for her.

All three children that we adopted were drug and alcohol exposed prior to birth. Our third and youngest (born less than a year after his sister who'd already been placed with us) came to us after we had been licensed just a year. Three FAE, & drug-babies within one year! Cheryl was right when she warned my husband about what she foresaw as a weakness in me. No, I could never turn these hurting children away. I love them and did so from first sight. However, the frequent screaming and howling from a child whose brain has been damaged by alcohol and drugs can unravel the nerves of the most patient and loving; these tantrums outlast the tantrums of normal kids and the decibels seem unnaturally high. The tantrums erupt quite suddenly—seemingly without cause; they can last for hours, and on some days, these explosions occur on several occasions. It's difficult for parents, siblings and even the pets during such times— and we didn't adopt just one, but three volatile, needy children.

My hope is in God and His love. We're still strong advocates of good nutrition and we believe nurture is powerful medicine, but now I know it'll take an all-out miracle to heal these kids. Adoption is not the end of the story; it is just a beginning. Each day is a challenge and some days are better than others. On our good days, I take heart; on the bad days, I sometimes wonder if I've made the biggest mistake of my life by taking on such challenges.

Am I a failure? Yes, but God is a winner and He saves failures like me. He gives beauty for ashes...My hope is in Him and Him alone. He uses the foolish things of this world to confound the wise, so I qualify. He can use me! I often think of the missionaries who gave their lives to bring Christ to the lost in foreign lands. Greater love has no man than He who lays down his life for His friends. We are not alone in the mission field...and this is my mission, but it's not at all what I envisioned! I pray that God—who called us to this new life—will sustain us till the end. Before adopting, I envisioned the blessings of happy little rescued babies...children laughing, babies smiling and cooing. Reality was something else entirely. Often, it feels like our marriage, our family and even our sanity is under crushing spiritual attack. I can relate to the words of Paul the apostle when he says:

"We do not want you to be uninformed, brothers, about the hardships we suffered. . . . We were under great pressure, far beyond our ability to endure, so that we despaired even of life. Indeed, in our hearts we felt the sentence of death. But this happened that we might not rely on ourselves but on God, who raises the dead."(2 Cor. 1:8-9)

I expected laughing, smiling and cooing. Instead, our days and nights are filled with inconsolable screaming, demands that cannot be met and needs that are overwhelming. These precious little children are very loved; they always have food, hugs, warmth and a mommy and daddy's love. However, they have intense needs, hurts and problems that the most loving mommy cannot meet or heal. But Mommy knows someone who can; so I will lead them to Him.

Sometimes I'm still ashamed that I'm not breezing through this. I don't always feel the assurance that everything will someday be okay, but I hope that you can glean from my story that this truly is a battle! As in other wars, without soldiers to stand and fight, there can be no victory. Also, without preparation, soldiers do not stand firmly in battle. Yes, I came into foster care and adoption wearing rose colored glasses, but I was warned. I brushed the warnings away. Now you, the reader, have the opportunity to hear this from an experienced mommy of five and now adoptive mommy to three. Adoption is a real ministry that requires more than you can imagine, even with advanced warning. These beautiful children are definitely worth fighting for. But understand, this is war you're waging! Be prepared and count the cost. If you have children at home, consider their needs and safety. I had no idea what this would cost my family. I expected we'd remain the happy family we'd always been and that these little ones would just add more joy. Had I known, I would have waited longer before I tramped into the battleground with my unsuspecting family. I would have been a whole lot less flippant. But I had no idea it was a battleground.

I want to encourage you to steep this decision in prayer and learn everything you can about FAES and other issues to which you will be exposed. With all that in mind, if the time is right and the calling is there, then gird yourself! Go to war and fight the good fight. There are children waiting for your loving arms. If you've been given marching orders, then march, but be prepared; put on the full armor of God. You're headed for the front lines and your very real enemy doesn't want to let these little souls go.

UPDATE:

It's been about ten years since Emily wrote her story. In the years that followed they struggled, especially with one of their adopted sons whose violent, uncontrollable outbursts were taking a huge toll on the family. I remember a time when Emily was almost ready to give up; it seemed hopeless. She asked for prayer time and again. Well, as you know, God is faithful; He answered her prayers! She began to realize God was directing her to experiment with nutritional intervention, something she hadn't previously believed in. In obedience she first tried using the GFCF (gluten-free, casein-free diet) with amazing results. Eventually she explored the Feingold diet as well. I remember when she'd been practicing nutritional intervention for a few months—I could almost hear Emily's shouts of *Hallelujah!* from a thousand miles away. Here's Emily's brief update, in her own words:

"One of the most positive lessons I've learned, that I believe will help many if they give it a try, is that nutritional intervention works! We saw many small changes at first, and some rather profound, but over time the positive changes multiplied. We soon noticed soy caused casein type reactions (extreme behavioral meltdowns), so we avoided that as well. My son reacted severely to berries and apples, and was sensitive to onions and garlic, so I learned to deal with that in my cooking routine. We eat a lot of turkey and salmon now; they cause a natural calming. Through allergy testing, plus elimination diets, we found triggers for our kid's extreme meltdowns. We avoid artificial colors and flavors as much as possible and try to keep our home free of toxic cleaners. I use more natural products that are better for people, pets and especially sensitive kids. We still face challenges, as all families do. But nothing like before. My son blessed my heart the other day when he said, "Mom, thank you for never giving up on me." I was so touched; I cling to those precious words. With all my heart I responded, "I love you, my son; I will never give up on you!!" His struggles have been difficult, but our family continues to seek the Lord's leading and go forward. My words to any that are in the midst of the battle, which may last till the Lord leads us to the other side is, from the mouth of my precious adopted drug and alcohol exposed youngest son: "Never give up."

The Hospice Survivor

By Cheryl Ellicott

The night was hot and I was cold. I stood in the dark as the ceiling fan spun above my head and my thoughts turned circles through my mind. *I'm tired and I've earned my rest — I'm four babies past my eighteenth year, and I'd like to sit down before I'm thirty.* Just as fast as I conceived one thought, another came whirling through:

Never grow weary of doing good, for in due season you will reap a harvest... if you do not give up.

Despite my uncertainty that hot summer night, I agreed to take a foster daughter into my home to live with my husband, me and our four small children. Not just another foster child, but a seventeen-year-old girl with a baby.

Never grow weary of doing good... for in due time you will reap a harvest.

I cradled the late night call in the palm of my hand, hesitating before I responded to the voice on the other end. I stared out the window into the dark Arizona night, remembering nights when I was zealous, when God's love was as real to me as the dark that now embraced the city. I recalled days when my faith seemed stronger, but those were hard times; while girls my age fretted over who they'd go to the prom with. I'd kept company with a hospice nurse. I held my own baby girl's hand as the cancer slowly took her from me... only faith in God's goodness, and in eternal life, kept me from despair.

Yet I hadn't felt drained back then. I wondered now if I were drifting toward the death of my closeness with Jesus—beyond the point of caring whether or not I would reap a harvest; sometimes I get tired like that. So tired. Usually it scares me; this time was no exception... I guess that's why I said yes.

"When will you bring them?" I held the phone up to my mouth now. The familiar voice of the CPS worker answered with the usual answer: "I'm not sure."

"Okay," I said, "I'll be ready." But I wasn't.

My foster daughter's name was Tia; she came to me because her mother had just died, leaving Tia and her baby on their own. At this time I was the only foster home in the city willing to take a teenager and her baby. So they arrived, and Tia began making herself at home. At nearly six feet tall and with a booming alto voice, she was accustomed to getting her own way. Even with her boyfriend—a drug dealer in jail for attempted murder—she was the boss. She hated healthful food and demanded canned corned-beef-hash and Pepsi. She wanted the bed disassembled so she could throw the mattress on the floor to sleep, like she was used to. She refused to put her baby, Danielle, in the crib or in generic brand diapers! Also, Tia liked to burn candles at night... thinking they would hide the smell of her marijuana smoke as it drifted through the halls of my home.

Tia was *"all ghetto,"* as she liked to say.

It took me a few crazy, everything-up-in-the-air days before I realized what was happening. My first thought came easily, You don't need this. Send them on their way. I was so tempted to have Tia and Danielle moved; let someone else worry about them. The second thought was harder... but I knew what God wanted.

Never grow weary of doing good... do not give up.

He wanted me to stand up tall, no matter how tired I was, and look this big girl in the eyes and act like a real mother to her. Maybe I wasn't feeling super zealous these days, but Tia needed love strong enough to tell her what to do... if not just for herself, for the sake of baby Danielle.

Standing beneath the thumping, rattling loose ceiling fan, I wondered if I could do what was best. *Lord? I'm not strong enough. She's too intense, too determined, too angry—too big! Surely you wouldn't expect me to bridle a bull. Did I forget to tell you how exhausted I am?*

I held my weary head within my small hands and sighed long and deep. I stayed there, praying, for longer than I'd prayed in a long, long time. My only other choice was to send them on their way...

In due time you will reap a harvest, if you do not give up.

So I gathered up my flimsy self and marched off to bridle a bull. I never did control her, but Tia opened her heart to me; that was something. Suddenly, all her anger and hurt came gushing out like a torrential flood, seeking to drown everything in its way.

Tia's mama had recently died from cancer; it was generally accepted that Mom's drug use could have caused the cancer. Tia sat beside me night after endless night and praised the virtue of her mother, but I saw anger just beneath her words. Maybe it was Mom's fault that Tia was abused and molested by the flow of messed up people in their lives. It probably was wrong that Mom allowed Tia to smoke marijuana to calm her frayed nerves. However, during those last days, after Tia had been nursing her dying mother for nine months, didn't Mom make everything right? Didn't she apologize for not being there when Tia needed her? How could you be angry with someone when you had changed their diapers and held their trembling hand as the cancer stole them away? Tia couldn't, but she could be angry with her foster mother. She could test her foster mom's love and expect that love to be strong enough to erase any neglect her own mother had shown her. Meanwhile, I could sit beneath my whining, squeaking ceiling fan. (which badly needed oiling) praying again, praying harder than I had since my own daughter was stricken with cancer, so many years ago. How I could possibly deal with Tia? I couldn't heal her pain.

Lord? I don't swim well enough to carry the weight of two! Oh sure, you've carried me through my valleys — even the shadow of death — but what do I know? Surely this broken child will pull us both under and we'll drown! She, scrambling and gasping for air; me, killing myself in an effort to hold her up! Or... maybe I'll be lucky and just be smothered to death...

Still the same answer came back to me:

Do not give up.

So, even though I felt guilty for my lack of fervor, I kept going. At the end of two months, I sat with the phone between clenched fists. I'd had enough. Sure, she was reading the Bible by then, asking questions, confessing newborn hope in Jesus Christ to forgive her and set her free from the crazy mixed-up emotions that tossed her about. Yet...

Tia was still an enormous brat; I was losing my patience and seeing a side of myself I didn't like — a side I hadn't even realized existed!

Tia whined day after day, night after night. "You need to tell me what Jesus says about this! I don't wanna read it for myself!" "You only love your kids; you don't love me!" "Why do you cook this stuff?" "Why do you wear your hair like that?" "I couldn't follow that rule because…"

Again and again, she had emergencies at curfew time and couldn't make it home. She was assaulted twice in two weeks; she totaled her car, and five times she went to the emergency room. She fought against everything I asked her to do. Oh sure, later she'd come back and tell me she was sorry. "I love you and you were right," she'd say.

But honestly, Tia was driving me crazy.

So that day came and I was sitting there feeling sick to my stomach, holding the phone and dialing the number to have Tia and her baby moved to separate shelters; there were no shelters or foster homes that would take both a teenage girl and her baby.

Why? Why are you giving up?

In my mind I answered, *What can I do for such a rebellious girl? Nothing I say helps her—she's in my face all day long! She's bigger than me, louder than me… and why do I wear my hair like this anyway?*

I wanted to scream, but held back.

Oh, I know she's hurting, but what can I do? I can't handle this disobedient girl.

Then the phone line was busy, so I picked up my Bible to pass the time. My bookmark lay inside the book of Matthew, in Chapter 21. I read the parable of the two sons, replaced the bookmark and dialed the number again. But as their line began to ring, I set the receiver back into its cradle.

"*Which of the two sons did what his father wanted?*" Jesus asked. The people answered, "*It was the first son.*"

My mind replayed the story as I sat and pondered, realizing what it meant: It wasn't the agreeable son, in the end, who did what his father wanted. The truly obedient son first said to his father, "*No! I will not,*" but later he changed his mind and went. Suddenly, I saw things as they really were.

Which child is Tia?

She's the first child, Lord. The one who says, "I will not!" and then later changes her mind and does what she should.

I smiled, pushed the phone away and the sick feeling in my stomach resided.

She's the obedient one.

With that realization came the shocking truth that Tia was sent to help me, not the other way around. Yet, she hadn't come to watch me die because I wasn't really terminal. I could see now that I'd never been more full of zeal, faith, and the power of God. No, I'd just been in circumstances that brought me shaking and crying into His strong arms. Maybe God had been missing our passionate, lengthy, late night talks... *Maybe* He brought me Tia so that our time together would become fervent once again.

So I kept her for awhile longer, though I couldn't change her. I spent many more days and nights leading her through the Scriptures to find answers. I prayed that God would comfort her and heal her broken heart. Yet even the Apostle Paul, each time he preached in a city, would eventually realize it was time to move on. In my case, there were no big rocks or death-threats involved, but when I felt my marriage and my relationship with my other children were about to crumble, I finally had Tia and baby Danielle moved. By that time, a shelter had agreed to take the two of them—together.

After they'd gone, I lay down, watching that silly fan sit there and do nothing on a cold night, and I was warm. I prayed and the presence of God surrounded me like a living blanket. Things had never been just about me or about how much I had to give. No, God's plans were always much bigger than that.

I kept in touch with Tia and Danielle for awhile, and it looked like Tia would just keep traveling the same path her biological mom took her down. I stood by helpless, watching Tia become the mother of two baby girls, then three... then four. Different fathers, never a husband. But eventually she moved far away and stopped calling or writing. I didn't hear from her for years and I wondered if my efforts were in vain. Had my prayers come to nothing? But then I realized that something amazing had *already* happened. My spiritual cancer was still in remission; God did a work in my heart, through Tia. Also, my prayers for Tia and her children were still there, permanently etched in the fabric of the unseen. They would be answered in God's perfect timing. Then one day, just before the final edit of this story, Tia found me again; a calmer, happier Tia; no longer quite as restless and troubled. She was now married, involved in a church, almost ready to graduate from college, and she still called me Mom.

I'm surrounded by miracles.

Update:

It's been about twenty years since I met Tia. Her own children are now adults and teenagers. I wish I could tell you that the months Tia spent in my home, calling me Mom, chased away all of her demons—but I cannot. After years of immoral living and addiction to illegal drugs, Tia finally *got clean* and got married. But then she became addicted to doctor-prescribed drugs; she's continued to suffer times of extreme mental instability. However, Tia hasn't let go of the faith that was born in her, inside our home; even when *out of her mind*, Tia resolutely claims Jesus as her Savior. Yes, I long for the day when her faith will finally grow up and free her from her self and the demons she inherited from her mother, and mother's lifestyle. But I know the story isn't over yet—and the harvest isn't mine to produce. I'm just a sower of seeds; God Almighty is the Lord of the harvest.

"... a man reaps what he sows... the one who sows to please the Spirit, from the Spirit will reap eternal life. Let us not become weary in doing good, for at the proper time we will reap a harvest if we do not give up . . ." (Galatians 6:8-9 NIV)

(Author's Note: The next two stories are from the perspective of grandparents who have helped raise their grandchildren and whose biological children were more difficult than some others.)

Refuge

By Karen Jessame

How can I explain my daughter Rhia? Wild as our New Zealand hills, like an untamed mountain pony… my sixth child was quite unexpected. It seemed she was born too soon after my fifth. Another baby so soon after the last one? I prayed, "Lord please protect this baby until I get my head around this and accept this as your plan for me…" After a hideously managed labour, Rhia arrived purple and exhausted. This merely hinted at what would come.

She's always been sweet, loving, gifted and intelligent, but also independent and self-assured like none of my other children; she brought drama to my once tidy life. So much drama. She stretched my parenting like none of my others—stupid, stupid girl, I have said at times—but which of my other children has caused me to pray so often? Which has, when they're grown, gifted me with a grandchild to help raise—turning my mature years to spring again?

Rhia stopped breathing at six weeks. Afterward, I stayed up night and day with her terrified she would stop breathing again. Alone with her in her battle, feeling emotionally distanced from my husband and other children, I sensed dark oppression around this baby… I was uneasy, unsettled, filled with dread and I thought the devil wanted to take her. Crazy thought, I told myself. I was postnatal and overtired. This is just mental exhaustion… Yet I prayed again and again, asking God to protect this baby. Eventually both baby and I were admitted to the hospital. After a week or so we came home and carried on as normal.

I remember Rhia at three, with wide eyes and windswept curls about her cheeks, prattling as she trotted along beside me to bring in the milking cow. She insisted on carrying a huge bucket. Suddenly the bucket flew into the air, the chatting stopped and Rhia was nowhere to be seen.

She had simply disappeared.

There was a hole in the grass alongside the track; I thought she had gone down a pothole in the limestone rocks. My own heart faltered; my sense of losing this child was overwhelming and unexplainable.

Then I heard a wee voice from far below, "Mummy," she said, "I am stuck and I am praying to Jesus cos I am scared!"

I followed the wee voice to where this tiny girl was—hanging onto a tree root, inside a rock cleft in the fluting of the limestone rock formations, on the bluffs below where we bring in the cow. I climbed down, reached out and pulled her into my arms and to safety. But strangely, this thick dread remained.

I know fear and darkness and I have struggled with something; I struggled with God. With no disrespect to my parents I will tell it how it was: I was beaten as a child; I was kicked, slapped, hit and otherwise abused. I believe my parents loved me and they did the best they knew how... they simply did not know how. Because of my childhood, I've wrestled with God being a father figure. I held back, wanting to be close to Him, but afraid He would reject me. With good reason, for I have done many wrong things. Yet, with Rhia as my daughter, I had no choice—even when I wasn't sure He'd respond to a mere farm wife who had not earned his attention, I cried out to Him anyway.

When Rhia first started school, she decided she did not like it. So she hid herself in the school mail box and arrived home with the mail man. At nine she went through a plate-glass window. I heard the crashing of glass and thought the dog had jumped on the table. But, no, there was Rhia lying on the floor covered in huge shards of glass, with blood on her face, feet, arms and legs. I picked her up and checked for any serious bleeding or glass in her body. We loaded her up traveled an hour and a half away to the doctor, with Rhia singing heartily all the way, *Jesus loves me this I know, for the Bible tells me so!* Her daddy helped the doctor sew her up and surprisingly there was little lasting damage.

One time the children had unexplained bruises. Rhia's bruises kept coming for days, so I took her to the Doctor. He questioned me closely: "How are things at home; how is your husband coping; is he well?" Blood tests were taken and I brought my bruised child home.

Two days later the Doctor rang. "Your little girl is very sick you must get her to the hospital immediately."

Again the feeling of absolute dread and boding evil that hounded me with this child. I could not shake it off. Hospital it was and on arrival we met three more children covered in bruises. Relief flooded over me and I was told it was Thrombocyto Paenia Pupura. The first of the affected children went home the next day, the second a day later and finally the third child went home. But Rhia stayed and stayed and stayed; blood test after blood test... day, after day, after day.

I had five other children at home, three hours away. My husband bundled them all up and came to visit. I missed them so much. I missed my home, my life... yet here I was bound to this child who would not cooperate on any level. After months of blood tests, bottles of steroids, absolute dread of her hurting herself and bleeding internally, I was done. The rest of the family was suffering, I was strung out and totally over it and the feeling of dread and anxiety was overwhelming. It was too much. I prayed, my Mum prayed, we all prayed—but blood test after blood test was bad, bad, bad. Finally my husband called the elders of our church and they came with a little bottle of oil—no fuss, no drama. They poured the oil on Rhia, put their hands on her and prayed.

I cry as I write this... the feeling of dread lifted immediately when they prayed. I saw that Rhia was not only our worry, she was the Lords! God would undertake for her... yes she might still be in danger and even obstinate, but the burden was not mine alone. Something evil and nasty and frightful went away that day and has never come back. I cannot explain fully; words cannot express the darkness I felt around this child—some of it was likely guilt, for I had not planned on another baby so soon. I didn't feel joy, excitement or need with this pregnancy. I had to pray for protection of an unborn baby in my own womb for goodness sake. I was so deeply ashamed of those feelings.

Gradually Rhia improved; the steroids were stopped, the blood tests were stopped and we went home to family and farm by the sea. Back home to carry on with everyday tasks, to be a cheerful Mum to the other children, enjoy and encourage my husband, run a house and a business, be a friend to many and have an encouraging word, to rejoice with those whose children do well and not let my sadness overshadow the other aspects of life. All the while feeling like I'm carrying a struggling child in my arms and heart all day long.

When Rhia was a teen, she started smoking pot. That was bad, but nothing so horrifying as the night my eldest daughter came running down from the shed screaming and crying saying that she thought Rhia was going to die. My niece, a troubled soul herself was staying with us; she was an influence Rhia didn't need. By the time I got up to the shed these two girls were staggering around incoherently and collapsing. Their eyes were bloodshot and they looked to be blind... they'd been sniffing petrol (gas). Even more shocking was the calf they were sitting with; he could not even get up. I thought they'd never be normal again; stupid, stupid girls... Afterward Rhia struggled along with a few brain cells missing and eventually regretted using drugs because it hindered her organisational skills and memory.

Our first five children were outstanding. Apart from the usual kid stuff there were no problems; they were highly respected, successful, lovely, steady and well-liked children. They were awarded prizes of achievement and took responsible roles within the school and polytechs. Both my husband and I also were involved in the school. We were well-respected and well thought of.

You may laugh, but within months of Rhia starting at the high school I was labeled negative, paranoid, aggressive and two other things I cannot remember. Rhia caused problems, but once she was labeled a problem, she was blamed for everything even when she was not involved. Our lovely model family was labeled dysfunctional and yes, I resented this. My other children deeply resented Rhia for all the drama and because the focus seemed always to have been on her. I resented Rhia for bringing such anxiety, shame and difficulty on our whole family, for awhile. But it was also easy to feel I brought it on myself, because I was lazy parenting a sixth child; I thought, Oh she will be alright; the others are all alright and she will get there... but Rhia really and truly was different.

At the end of my rope I could not cope any longer and we got the help of an advocate from the child and mental health unit. Rhia was diagnosed with Aspergbergers Syndrome and a programme was put in place at the school. It worked very well, but only until she had no incidence of bad behaviour within a certain time period. Then the support was withdrawn, the teachers went back to treating her like before and at 15 years old Rhia was chucked out of school.

Just before she left school she took on work experience at a racing stable and came home the proud owner of a chucked out horse. That horse became her focus, her love and the path to a more positive life. She threw a saddle on him took him to the beach and galloped into newness. She stayed at home, kicked the drugs, worked in town and saved her money. Then a few days before her 18th birthday Rhia was in a vehicle accident and her foot was severed except for a small piece of skin and ligament. We gathered at her bedside and prayed; after hours of surgery her toes were pink and she still had a foot.

Months of recovery followed. Her determination was incredible. She stumped around, rode her horse, treasured her pins and screws and plates and x-rays and at last, was hired on to her first job away from home. She was so excited; she tossed her belongings into the car and away she went to a job of breaking horses.

Turned out she was not paid and her boss was little more than a pedophile. After much drama and anxiety our girl came home and started polytech. She did well but something was wrong...

Then one night she rang and told us she was pregnant. She did not tell us then that her boss had raped her. She only said she was four months pregnant and was booked to travel to another town to have an abortion. For us at the time it seemed so huge, so dreadful — the ultimate insult, the stupid girl. We had no idea... What I did know was I wanted that baby so badly. Already it was part of our family; if the decision was to kill that baby it would never mean it was not there. My feelings were so intense — as if the baby had already been born and I was holding it, having to give it up to be killed... and yet... it was not our decision to make. So I fell back onto my rock in Christ.

"If any man lack wisdom let him ask of God who giveth freely to all men..."

"Oh God in Heaven I need your wisdom," I prayed. "How do I plead for the life of this child and yet give my daughter space? This child will always be ours for years to come. If it's killed now there will be a hole in our family."

I told Rhia if she chose to abort the baby that there would be no going back. If she chose to have this baby—whether to adopt out or keep it—there would always be an opportunity to save or settle the issue. But once the baby was killed she would have no options. We promised her our unwavering support and that we would help in every way possible. We told her we loved her and that we would love her baby as well.

Over the next few days we waited and worried. Everyone had their ten cents worth on the situation and their perspective and thoughts. Another overwhelming drama. I began to feel isolated again as when Rhia was a baby and so ill, or when she was at school and using drugs and so needy. I felt again the dread of having done things wrong, of blaming myself. Was I overcompensating for the bad feelings I'd had over becoming pregnant again so soon after a last baby? The last straw was when my husband said abortion might be the best solution. I was furious with him, recalling all my old wounds and every time I'd felt he was not with me in Rhia's battles.

So there I stood one day, hanging out yet another load of washing, with snot and tears running down my face; what a mess. Then suddenly the lights went on in my soul. Dear God, you care for this child far, far more than I ever could! I felt a lightening and laughter welled up within me. The burden lifted away just as it had when the elders prayed over our sick little girl. *Sweet Lord, I give the whole thing to you!* I realized this was the Lord's burden, not mine.

"Dear God, you see the end from the beginning. You are trustworthy. You make no mistakes. Even when you seem silent and we are disappointed with this silence, struggling with it and angry, you are every bit the same God as of our joys and incredible experiences. Nothing about you changes; we can trust you. Please let us honour you with how we handle ourselves through this experience. People will be watching, trying to find an excuse to discount God in their own lives. Do not let us give them reason."

I felt great excitement and anticipation, wanting to see what God could do. I grew, I flew, my soul just lifted and I ended up praising God and feeling a real sense of wonder. I had struggled with seeing God as a good Father because if I was naughty as a child there was no going back; wrongs were heaped up, days could go without being spoken to, there was no way to make amends or put things right. I did some real, real bad things at times and lived with a sense of fear and dread. I put this on God too, feeling very uncomfortable asking for things—I thought I had to earn the right to ask. But at last I saw something: the eternal God is our refuge and underneath are the everlasting arms. God is in His heaven above us. God reaches down to men in grace and love and mercy. Who needs refuge? A refuge is a hiding place, a place of healing and provision. Everything is there for us in God; we hurt, we cry, we do things wrong, we are attacked, we are challenged, we are scared. If we fall, His everlasting arms are underneath us—not on top to shield up from every trouble, not raised up to strike us for doing wrong things, not behind his back to ignore us because we are naughty or disobedient, but underneath us to catch us. I'm no longer afraid to feel a sense of excitement even in the darkest hour, because He is a good Father. Yes, Satan means this or that for evil, but God can and will use it for good.

Not long after that Rhia told us she'd decided to keep her baby. In due time she gave birth to a beautiful baby girl. Our granddaughter is four years old now. She has lived with us and with her Mummy. Things have been tough—real tough. There have been tears, laughter, joy, sorrow… and some dread. I still feel all these things from time to time. But our grandbaby is such a lovely little girl; she has fitted into the family like the precious gift she is. She is dearly loved by all her aunties and uncles and has a very special bond with her granddaddy. She brings us much joy and delight.

When my daughter stumbles, I recall God's arms are holding me, catching me when I would fall. I remember Rhia's wee voice from far below saying, "Mummy, I am stuck and I am praying to Jesus cos I am scared!" I remember when I was that wee child, but I did not cry out—afraid that only beatings would come. My parents would not beg God to protect me, but might likely hurt me. Maybe the sense of dread I experienced was tied to guilt; maybe it was about what might have been, without Jesus; but He is here and we are calling out to Him… because we are scared. So, even today, I will climb down, reach out and pull Rhia into my arms and to safety—for as long as she needs me to.

Update:

It's been about ten years since Karen wrote her story. She and her daughter Rhia have continued to co-parent... It has been challenging, and Rhia has continued to have ups and downs. But the hardest part has been the judgment and criticism from other family members who believe Karen does too much to help. Nevertheless, Karen knows that each child needs something different, and she is willing to give what's needed, despite criticism. She says they have been blessed by God; she's peaceful about the future. Rhia has recently applied for a job that would require her (and her daughter) to leave the farm; Karen says the thought of them moving on is very hard. She has loved the company and excitement of being part of her daughter and granddaughter's lives.

Grandbaby's First Best Friend

By Elaine Lambert

"Greater love has no one than this, that he lay down his life for his friends." John 15:13

Our second daughter was an enigma from the start. An amazing little blessing, a gift from heaven that filled me with joy, but also surprise. For starters, I expected a baby boy. Just a hunch, but I was convinced I was carrying a brown-haired, brown-eyed boy; her daddy and I are both brunette. Yet there she was; beautiful chubby cheeks, little button nose, sea blue eyes and sun-kissed copper hair... yes, red. Who'd have ever thought? What a shock. What a gift! So we called her Peaches, with sugar and cream. Yet for all her baby sunshine, there was always the sense of a coming storm.

"She's so serious," said my own mother. "I've never seen a baby worry so much."

What could I say? It was an understatement. Highly intelligent, precocious, overflowing with vibrancy, imagination and potential — yes. But our little girl rarely relaxed and enjoyed life. She was either laughing too loudly or in a state of panic. From the beginning, she struggled to find a balance. At least I think that's what was happening. I was struggling too, trying to understand her. When she was learning to talk she panicked if we didn't recognize every word she said. Later, if I told her she'd done something wrong, she'd start screaming... at herself. As she grew, she was always the loudest, liveliest, most fun person in the room — or she was the darkest rain cloud.

Then she hit puberty and entered a new level. She was a three-ring circus with clowns and dancing bears... sometimes the whole carnival: balloons, cotton candy, roller coaster... and a haunted house. Suffice to say, her teen years were turbulent. I've lain awake more nights than I can count praying our daughter is alive. Yet when she finished high school and went off to college, I was hopeful.

A couple of months later, she'd been kicked out of college and banned from the campus; she was drinking heavily, using drugs and doing literally everything else we'd raised her to avoid. She came home in tears and saw a little brown puppy in my living room; not just any brown puppy—a fifteen-hundred-dollar puppy named *Amazing Grace.* I sometimes have show dogs and this pup was just passing through on her way to a family.

My daughter loves dogs; I wasn't surprised when her face lit up. She stopped crying and asked, "You got me a puppy?" Of course I thought, *No way! I love you dearly but this puppy is most definitely not for you.* Yet when I prayed, I felt sure that God was saying, *Yes. The puppy is for her.*

It made no sense, but I gave her the puppy. She absolutely adored little Gracie. She was touched that I would give her a puppy after she'd bombed on her first try at independence. She and Gracie were inseparable, for a time. Again I was hopeful.

Then she began leaving Gracie with me for extended periods while she was out doing who knows what and staying God only knows where. Eventually she rarely came around and she realized she was neglecting Gracie. She had intense feelings of love for her puppy, yet her lifestyle wasn't suited to nurturing anything. In tears she asked me to find a new family for her sweet, lonely little dog. So I did.

In my prayers I sometimes asked, and wondered, if I'd been wrong. *Father, did I mess up? Was I not supposed to give her the puppy?* It seemed like such a mistake. In the end she had more remorse and heartache because she'd lost something she loved and failed again. And yet ... if I heard any reply to my prayers, it was this: *You didn't give her Grace, I did.*

Then I had a dream.

In my dream, I took a pregnant young woman to the doctor; she was someone close to me, but I couldn't see her face. I sat in the room while she had her ultrasound.

Then suddenly, in my dream, I realized I too was expecting a baby. I decided to have an ultrasound as well. As the nurse ran the probe over my stomach, the baby began to move; I could feel it so well. I reached down to see where its hands were; they were on either side of my abdomen. Then the baby stood up as the skin on my stomach cleared like a mist and became translucent as glass. My skin thinned to a film and the baby put its hands in mine and held me tightly. It struggled and lifted its head to gaze up at me. Then my husband was there, and the baby gazed from me to him. The face was tiny, with huge eyes and an ethereal gaze.

I dream a lot, but rarely so vividly. When I do, the dream usually foreshadows coming events. This dream unsettled me; I talked with close friends and we prayed God would prepare my husband and I for whatever was coming.

Nine months later our daughter got pregnant.

She had a steady boyfriend and they were happy about becoming parents. She stopped drinking and doing drugs as soon as she knew she was pregnant. Her boyfriend didn't quit, but he cared enough to leave her home alone while he partied. She accepted this, somewhat, and seemed like an excited, expectant mother. She knitted baby blankets, planned a baby-shower and kept a baby book. She talked about how much fun they'd have with their child, but I had a deep sense of foreboding...

When the baby was born, his parents took a step toward stability and got married. To celebrate, they got drunk... and stayed that way. They still talked about the fun things they'd do with their child. They were hopeful, but I really was not. I'd been in their apartment where the shades were always down; there were empty booze bottles in the corners; shadows and piles of trash everywhere; and smells and feelings that were far from comforting. It was more like a haunted house than a baby's nursery. No, I was not hopeful. Some clowns scare little children, and bears are not safe playmates—not even dancing bears.

Because baby was born prematurely, he stayed in the hospital for over a month. In the beginning his mommy was heartbroken that she had to leave him; she returned to the hospital for all of his waking and feeding times. However, things changed when her drinking and drug usage resumed. We didn't realize right away. As grandparents, we visited a couple of times per week at first, trying not to get in the way or threaten the new parents' connection with their child. But when we found out his parents weren't consistently showing up, we increased our visits—no longer worrying we'd step on toes. Our concern was now for this precious infant waiting in the hospital, alone.

Born two months early, with parents who'd taken leave of their senses, he was a delicate little person in an uncertain situation. I nearly cried when I held him. I begged God to protect him and make him big, healthy, and strong—to shower him with love and shield him from the harm and heartache stalking him.

By the time baby was ready to be released from the hospital, his parents' lives and marriage resembled a train-wreck and Child Protective Services were investigating them, concerned they were unfit. I stood beside my daughter in the hospital, promising CPS and everyone else involved that I would closely monitor the baby and his parents. I didn't need the State to ask this of me, but without my promise they wouldn't release the baby.

Later, when I was alone with my daughter and grandson, I held him closely, watching as he struggled to lift his head and gaze around the room—it was the same exact face I'd seen in my dream. Premature babies have a bony little face with big owl eyes. I'd never seen one before, outside my dream. Still holding the baby, I spoke to my daughter, hoping she was listening. "I'll be here to help you. You can ask me anything, anytime. I'm always on your side. Do you know that?"

"Yes, I know," she said, not looking at me, but not exactly looking away.

"From now on," I said, "this baby needs you always on his side—as his best friend. He needs you to take care of him, protect him and think he's wonderful—when you feel like it, and when you don't. Sometimes you might be his only friend, that's why it's so important." She was looking off into the distance now. "Do you understand?" I asked.

I don't think she heard me. I was talking to myself.

I was talking to myself.

At that moment, I knew I really was talking to myself. I looked down at the perfectly formed infant in my arms; he looked my way and then slowly up toward the ceiling, as if seeing things I couldn't. I believed his mommy would cherish him and they'd have a beautiful relationship... when her mind cleared. But he couldn't wait.

God foresaw this; He knew all along who our grandson's first best friend would be. He even shared His secret with me... in a dream.

Our grandson is older now. He's happy, smart, well adjusted—maybe a little spoiled and certainly a lot cherished. Plus, he's by far the biggest, strongest toddler I've ever known. When God answered my prayer, He really answered it.

When the baby was just a few months old, I knew God had prepared me to get a lawyer and take legal custody of him. With his parents lives out of control, it was just a matter of time before CPS would step in again. Would they know or believe the baby had been in my care most of his life and that he was safe? I couldn't take that chance; without legal custody I was powerless to protect the baby in my arms. His parents wanted the best for him, but in their youth and with their serious issues, they were barely managing to keep themselves alive. They saw this and didn't argue when I proposed third party custody.

As time flows on, I hold my breath, watching my daughter's life. I wish I could tell her, "I understand." But I don't. She's still an enigma to me—adrift inside volatile and conflicting emotions, alternately struggling to right her life, then racing headlong toward self-destruction... and I don't know why. The best I can tell her is, "I love you."

I hope she knows I'm still on her side—always loving her, believing and hoping. I'm fighting her battles with her, though it often looks like I'm against her. Some time ago, her enemy became herself. So as much as I want to, I won't take her side if it means she, or her beautiful baby, will suffer. When she's in her right mind, she wouldn't want me to anyway.

I've seen God heal her from incurable disease, grab hold and remove her from fatal circumstances and even speak to her in dreams. God gives her grace again and again and again. She accepts his grace with gladness, then tramples it underfoot. God has grace abundant and mercies without number. I pray that He'll continue to be patient, keep holding out His mighty hand and offering her His heart. However, He showed me what would happen if my daughter—in her current capacity—were entrusted with a precious life to nurture. If I stood by and did nothing while she neglected a puppy, I'd feel very badly and would bear the guilt. But God help me if I ever have the power to intercede, yet stand by while my grandchild's cries go unanswered.

I don't understand, I don't know the rest of the story. But for now I know I must be bold, be strong and be filled with the power that God offers me. In His strength and with His wisdom, I can be a steadfast best friend to my daughter and to my grandson. I believe that in their lifetimes they'll have more best friends; it's been an honor, a privilege and my divine commission to be their first.

"Speak up for those who cannot speak for themselves, for the rights of all who are destitute. Speak up and judge fairly; defend the rights of the poor and needy." Proverbs 31:8-9

Update:

Many years have passed since Elaine wrote about her daughter and grandson. Here's an update, written by the daughter in her story:

"Victory in Jesus! My Mom wasn't the only one who dreamed about my baby before he was born. In my dream I had just woken from a coma. I walked into a small church and saw my parents sitting in a pew near the door. Overjoyed to see me, they jumped up and ran to greet me. They had a sweet, little blonde-haired child with them who was running happily up and down the aisle.

"Who is this?" I asked them.

"This is your child," they replied.

The year after my strange dream, I became pregnant with my first child. Just before my little boy was born I was warned to repent of my sins. I didn't listen; I didn't repent.

My baby was born very prematurely and I was over-medicated at the hospital. I couldn't wake up, or breathe alone, for two days. Afterward I started drinking again, this time more heavily, and using harder drugs. Baby's father and I split up (he took the dog and the car; Mom and Dad kept our baby). But my family loved me. They loved me enough, not only to care for my precious boy, but also to pray for me. My dad even fasted for me on numerous occasions. They put me on every prayer chain they knew of.

They prayed, they loved me and they believed in miracles. Then one day my miracle came: I "called to God for help, and He healed me." He even sent a group of born-again believers to lay hands on me—I met them while wandering through the park. They called me over and asked if they could pray for me. When they surrounded me and began to pray, I felt something swirling above my head, being pushed upward, as if it had come out of my body. Then *whatever it was* left. I screamed at the lady beside me, "What are you doing to me?" She smiled in response.

I gave my life over to Jesus shortly after, and soon I was reunited with my baby boy. I will never forget walking into that little country church to sit with my parents and my sweet little blonde-haired boy, who couldn't stay in our pew near the door. He insisted on running up and down the aisle

But my story isn't over. Not all *unfit parents* have godly people praying for them, as I did. The "messed-up mommies" need our love as much as their children do. They need our prayers and our faith in God's miraculous power. Consider, for example, my friend Anna-belle. I met her during my prodigal years. Annabelle didn't have praying parents. As far as I know, no one prayed for her. I sat with her after she delivered her sixth child, a beautiful brown-haired baby girl whom she named Jewel. Looking at that sweet, precious infant, I couldn't help but think that once-upon-a-time Annabelle was just like her. However, my friend didn't get to keep her baby. Little Jewel was born addicted to heroin, so she went directly into the state's care to be adopted—as Annabelle's other children had been.

It's been years since I've seen Annabelle, but I pray for her now—often. If God can save a wretch like me, he can surely save her. He can also save the parents and families of any needy child I cross paths with, if I'll pray for them. He can save the parents who you pray for! But we must love them, while we love their children. When I was lost, no one ever said a negative word about me to my little boy. Words can't express how happy and thankful I am that my son was protected, nurtured and deeply loved while I was out "writing my testimony"—and that he wasn't turned against me. He wasn't the only one who was cared for; I was also deeply loved—and I knew it.

No, not everyone I pray for will be saved. Some of them may always reject the Lord's drawing. But who am I to say who will, or will not, be saved? God's command to us is to love deeply—from the heart—and to pray without ceasing. The rest is up to Him."

Children of Goshen

By Bigimba Ngabo

I was born in the eastern part of Democratic Republic of the Congo. As a young boy, due to civil and political wars which started in 1996, I fled from my home village with my parents and siblings. We went to another village very close to the border of Burundi. I was there for several of my teenage years, but we didn't stay. In 2004 another war started, and we fled to a refugee camp in the country of Burundi.

I was Christian, and my family was Christian as well. However, I didn't realize much about God until God appeared (became more relevant) to me in those difficult times in Burundi, when the genocide—the killings—started. It was a Friday night, August 13, 2004, when the enemy came into the refugee camp. They killed 200 people in two hours. It was not an easy time for me, or for the other survivors. The leaders, and even the pastors, became very shaken in their faith. Nevertheless, I didn't give up. I prayed and asked God why this was happening.

From that time, God heard my heart and gave me a revelation: He wanted me to do something for the people. The revelation to begin *Goshen Ministry* came from the Bible—from the story of the Israelites in Goshen, Egypt, in Exodus 8:22. I saw there how God had helped, was gracious to and protected the children of Israel when they were enslaved in Egypt. I realized that even in hardships and obstacles, He is still a God of Restoration and Protection. He is a God for needy people! So, I started *Goshen Ministry* in Burundi in 2004, along with my three brothers. We wanted to address both the spiritual and physical needs we saw.

That year I recognized the need for children in Bujumbura, Burundi, to be fed and sheltered. There were many displaced and abandoned children, orphaned during the Civil War, or by diseases associated with poor living conditions. They often ate at the garbage dump sites and some turned to crime to survive. Initially there were ten children for whom we took the responsibility to provide their necessities of life. By February of 2006 *Goshen Ministry* was registered with the Burundi government to care for children and fifteen children were being cared for daily. However, there was not any particular place for them to live; they were just living from place to place as shelter could be located.

In 2007, my family had the opportunity to come to the U.S. as refugees. God gave Tucson, Arizona as a hometown for me; I realized it was God's plan for my life. When I arrived, I didn't feel like I was ready, but I felt in my heart again a calling. Because we had to meet many refugees from all over the world, God spoke to my heart again to do something—to continue a ministry in Tucson. Three months later, I started a prayer and worship gathering in my apartment building. My plan was to reach out to the refugee community in Tucson—different areas, different cultures and even different beliefs.

After coming to the U.S. I also continued to help the orphans in Bujumbura. Then in March 2009 a terrible thing happened. The temporary shelter where the orphans were staying accidentally burned down. The fire claimed the life of Grace, who was just two years of age. After this, by God's goodness, we received donations to purchase a small three room home in Burundi. The children finally had a home of their own! It was named the *House of God's Grace*, in memory of Grace. With this provision, God made it possible for the children to have electricity and running water. Another home was established in 2014, called *House of God's Mercy*. And later a third home was opened and called the *House of God's Blessing*.

Soon there were forty, and then fifty children the Lord enabled us to provide for. The "provisions" were more than food and shelter; we met the children's educational and spiritual needs in a family setting! The homes had house parents, tutors in the afternoons after their regular school was dismissed and an English teacher on the weekends.

But in April of 2016 the term *Goshen* took on more meaning as political strife and violent, deadly, public demonstrations broke out throughout Burundi. Tens of thousands of people fled the country. At the end of April the violence surrounded the Goshen children's homes. They and their houseparents also fled, on foot, to the Congo, with the hope of getting into Rwanda. The children finally made it into Rwanda, although they could not stay, and then eventually into Uganda where they have now received asylum. Glory to God who has enabled us to care for the children.

Right now, Goshen Ministries has the Tucson church, and a ministry to the refugee communities—it is growing fast, and God has blessed us on every side. We also have a church in Bujumbura, Burundi, another in a nearby province associated with a large refugee camp, one in Rwanda, and a new church has just been started in Uganda also. Our long term goal and hope is to plant more churches and to care for more children in the Central African region. We would also like to host medical clinics and a vocational education center, not only to help the children, but also the impoverished of Burundi. And we would like to open a school to assure the children will get a good Christian education and not have to worry about tuition costs.

However, for now the situation in Burundi is still unsettled, and our monthly expenses have increased, due to the exodus of the children to find a safe haven. They literally fled with only the clothes on their backs (and they grow quickly). Our vision is to see them mature to be God honoring adults able to care for themselves and others—and we see this vision becoming reality. The Goshen children are amazingly resilient and brave, and they really care for each other. They consider themselves to be one big family. God has been an amazing God to us. But through this exodus we have added homes, widows, more children and private schooling—this means that we need more believers to help support this kingdom work. Over sixty children and four widows are now being supported by this ministry.

I am blessed to be the Goshen Ministries' leader. I am very confident that God is God, that He is God for all situations. He is my God.

†

Can you help support the Goshen children? For information, contact: Goshen Ministries, P.O. Box 32032, Tucson, Az 85751
Phone : 520-444-8765 or GoshenMinistries.org

Invisible Ranch

The story of All The King's Horses Children's Ranch

In 1993 the Lord called Ana Lucore to Himself. After receiving free-grace to fully repent of a life of self-destructive sins, Ana asked the Lord if she might work for Him full-time. He agreed and began her missionary on-the-job training in New York, at a ministry center for women and children in crisis.

Five years later Ana had just finished a ten-month missionary venture in South Africa. At an age where others might consider retirement, instead Ana prayed, "Where do I go from here, Lord?" As she waited, she saw in her mind's eye a ranch for abused children, with ponies, puppies and a river running through it. This new direction settled into her heart: she was to return to her own country and help needy children.

Back in America, Ana shared this vision with Christian friends who began to pray. She researched the needs of abused and neglected children and the overwhelmed US foster care system. The idea of having ponies, and a puppy or two, took on more meaning. Ana learned that to remove a child from their home (no matter how virtuous the reason) is traumatic. Even if their homes are unhappy or dangerous, it's their comfort zone, their culture—their "home country." Another place (even a safe, loving place) is a foreign land, with a foreign culture. Ana remembered being comforted by the presence of a horse and a dog when on mission in South Africa, because animals remain unchanged regardless of culture. Likewise, these creatures would comfort children at the ranch.

Soon the Lord established Ana and another missionary, Susan, in Benson, Arizona. Keeping first things first, the ladies spent their mornings marching through the desert, calling out prayers to God for their new neighbors. Determined to meet needs where they found them, they began rounding up unsupervised children and asking their parents if they could take them to church. Most parents were grateful for the offer. However, the pastors and congregations of the churches they visited were not so agreeable. After many discouraging tries, they finally found a church whose members extended the love of Christ to the unruly youngsters following Ana and Susan down their aisles.

Whenever Ana heard of a family bombarded with the world's addictions, she prayed for an opportunity to introduce herself. On occasion she'd pull up in front of their house, stand beside her car, lean on the roof and yell, "Hello in the house!" Then she'd wait a few minutes while the people inside checked her out, hid things they didn't want seen, and prepared to answer. Usually their front door opened when she walked around the front of the car.

"Yeah? What do you want?" they'd ask suspiciously.

"My name is Ana. I want to be an extra grandma to your child," she'd answer, mentioning their child by name. "I'm not here to tell you what you should and shouldn't do—you know that already—but I will tell you this: Jesus can set you free." At this their looks of suspicion usually changed to mere curiosity. "In the meantime," she'd continue, "why don't you let me take care of your child for awhile and get him out of here?" Word quickly spread around town that there was a woman willing to baby-sit for free. So in addition to taking groups of children to church, Ana opened her home to many children who'd never been to church or heard the Bible read. Some hadn't even heard of Jesus.

In time they had a board of compassionate believers who supported the vision of a ranch for abused children. They named their ministry *All the King's Horses Children's Ranch*. Volunteers and church groups even traveled from other states to help them minister to local children. Yet the ranch Ana had envisioned was still invisible. While they waited for the Lord to show them where the ranch would be, Ana and Susan determined to remain faithful, meeting needs wherever they found them. Still sharing a home, these *sisters-in-Christ* determined to be a witness to the purity of such relationships in the Lord. And because of their singleness, they had time and attention to spare. Therefore, despite hindrances and trials, in the year 2000 Ana and Susan decided to help even more children by becoming foster parents.

A vibrant teacher named Kris (one of their board members) had adopted three siblings through the foster care system. Kris and her husband Andrew were raising the boys on a ranch not far from Benson. Kris was always willing to answer Ana's questions (or to get on her knees and pray when she didn't have the answers). Kris greatly encouraged Ana as she and Susan navigated the lengthy foster care licensing process.

In January of 2001, Ana and Susan received their foster care license. In their first six months as foster parents, a string of teenagers came and went in their home. Some were inconsolable and talked non-stop, some were rebellious and sullen, and one young man was cheerful and friendly—but he ran away from their home. They were reaching out to many children, but still Ana wondered when the very detailed ranch she saw in her mind (and held in her heart) would appear. Through snake bites, lost children, broken bones and a bar- rage of other mishaps, Ana perceived that a very real spiritual enemy fought against their attempts to bring the hope of Jesus Christ to children; she prayed for the strength to remain faithful.

In June 2001, Ana and Susan received two more foster sons, pre-teen brothers. The older of the boys, twelve-year old Jeremy, was especially withdrawn. Ana wished she could connect with him. When she took the boys to ride horses with Kris's sons, Ana marveled at how Kris patiently tutored the oldest of her adopted sons, Jona- than. Watching Kris gently encourage fourteen-year-old Jonathan (while he sat with a semi-glazed look on his face) gave Ana hope for the children in her own care. Jonathan had been born brain-damaged because his biological mother abused alcohol every day of her preg- nancy. As a young child Jonathan endured starvation and beatings. With dreadfully flawed, alcohol-induced ingenuity, Jonathan's fami- ly attempted to manage their out-of-control, special-needs child by chaining him to a doghouse in the back yard. Now under Kris's good care, Jonathan still struggled with moderate learning disabilities and serious emotional problems, but (given his past) the boy was doing miraculously well.

A few months later, Ana and Susan's foster sons went for a *sleepover* at Kris's house. They got along well with Kris's sons and were attending a distant charter school with Kris as their teacher.

Because Susan had to work and Ana had recently broken her arm and wasn't yet driving, the sleepover would help with early morning testing. But that night Ana was woken by a phone call from the police: fourteen-year-old Jonathan had shot and killed his adoptive mother, Kris. He had also shot one of his younger brothers and Kris's husband, seriously injuring them. Then Jonathan and Ana's twelve-year-old foster son Jeremy had stolen a car and disappeared.

In time Jonathan and Jeremy were located and locked up, and Jonathan's brother and adopted father recovered from their gunshot wounds. But a deep wound and dark haze covered the hearts of those involved with *All the King's Horses Children's Ranch.* Inconceivable evil had hatched in a time and place set apart for love and healing. They lost a board member, they lost two children to the consequences of a terrible crime, and now they were also in danger of losing their vision and hope.

In the months that followed, amidst grieving and court appearances, they all stepped back for a time of grave consideration. Ana knew that her life, and her life's mission, were of God. She was also convinced that Kris' death was what the dictionary called being a "martyr". Therefore, after a long period of prayer, Ana concluded that she too was willing to be "one who suffers much or makes great sacrifices in order to advance a belief, cause or principle." She desired to live for Christ by serving children, and also by dying for them if need be. Refocused, Ana and the board of *All the King's Horses Children's Ranch* renewed their dedication to the vision and began to rebuild their hope. Ana and Susan resumed their lives as foster parents and extended grandmothers to neighborhood children whose families were in a state of obvious dysfunction.

Then one day in 2003, Ana and Susan finally saw the ranch outside of their mind's eye. Between a woman who believed the Lord wanted her to purchase property for the ministry and another who wanted to bless children by offering her family's land at a greatly discounted cost, Ana and Susan found the land that would become the children's ranch. On their first visit they pulled onto the barren 89 acres cautiously. It was an illegal desert dumpsite; hordes of vultures perched atop the garbage piles while others circled above them. Draped over the low limb of a nearby mesquite tree hung a long, beheaded rattlesnake. Their first glimpse of the ranch didn't exactly lift their spirits. But a river ran through it—and there was room for a great herd of ponies!

Thirteen years and a lot of hard work later, the ranch is home to many children (placed through the foster care system)—but it could fit even more. Ana believes they'll have funds to build some day, but for now they're blessed with comfortable manufactured homes. The rural setting allows for much roominess, and the homes on the ranch support one another—house parents act as aunts and uncles for the children in the other homes. House parents care for just four to six children, of their own choosing, so the children can feel the intimacy of family. When asked about their most pressing need, Ana says, "The Ranch's need for more house parents is immediate. We have a home ready for four children—and it sits empty as we wait on the Lord. Please join us in the prayerful search." And yet, Ana cautions that the setting isn't right for every family, nor every season of their family. Regarding rose-colored glasses, the ranch seeks to heal children, but not at the expense of other children. For example, parents want to bring their young children to rub elbows with damaged kids, who don't even know they're behaving in depraved ways, are not what the ranch is looking for. Ana adds, "Also, parents must be able to accept a child without receiving appreciation in return. If someone needs to get their self-worth from these poor war-torn children, then they have their eyes off of the One who calls us *Accepted in the Beloved*."

When asked how many ponies and puppies the ranch currently has, Ana cheerfully answers, "The ponies and puppies remain invisible, for now."

†

To find out how you can support this ministry, contact them at:
All the King's Horses Children's Ranch
543 Grapevine Loop
Benson, AZ 85602

Ana's book, *From Invisible,* can be ordered at their website:
www.atkhchildrensranch.org

Epilogue

*F*riends, thank you from the bottom of my heart for reading through this entire book. I pray it's given you insight into some of the difficulties in orphan care or ministry to street children. Above that, I hope it's prepared you for eternal victory.

Since you finished the book, I'll let you in on a secret: Many people were scared, so they turned back. Others aren't sure they've been chosen to fight this battle, so they also went away; don't judge them. The Lord doesn't want us claiming our victory was due to our *huge army*.

When I started this book, I knew the Holy Spirit was strongly urging me to write. I'm sorry, but I became discouraged or distracted many times. I almost quit. Yet each time the Lord sent someone to me with a message that spurred me forward. These were strangers, Bible study leaders, pastors, writers, friends etc.. They were unaware of the book and not always specifically talking to me—but *God was.* Without fail they'd say the exact words that were in my mind and heart all day, all week or longer—words I hesitated to write because they were *controversial;* or those I'd just written and then prayed about, asking God, "Did I understand you correctly? Was this really You, or was it my imagination?"

As I wrote the sections that intimidated me most, God seemed to speak the loudest. He'd biblically explained these things to me for years—I took notes multiple times. But when it was time to actually take a stand, publicly, I was afraid. Who am I? I'm the *most fearful child.* What right do I have to say such things? I'm no one, and I've made mistakes.

Not only did these words fiercely oppose things the majority of society loves, but also the lifestyles of many church-going people. I'm not fierce and I don't wish to oppose anyone, least of all *church-going people.*

One day I had this discussion with God, *fervently*, and then picked up my Bible to resume reading where I'd left off the day before. I just happened to be reading in the book of Judges, chapters 6 and 7.

In these chapters, the children of Israel were being abused by the ruling society and crying out to God. So the angel of the Lord came to Gideon, where he was hiding (so the enemy wouldn't steal his food), and He told Gideon to go and deliver the people. When Gideon questioned how this could be possible, the Lord answered, "Am I not sending you?"

"But Lord," Gideon answered, "how can I save Israel? My clan is the weakest . . . and I am the least in my family." In other words, *Who am I? What right do I have?*

Again God answered: "I will be with you . . . " He agreed with Gideon: *You're correct; you aren't adequate and you don't have any right to tell people what to do.* But "I'm sending you, and I will be with you." That makes all the difference.

As I read these verses, I could relate to Gideon. Then when Gideon asked, "How can I be sure it's really You talking to me?" I believe I laughed out loud. And bless Gideon's heart; when he decided to obey God, to go out and fiercely oppose even his father's culture (by tearing down an altar to a false god and smashing a totem pole), he went at night, so nobody would see him! Here's a man after my own (natural) heart. Of course it didn't work; his neighbors found out and tried to kill him anyway.

That night, after I read those chapters, we went to a Bible study group. They'd recently finished a guided Bible-study booklet together and were trying to decide which lesson-book they'd use next. But in the meantime—the leader half-apologized about this—they were going to do a one-night, *random* study of the Bible. "I don't feel qualified," he said, "and I have no idea why we're looking at this subject and this book of the Bible, but I'm just sure God's been laying this on my heart. So open to the book of Judges. We're going to read about Gideon, in chapters 6 and 7," he said.

So I just *randomly* happened to study the same chapters for the second time that day.

After God called Gideon to deliver His children from oppression, Gideon called together a mighty army. Tens of thousands of fighting men rallied together. But God told Gideon that his army was too impressive; when He gave them the victory, they'd think they were awesome. God wasn't willing to share His glory. He wanted them to understand that it was *His* victory and that *He was awesome!*

So the Lord stripped Gideon's army down to almost nothing. Meanwhile, their ruthless enemy swarmed into the region, thick as locusts, and filled the valley. During the night God told Gideon, "If you're afraid to fight this battle, sneak down into the enemy camp tonight and listen to what's being said." Gideon arrived just as one man was telling his friend about a dream he'd had. The friend interpreted the dream this way: "This can be nothing other than the sword of Gideon . . . God has given the whole camp into his hands!"

As I sat quietly through Bible study group that night, the leader said many things, word-for-word (not related to Gideon), that I'd written that same day. Meanwhile, from across the room, another gentleman kept giving opinions which were the rest of what I'd written, also word-for-word—about the false gods and unholy altars in our land, the very ones I'd been tugging at earlier, unseen and (as of yet) unheard. And the Lord was speaking to my heart: *If you're afraid to fight this battle, go down and listen to what's being said tonight.*

When Gideon's army was finally small enough, and when he'd received courage, he rushed out to battle. Each of Gideon's men carried a trumpet and a jar with a candle inside. In essence, Gideon gave them these commands: "When we face the enemy, make a lot of noise and *let your little light shine!*" God defeated the enemy that night, and He alone received the glory.

No, I don't want to fight, tear down altars or bring an unpopular message. But the message of God and the lies of ungodly cultures have always been enemies; they always will be. God will never stop fiercely opposing spiritual oppression, idolatry and wickedness, for these are the enemies *that make children cry out.*

He's the great deliverer; He'll always be victorious, so I want to be on *His* side in every battle. And He delights in doing things *His* way, which usually seems upside down and backwards compared to the methods we need for success. Only God brings victories through tiny remnants, tumbles walls with shouts of praise and sends great armies running before a little band of trumpet players. By using the faithful, available *weak*, God Almighty confounds the wise.

So as you follow the Holy Spirit toward orphans, foster children and street kids, intent upon bringing them Christ's eternal riches—not just temporary comforts—don't expect a vast army to go with you. It's okay; He can give the victory with many, or with few. And if you're afraid to fight this battle, listen to what I'm saying: If you're being called, God is the one sending you; He will be with you. Praise Him with *all of your breath*; be filled with *His Holy oil* and *keep your fire burning.* The joy of the Lord is your strength, so get your *Jesus-Loves-You* T-shirt on, hold your candle way up high, and let's go make some noise! When the dust is no more and the *Morning Star rises with healing in His wings,* I'd love to hear about the miracles you've seen and the children He's delivered—*just because you bothered to fight for them.*

"But thanks be to God! He gives us the victory through our Lord Jesus Christ. Therefore, my dear brothers, stand firm. Let nothing move you. Always give yourselves fully to the work of the Lord, because you know that your labor in the Lord is not in vain."
(1 Corinthians 15:57-58 NIV)

"While women weep, as they do now, I'll fight; while little children go hungry, I'll fight; while men go to prison, in and out, in and out, as they do now, I'll fight — while there is a drunkard left, while there is a poor lost girl upon the streets, where there remains one dark soul without the light of God-I'll fight! I'll fight to the very end!"
— William Booth, founder of the Salvation Army

"Make search for the Lord while he is there, make prayer to him while he is near: Let the sinner give up his way, and the evil-doer his purpose: and let him come back to the Lord, and he will have mercy on him; and to our God, for there is full forgiveness with him. For my thoughts are not your thoughts, or your ways my ways, says the Lord. For as the heavens are higher than the earth, so are my ways higher than your ways, and my thoughts than your thoughts. For as the rain comes down, and the snow from heaven, and does not go back again, but gives water to the earth, and makes it fertile, giving seed to the planter, and bread for food; So will my word be which goes out of my mouth: it will not come back to me with nothing done, but it will give effect to my purpose, and do that for which I have sent it. For you will go out with joy, and be guided in peace: the mountains and the hills will make melody before you, and all the trees of the fields will make sounds of joy."
(Isa. 55:6-12 BBE)

Bible Basics

"Do you believe that there is only one God? Good! The demons also believe---and tremble with fear." (James 2:19 GNT)

Do you believe in God? Good. But the demons believe it even more. Are they forgiven and saved? Are they God's friends? Of course not. There's something more. That something more is explained very clearly in the Bible -- but many people are afraid to read their Bibles; they think they won't understand it. For those who want to read the Bible but get overwhelmed or don't understand it, this simple Bible Study highlights the main points of the Bible. Children and adults alike may use this to jumpstart their Bible reading. Pray for understanding before you begin and you'll find it even easier. Be sure to look up the scriptures listed.

God loves you

He loves you more than anyone ever has or ever will. He made you to be His friend. He thinks about you more than you think about yourself. He wants you to know him, like He knows you.

He has a beautiful and important plan for your life.

"God so loved the world that He gave His one and only Son, that whoever believes in Him shall not perish, but have eternal life." (John 3:16 NIV)

"How precious concerning me are your thoughts, O God! How vast is the sum of them! Were I to count them, they would outnumber the grains of sand..." (Psalms 139:17-18 NIV)

[Christ speaking] "I came that they might have life, and might have it abundantly" [that it might be full and meaningful]. (John 10:10 NIV)

God is good. We are not

Most people aren't living a meaningful life as God's friends. We have a big problem; God is all things right and righteous. He is love and truth; He is holy and perfect--we're not.

We've done wrong things (sin); it came natural to us...

Our sin separated us from God; now we can't hear Him when He calls and our guilt makes Him turn His face away when we pray.

"All have sinned and fall short of the glory of God." (Romans 3:23 NIV)

"The wages of sin is death" [spiritual separation from God]. (Romans 6:23 NIV)

"...the eyes of the Lord are on the righteous and His ears are attentive to their prayer, but the face of the Lord is against those who do evil." (1 Peter 3:12 NIV)

Our sin has condemned us

We might try to convince ourselves that we're okay. We may compare ourselves with others and say, "See? I'm not *that* bad." The world is filled with false religions, psychology, and philosophies that tell us we're good enough; we may believe and try each one, but they won't set us free.

No, not even religion can save us - we've already broken one law thus we might as well have broken them all; we can't be good enough to make up for it. Even if we're good compared with most people, there's still a canyon of guilt between our perfect God and us. Our souls remain hopeless; our spirits lifeless and lonely.

"For whoever keeps the whole law and yet stumbles at just one point is guilty of breaking all of it." (James 2:10 NIV)

"My guilt has overwhelmed me like a burden too heavy to bear. My wounds fester and are loathsome because of my sinful folly. I am bowed

down and brought very low; all day long I go about mourning." (Psalm 38:4-6 NIV)

God offers an escape from condemnation

Despite our sin, God loved us (enough to die in our place) and He's made a bridge over the canyon of guilt that separates us from Him. God sent a savior to suffer and pay the penalty for our sin.

"...the law requires that nearly everything be cleansed with blood, and without the shedding of blood there is no forgiveness." (Hebrews 9:22 NIV)

Jesus Christ was the only person who ever lived a perfect and sinless life. He claimed to be God in human form. He proved it by fulfilling hundreds of prophecies concerning the coming Messiah--or savior--who was promised to be "Almighty God" and "God with us." He healed the sick, cast out demons, brought dead people back to life and He rose from the dead himself.

Jesus' death was an acceptable substitute for ours, because unlike everyone else, He was not dying for His own sins; He was dying for ours. There are many false beliefs and useless religions, but (this is important!) there's only ONE bridge to God! Jesus Christ, the promised Messiah (Savior), is God's ONLY provision for forgiveness from sin; through Him, we can know God's love and plan for our lives.

Christ Died in Our Place:

"God demonstrates His own love toward us, in that while we were yet sinners, Christ died for us." (Romans 5:8 NIV)

Christ Rose From the Dead:

"Christ died for our sins... He was buried... He was raised on the third day, according to the Scriptures... He appeared to Peter, then to

the twelve. After that He appeared to more than five hundred..." (1 Corinthians 15:3-6 NIV)

Jesus the Christ (Messiah) Is the Only Way to God:

"Jesus said to him, 'I am the way, and the truth, and the life; no one comes to the Father, but through Me.'" (John 14:6 NIV)

"'Where, O death, is your victory? Where, O death, is your sting?' The sting of death is sin, and the power of sin is the law. But thanks be to God! He gives us the victory through our Lord Jesus Christ." (1 Corinthians 15:55-57 NIV)

If we don't know Jesus, we are not God's friend yet because we're still stained by the things we've done wrong; we're separated from God who is perfect; we can't be good enough. However, we can cross over on the bridge God worked so hard to give us.

"Therefore, my brothers, I want you to know that through Jesus the forgiveness of sins is proclaimed to you. Through Him everyone who believes is justified from everything you could not be justified from by the law of Moses." (Acts 13: 38-39 NIV)

"...a man is not justified by observing the law, but by faith in Jesus Christ. So we, too, have put our faith in Christ Jesus that we may be justified by faith in Christ and not by observing the law, because by observing the law no one will be justified." (Galatians 2:16 NIV)

Through Jesus, We can be God's friends

We can be set free from our sin, guilt, and shame. We can accept Jesus' payment for our sin. We can be forgiven and considered righteous, because Jesus wants to share His righteousness with us. What does He ask for in exchange? Us! He wants us wholly; hearts, minds, bodies and souls.

"Love the Lord your God with all your heart and with all your soul and with all your mind and with all your strength." (Mark 12:30 NIV)

We must believe. We must ask Jesus to take away our guilt, give us clean hearts, and carry us over the bridge and into friendship with God.

[Jesus said] "I tell you the truth, whoever hears my word and believes Him who sent me has eternal life and will not be condemned; He has crossed over from death to life." (John 5:24 NIV)

"He commanded us to preach to the people and to testify that He [Jesus] is the one whom God appointed as judge of the living and the dead. All the prophets testify about Him that everyone who believes in Him receives forgiveness of sins through His name." (Acts 10: 42-43 NIV)

"If we claim to be without sin, we deceive ourselves and the truth is not in us. If we confess our sins, He is faithful and just and will forgive us our sins and purify us from all unrighteousness." (1 John 1:8,9 NIV)

God will be with us, and in us

If we believe, are forgiven, and ask, God will send His Holy Spirit to live in our hearts. The spirit will explain spiritual things to us, give us power to obey and change, and help us discover the important plans God has for our lives.

"At one time we too were foolish, disobedient, deceived and enslaved by all kinds of passions and pleasures. We lived in malice and envy, being hated and hating one another. But when the kindness and love of God our Savior appeared, He saved us, not because of righteous things we had done, but because of His mercy. He saved us through the washing of rebirth and renewal by the Holy Spirit, whom He poured out on us generously through Jesus Christ our Savior, so that, having been justified by His grace, we might become heirs having the hope of eternal life." (Titus 3:7 NIV)

"I will pray to the Father, and He will give you another Helper, [the Holy Spirit] that He may abide with you forever." (John 14:16 NIV)

If you believe the things you've read in this Bible study, talk to God about them. Ask Him to forgive your sin through the work Jesus did. Ask Him to fill you with His Holy Spirit and open your eyes so you can understand him. Begin to read the Bible and pray that He will explain it to you.

www.ingramcontent.com/pod-product-compliance
Lightning Source LLC
Chambersburg PA
CBHW030921090426
42737CB00007B/271